The Arab and the Brit

The Arab *and* the Brit

THE LAST OF THE
WELCOME IMMIGRANTS

Bill Rezak

SYRACUSE UNIVERSITY PRESS

For a listing of books published and distributed by Syracuse University Press, visit our
website at SyracuseUniversityPress.syr.edu.

ISBN: 978-0-8156-0974-2

Library of Congress Cataloging-in-Publication Data
Rezak, Bill.
    The Arab and the Brit : the last of the welcome immigrants / Bill Rezak. — First edition.
      pages cm
    Includes bibliographical references.
    ISBN 978-0-8156-0974-2 (cloth : alkaline paper) 1. Rezak, Bill—Family.   2. Palestinian
Americans—Biography.   3. British Americans—Biography.   4. Immigrants—United
States—Biography.   5. Indentured servants—Canada—Biography.   6. Palestine—
Biography.   7. England—Biography.   I. Title.
    E184.P33R38 2012
    304.8'205694073—dc23   2012040261

Manufactured in the United States of America

Give me your tired, your poor,
your huddled masses yearning to breathe free.
The wretched refuse of your teaming shore.
Send these, the homeless, tempest-tossed to me,
I lift my lamp beside the golden door.
                    —Emma Lazarus, "The New Colossus"

Bill Rezak was president of the State University of New York College of Technology at Alfred (Alfred State College) from 1993 to 2003. He was instrumental in transforming Alfred State from a two-year technical college into a baccalaureate polytechnic. Before his time at Alfred State, he was dean of the School of Technology at Southern Polytechnic State University in Marietta, Georgia.

Rezak also spent eighteen years in engineering, design, and construction of power-generation facilities, both nuclear and fossil fueled. He earned a bachelor's of science in mechanical engineering from Lehigh University, a master's in mechanical engineering from Stevens Institute of Technology, and a PhD in human resource development from Georgia State University. He was a registered professional engineer in several states.

Contents

Illustrations

Preface

FOR YEARS, when asked my nationality, I responded that my father was Palestinian, my mother was British, and I am American. My American family and I would not exist were it not for my paternal grandmother's wisdom, maturity, tenacity, strength of character, and influence over her Arab spouse or for the courage of my maternal grandfather, who was an indentured servant.

My grandmother, Radia Khouri Rezak, was one of the strongest and most determined people I have ever encountered. She died of cancer at age seventy-one in Syracuse, New York, in 1951 when I was eleven years old. At the time, I had no idea of the significance of her passing—of her immense contribution to my family's development in America.

There were no countries as we know them today in the Middle East prior to World War I. The vast region across North Africa and the eastern end of the Mediterranean Sea was simply "Arabia." Many Arabs were wanderers who moved freely from place to place much as Native Americans did before foreigners barged into *their* homeland.

In the early sixteenth century, the Ottoman Turks—invaders from Turkey and Muslim by religion—ruled by force the region from the western mouth of the Mediterranean Sea to Persia (today's Iran, which is not an Arab nation) on the east.

Not until World War I ended in 1918 did the Allied forces France, Great Britain, and the United States draw arbitrary "lines in the sand" in Arabia to create countries according to *their* preferences. These capriciously drawn boundaries paid little heed to Arab tribal, religious, or economic common denominators. Arab allegiance has not been traditionally to nation. It has been to family, tribe, and clan. My paternal grandfather was a Bedouin wanderer at the turn of the twentieth century who raced his Arabian ponies for pleasure and profit. He achieved no small amount of notoriety in and around Nazareth, which lay in the region called Palestine, by harassing the occupying Ottoman Turks whenever he could. But when he ended up on the invader's "list," my grandmother insisted that they flee to America with their family. My father was four years old at the time.

Great Britain in the late nineteenth century was a contrast of extreme wealth concentrated among a few at one end of the economic spectrum and abject poverty for the masses at the other—with a very small middle class in between. Homelessness was chronic in this society. Unless born into affluence, the British pretty much lived in squalor.

My mother's parents were sent to Canada from Great Britain into indentured servitude separately and alone at ages ten and sixteen. They worked off their servitude, met, married, and moved to New York State, where my mother was born.

These two distinctly different families combined in their struggles to succeed in their new circumstances in upstate New York and achieved remarkable success. My parents met at Syracuse University prior to World War II. Their experiences during the war as part of "the Greatest Generation" were typical of many of their contemporaries—that is, long periods of separation, sacrifice, and hardship.

My father's ancestors were highwaymen on the Arabian Peninsula in the eighteenth century. They evolved as priests in the Eastern Orthodox Christian Church. They sparred with the Ottomans and brought their family to America.

My British ancestors' story commences in the mid–nineteenth century in London, from where my ten-year-old maternal grandfather sailed alone to Canada and grew into a farmer, carpenter, and railroader, all while becoming a formidable lacrosse and hockey athlete with the native Iroquois. My British grandmother's story is equally harrowing, as she entered servitude at sixteen.

This book is a nonfiction narrative. But because many of the events depicted are from 100 to 250 years past, their retelling relies on family lore. I have taken liberties with history when I was unable to establish a factual basis.

Thanks to a great deal of research accomplished by my parents and to the existence of many pieces of correspondence, I have reconstructed the lives of a number of my ancestors. Where there were gaps (there were many), I took literary license to convey the circumstances as best I understood them. Recognizing that the written word sometimes becomes "the truth," I don't believe that I have strayed too far afield from the facts.

My perception of the people in this book is mine alone. All of the dialogue is fictitious.

My parents believed that service to humanity was the best work of life. The story of this family provides the foundation for this belief system. They never would have made it had it not been for a helping hand every step of the way. They lived and breathed the "pass it forward" philosophy of life. It is my hope that this account will bear witness to that fact.

The reader may wish to refer to the appendix for a briefing on the regions of the world discussed herein and for my family tree. It may assist in establishing a context for the story.

Acknowledgments

I DECIDED THAT MY FAMILY had an interesting story when I began to realize as a teenager that I didn't know anyone else who had a parent from the Middle East or who had a grandparent who came to the Western Hemisphere as an indentured servant when still a child. During my parents' retirement years, they researched their family histories. Much of their work is reflected herein. There would be no story without the research and notes provided by Nicholas H. Rezak and Frances Pauline Curnick Rezak. This humble endeavor is dedicated to them and their parents. Their courage and grit will amaze the reader, as they have me.

My cousin Louis Rezak is responsible for the thoughtful account of life in Dave and Mary Rezak's family. Cousins Helen, Robert, Jack, Barbara, and Chris added to this fine fabric.

While I was doing the research for the book, my uncle Dick Rezak was still alive for me to interview for the details regarding his and his family's life. My brother, David M. Rezak, who is currently a faculty member at Syracuse University, has helped fill in blanks and visited Barnardo's Home in London to obtain countless details regarding our maternal grandparents.

I was astounded at the records and photographs that Barnardo's Home had kept regarding my grandparents. This material facilitated a re-creation of their lives and helped make the endeavor a fascinating experience.

My editor at Syracuse University Press, Mary Selden Evans, has the patience of Job. She found critical readers, all of whom provided valuable feedback and encouragement. Her support has been key to the completion of this endeavor.

Mary's editorial assistant, Kelly Balenske, gracefully accepted the role of technogeek in helping this old dinosaur to format things. And Annie Barva tried to reteach me English grammar and helped make the language flow.

The Arab and the Brit

1

Nazareth

THE LEAKY LITTLE LIGHTER began to row from the wharf in the Arab port of Haifa into the harbor. A small rusty freighter lay at anchor a few hundred yards away. She had a single smoke stack and was about two hundred feet in length. A sagging rope ladder with wooden steps descended down the outside of her hull from the main deck to the water. She flew a Liberian flag and was *not* a pretty ship.

It was just after dawn in early June 1913. The city of Haifa was then in the region of the centuries-old Ottoman Empire known as Palestine at the eastern end of the Mediterranean Sea. Little four-year-old N'cola ibn Habeeb el Rizk el Khleifi al Nasirah sat on his grandfather Eassa's knee amidships in the lighter. He wore a small, dark wool Western suit hand crafted laboriously by his father, a tailor by trade. N'cola had a round face and almost no forehead because his hairline sloped low across his temples. His skin was the shade of dark olives. His large black eyes alertly assessed his surroundings.

N'cola's brother, ten-year-old Daoud, stood in the prow of the lighter. He wore a similar dark wool suit hand tailored by his father, whose craft had been honed creating flowing Arab robes rather than Western suits. Daoud was tall for his age and slender, with features similar to N'cola's. He had a sharp nose and a strong chin. Daoud was excited about the impending adventure, yet he maintained a peaceful assurance that belied his meager years.

The boys' parents, Habeeb ibn Daoud and Radia bint Eassa, traveled with them. Habeeb, the tailor, was forty-seven years old and a proud horseman. He would rather have been leaving on one of his extended ride-abouts than on this excursion by sea. Habeeb was five feet, ten inches tall and of strong, wiry build. His thick, black hair was combed

1

straight back. He had a swarthy complexion and a beaked nose, and he sported a mustache. He wore an Arab robe—a black one for this somber occasion—because he did not like Western suits; he also knew he lacked the skill to tailor them well. Besides, this whole undertaking was Radia's idea, and he did not want to indicate too much enthusiasm by adopting Western clothes.

Radia, at thirty-three, was aglow with hope and anticipation. Her press to strike out for America was about to unfold. She wore a blouse with a choker neckline and a floor-length gray wool skirt. She had large expressive dark eyes, smooth olive skin, and long, curly, dark brown hair of very fine texture. She could hardly contain her joy and excitement. She realized, however, that now, in front of her husband, Habeeb, and her father, Eassa, would be the wrong time to display these emotions. Radia's mother, Nasra el Tannous, was also aboard to escort them as far as the freighter.

The mist lay heavy in billowy clouds over the dead calm harbor as the little lighter parted its way toward the larger ship. N'cola couldn't understand the fluffy puffs of fog. He had lived all his life in arid Nazareth to the east. This moisture was a novelty. As the lighter penetrated each new cotton ball, N'cola attempted to catch some of it in his hand. And each time he came away empty.

Daoud chuckled at his little brother.

"You can't catch the air, N'cola. You can only breathe it!"

N'cola looked at him with wide-eyed disbelief.

"I am *not* breathing it," he said. "I'm going to hold it."

He grabbed at the puffiness again, with the same result as before.

"Silly camel," said his brother. He turned his attention back to the steamship looming ahead.

N'cola glanced up at Cedo Eassa and saw a tear run down his nose. He had never seen his grandfather cry. Something must be amiss!

"What's the matter, Cedo?" N'cola exclaimed.

Khouri Eassa sat stiff-backed in his black robe and high black hat. He was a priest in the Eastern Orthodox Christian Church, as had been the first-born males in his family for six generations. He looked down at the little boy sitting in his lap below his flowing beard.

"I am sad because I will never see you again," croaked the priest.

"Why *not*, Cedo?" The child tried to digest the troubling revelation.

His grandfather could not answer. N'cola stared into the mist. Cedo was correct; they never saw each other again.

N'cola's father, Habeeb ibn Daoud el Rizk el Khleifi al Nasirah, was the quintessential Arab male of his time. Arabs have historically been a nomadic people, wandering from fertile valley to fertile valley throughout the Middle East. Desert Bedouins were isolated, self-reliant, and ready to take the initiative whenever the need arose. They were headstrong, resisted authority, and lacked communal spirit. They loved challenge, glory, romance, and poetry.

Habeeb had been trained as a tailor of men's clothing, which in his part of the world meant he was skilled in the sewing of flowing Arab robes and headdresses. Sewing, however, was not his first love. Habeeb's business partner, Georges, a Jew who also lived in Nazareth, was the better tailor. It was not unusual, one hundred years ago before the post–World War I Western powers' intervention in the affairs of the Middle East, for Christians and Jews and Muslims to live and work harmoniously in close proximity.

Habeeb's special talent was "the gift of gab." He loved people and especially enjoyed making and influencing new acquaintances. The partners struck a bargain of convenience: Georges loved to sew and was a homebody; Habeeb, a wanderer, loved visiting new and interesting places and persuading people to place orders for Georges' fine work. He also had another reason for preferring this lifestyle: he loved horses almost as much as he loved his family. Since his youth, he had raised two or three at a time for his own riding pleasure and for sale. As he traveled about peddling the clothing that Georges created, Habeeb rode his ponies. The little Arabian horses were quick and agile. He prided himself on keeping them in top form.

It was Habeeb's habit to gather his ponies and ride off into the desert for weeks at a time, wandering from village to village and *bedou* camp to *bedou* camp selling his wares and visiting with new acquaintances and customers. During the late nineteenth and early twentieth centuries, there was little communication between villages and tribes in the Levant. There were no borders to cross, no separate countries, no national identities—just Arabia. It was a wanderer's paradise.

Visitors were the source of most news, and Habeeb enjoyed being the center of attention. He was well read in matters of current interest (Nazareth was close to the region's intellectual center) and skilled in the use of the Arabic language, which is rich with rhyme and melody. He loved the way the language flowed and sang. During his travels, he was appreciated as a spinner of tales of the happenings of the day.

Habeeb would ride out to sell, tell tales, visit, make new friends, enjoy his freedom, and prove his ponies the fastest, most graceful steeds in the region. He always challenged his hosts with a bet on his mounts' prowess.

A small white pony named Yallah was his favorite. She was the fastest filly he had ever seen, let alone ridden. She simply could not allow another horse to beat her. Habeeb admired that trait in people as well as in horses. He was highly competitive in business sales, in games such as backgammon and whist, as well as in horse racing. He could not tolerate losing.

Habeeb was fourteen years older than Radia bint Khouri Eassa. He had first encountered her in the Church of St. Gabriel in Nazareth, where he attended the Eastern Orthodox liturgy. He was a Christian, and Radia's father, Khouri Eassa al Nasirah, was the priest of St. Gabriel's, the church that their common ancestor Khleif (who was buried within) had established in the mid–eighteenth century. At the time of their meeting, Nazareth ("Nasirah" in Arabic) had a population of about six thousand. Most were Christian.

It was not Radia's beauty that had drawn Habeeb's attention, although he found her attractive. There was much about her that commanded his attention. She was as tall as he, with a broad face, an ample nose, large dark eyes, strong features, and that incredibly fine, long, wavy, dark brown hair. She had an assurance that he found both confusing and alluring. She was intelligent and had been educated in a Russian convent. This was unusual for young women of her era, and she had achieved this advanced education because her father was an influential priest. She was fluent in

Russian as well as Arabic. He had never known anyone who could speak a language other than his beloved Arabic. He thought it must be fascinating to be able to communicate with foreigners in their native tongue. He could not imagine doing so himself.

Radia was quick to speak her mind—to offer her opinion on politics, religion, and the events of the day, which amazed Habeeb. He had never been around a woman so young, so outspoken, and so confident. The young women Habeeb knew were shy, demure, and even subservient, qualities that most men found endearing. The older women he had come across were cranky and dismissive.

Habeeb had long ago decided that he wanted to find a woman to wed who was like his older sister, Leah. Leah, who never married, was the principal of a private school in Ramallah owned and operated by a British woman named Mrs. Morpheu. Mrs. Morpheu eventually passed away and, having no heirs, left the school to Leah, who owned and operated it. The school had several buildings and a large campus. (The campus was seized by the Israelis in 1948. Neither Leah nor her family was ever compensated.) Leah was an extraordinarily well-read woman with an air of authority that Habeeb admired. He saw these qualities in Radia.

At age thirty-four, Habeeb asked his father, Daoud, to speak to Khouri Eassa about the possibility of his courting Radia. He was a man with a trade. His partnership with Georges was successful. He could afford to support a family, which made him desirable. For him to marry into the family of a priest would provide him influence and prestige in Nazareth.

Radia, for her part, found Habeeb enigmatic. He was a gifted debater and held strong opinions regarding issues of the day, about which he was well read. These opinions were similar to her own. At the same time, he had a reputation as a bit of a wanderer and gambler.

They both deeply resented the occupying Ottoman Turks. Habeeb was persuasive and enjoyed arguing political issues regarding the Turks with his male contemporaries. This drew Radia's interest and admiration. She believed that if she were to partner with a man whose values and opinions were similar to her own, she would be able to thrive and achieve influence in the male-dominated society in which she lived. So when her father advised her that Habeeb ibn Daoud was interested in seeing her, she thought to herself that, at age twenty, she was probably this mature man's equal; and if he thought so too, well, all the better.

In 1901, a year later, they were married by her father in St. Gabriel's. The ceremony was beautiful, with all of the symbolism and joy fitting the occasion. Radia wore a white gown of her own creation, with intricate embroidery appropriate for a wedding. She was an accomplished seamstress and lace maker. Her long, fine, dark hair hung in tight waves down her back. Her beauty and dark olive coloring set off her impressive amber jewelry. Habeeb wore a black flowing gown of his own creation. He was handsome, if a bit sobered by the occasion. They were well matched.

Khouri Eassa and Radia's mother, Nasra bint Ibrahim el Tannous al Nasirah, had always encouraged her to think expansively about her life. She had felt free to study whatever she desired. She undertook the only higher-education experience available to women of her generation in Ottoman-occupied Nazareth where a Russian Orthodox Church convent operated a postsecondary college for women. Radia relished her studies, graduated with distinction, and became fluent in Russian in the process. She was interested in social issues, and because she was incensed with the Ottoman Turks, she learned as much as she could about the politics of the day.

Habeeb was overjoyed to find a woman with whom he could communicate regarding his favorite subject—ousting the Turks. The Ottomans were shrewd in their approach to occupation and control of their empire. In the early fifteenth century, their military overran the Arabian Peninsula, but they did not attempt to reconstruct Arab societies to fit their own ideology. They instead left local Arab chieftain leadership in charge of families and clans and solicited taxes to enrich their kingdom and to pay for their occupation.

The region had been under Ottoman control for more than five hundred years. The Turks were ruthless rulers. If they encountered resistance to their occupation, they brutally suppressed it. They treated the Arabs as serfs who existed for their aggrandizement and, in doing so, fomented massive resentment in the population.

Arabs not only hated the haughty occupiers but couldn't gain in an economic sense. Every time they began to get their feet firmly planted financially, the Turks raised taxes. This combination of psychological abuse and economic constraint made life almost intolerable, especially for Arab men responsible for earning a living.

2

Bill Curnick and Barnardo's Home

THE INDUSTRIAL REVOLUTION in the second half of the nineteenth century accelerated the migration of the population in Great Britain from the countryside to the cities, especially London. The result of this movement was the development of horrific slums and cramped row housing. The wealthy lived well, and the poor hardly lived at all. Cholera, tuberculosis, and typhus were common and frequently fatal. Public and charitable institutions were constructed to care for the poor, including hospitals, workhouses, orphanages, and asylums for the most vulnerable members of society. If it weren't for these institutions, my family would never have made it to the America—indeed, would not even exist.

Thomas J. Barnardo of Dublin decided at age sixteen that he wanted to be a medical missionary. He aspired to provide medical expertise and spread Christianity in China. In 1866, at age twenty-one, he went to London Hospital in Whitechapel to undertake medical missionary training. Shortly after his arrival in London, there was an epidemic of deadly cholera. Barnardo helped treat the sick and dying and realized that there was a great deal of suffering and poverty to be addressed right at home. In 1868, he began to teach a group of destitute London boys ages eight to ten. He held evening classes in a space he arranged in a donkey shed.

One night after class, one of the lads, Jim Jarvis, remained behind, as recounted in *Barnardo's, Jim Jarvis, and the Biggest Family in the World* (my rendition given here).

"May I stay 'ere for the nigh', please, sir?" he pleaded.

"Gracious no, Jim! Your parents would be worried to death!" exclaimed Dr. Barnardo.

"Ain't got no ma or pa," stated the boy.

"Nonsense! Where do you live, boy?" queried the dumbfounded Barnardo.

"Don't live nowhere," came the response.

"Well, where do you sleep?" Barnardo half asked, half exclaimed.

"Slep' in an 'ay cart las' nigh', sir," Jim shared. "There's 'eaps of us 'omeless kids out there!"

"Show me!" demanded Dr. Barnardo. "But not until after you've eaten. When was your last meal?"

"Yestidy, sir. I'm pow'ful 'ungry!" the boy smiled in anticipation.

As Jim ate, he recounted to Dr. Barnardo how the homeless boys lived—hanging out on the streets by day begging or stealing food and sleeping on rooftops warmed by the fires within at night. After his meal, he took Barnardo to the roofs to show him.

Dr. Barnardo found a widow woman willing to board Jim, then he worked tirelessly trying to find similar accommodations for other homeless boys. One day after he had placed fifteen boys in foster homes, he was asked to speak about his endeavors at a missionary conference for global caregivers. He began by telling the gathering that he had nothing to share with them about missionary work in far-off lands, but that he had discovered a serious social problem right in London. His audience was spellbound. After the conference, he began to receive donations in support of his work.

As the contributions grew, Barnardo was able to purchase housing for his boys. His first such home was at 18 Stepney Causeway in 1870. By 1877, he had six homes along the Causeway, accommodating almost 250 boys. At the homes, the boys learned trades such as wheel making, carpentry, baking, shoe making, and printing.

One winter night when all of the beds were full, a new red-haired boy named John Somers, known to his pals as "Carrots," asked Dr. Barnardo for lodging. Barnardo had to turn him away, telling him that there was no more space and that he would put him on the waiting list for the next available bed. Two nights later Carrots froze to death on the streets of London. Dr. Barnardo was heartsick.

"Never again!" he vowed.

The next day he erected a sign at the home that read, *"No Destitute Child Ever Refused Admission."*

By 1876, Dr. Barnardo had married. He and his wife purchased a home in Barkingside, Essex, where they began to house destitute girls as well.

Barnardo learned of a need in Canada for English-speaking farm labor. He hit upon the idea of placing boys and girls in foster care there. The children would go to Canada at age ten and agree to work at farming (boys) or domestic endeavors (girls) for seven years of indentured servitude. In exchange, they would be fed, clothed, and sheltered, go to school for six months in the winter, undergo a Christian upbringing, and receive a small monthly allowance. At age seventeen, they were free to strike out on their own.

By 1940, Barnardo's Home had sent about fifty thousand children to Canada as indentured servants. Dr. Barnardo visited regularly and hired people in Canada to place the children and to travel from child to child to assess their well-being in their new surroundings. There were as many stories of abuse and neglect as there were successes. Almost 25 percent of the girls were pregnant out of wedlock before completing their indenture. Nonetheless, thousands of young lives were saved by Dr. Barnardo and his visionary initiative.

Today Barnardo's raises money to support delivery of social services to youth in need in Great Britain, Australia, and New Zealand. It has almost five hundred employees in offices worldwide. Dr. Barnardo died in 1905. His legacy lives as a testament to his vision and caring. Many of us owe our very existence to his foresight.

In the mid–nineteenth century, Thomas and Ann Curnick resided above and operated a chandler's shop at 1 Broadbank Cottages, North Woolich, East Ham, Essex County, Great Britain. Chandlers stocked and sold nautical fittings and items needed for maintenance and repair of the ocean vessels of the day.

The shop provided an excellent living in Victorian England, and the Curnicks were well off. They were said to be descendants of John Milton. A son they named John Robert Milton Curnick was born to them in 1854. John Curnick, their only child, grew up to be a merchant mariner. He loved the sea, and it was understood that when his seafaring days were over, he would inherit and operate his father's chandler's shop. A sound appreciation for ocean-going vessels and their needs was requisite to becoming a successful chandler.

Sarah Patience Cooke was born to Mr. and Mrs. George Cooke on December 30, 1854, in Highsworth, Swindon, Wills County, Great Britain. The Cookes were people of meager means, and Sarah was not well educated.

Both John Curnick and Sarah Cooke were tall and handsome. He stood taller than six feet, and she was five feet ten inches. With his preparation for a life at sea, John was considered a most eligible bachelor. He had excellent earning potential with the Merchant Marine and would one day take over the lucrative chandler's shop from his father. He could have his pick of any number of prominent, well-educated young women.

John first noticed Sarah in church. She was the most beautiful, statuesque woman he had ever seen. She cut a lovely figure in her tight, high-waisted skirts and snug blouses.

"Mother, Father, who is that *gorgeous* girl?" John excitedly pointed out Sarah to his parents.

"She *is* lovely," agreed his mother. "However, her family has nothing. Your interest in her would not build the wealth of your family or contribute to your place in society. There are many other beautiful, intelligent, and well-educated young women for you to choose from, John. Why, she doesn't even have a secondary education!"

"Mother, I want to meet her, please," insisted John.

"Then you'll need to find someone else to introduce you, Son," stated his father emphatically. "She just isn't up to our standards for you!"

John was not deterred. After Sunday services the next week, he asked the Episcopal priest for an introduction, and he began to court Sarah. Even though she was not well educated, he found her to be bright, interesting, thoughtful, caring, and sensitive, with a lively sense of humor. And he was mesmerized by her beauty.

Courtship in Victorian England was considered more of a career move than a romantic experience. A woman's property went to her husband upon marriage. From the time she was a young girl, a woman was groomed for the role of wife and mother. Properly trained—which Sarah was *not* because of her family's lack of wealth and relatively poor standing in society—a girl learned to sing, play the piano or guitar, dance, and be conversant about light literature of the day. She also learned French and the rules of etiquette as well as the art of conversation *and* the art of silence. Sarah was not sophisticated, but she was an astute observer and picked up on much of the appropriate behavior for a young woman of the time.

Courtship advanced in stages, with couples first speaking, then walking together, and finally keeping company after mutual attraction had been confirmed. Chaperones were present until a couple was engaged.

Most of Sarah and John's meetings took place at Sunday services, church suppers, and holiday balls. John's parents disapproved of his relationship with Sarah. They warned him that he could expect no financial help from them if he were to marry her. They believed her to be well below their son's social status. This disapproval only worked to make John more determined to pursue her.

With the knowledge that his parents did not support their relationship, John and Sarah eventually traveled to Plumstead on July 24, 1875, and eloped. Both were twenty-one years old. The senior Curnicks never forgave their son. Nonetheless, John and Sarah moved in two doors down the street from them at 3 Broadbank Cottages, and John went to sea.

He sailed on steamships, primarily back and forth between London and New York City. He worked in the engine room and was gone for as long as four weeks at a time. Then he would be at home for a month as the crews rotated on and off duty. John and Sarah were happy and excited to be together. They decided to start a family immediately. A son, William John Thomas (Bill) Curnick, was born on May 24, 1876. Even this joyous event failed to warm Tom and Ann Curnick to their son's family.

By the time their second child came along, they were living at 17 High Street, East Ham, *away* from the senior Curnicks. Ellen Mary (Nell) Curnick was born there on January 3, 1878. Harry David Cecil Curnick was born on August 11, 1879. Poor little Robert Edward (Robbie) Curnick came along in 1881 and died on March 22, 1882. Ada Louise (Lou) arrived on August 18, 1883. Another child, Emily, was born in early 1885 and lived only a short while. So of six children, four survived to adulthood—not unusual for the time, but difficult for the young parents.

Sarah vowed that her offspring's well-being would be first and foremost in her life. John was a successful merchant mariner, and Sarah settled in as mother and homemaker for the family.

An easy life was not to be theirs. John's health began to fail when he was in his late twenties. He experienced a great deal of chest pain, shortness of breath, and weakness. He may have been a victim of genetic Marfan's syndrome, a connective-tissue disorder that sometimes skips generations. Connective tissue exists between tendons, ligaments, blood vessel walls, cartilage, heart valves, and other body structures. In a Marfan's victim, this tissue is not as strong as it should be. Marfan's syndrome is most serious when it affects the aorta, the major artery to the heart. The wall of the aorta where it connects to the heart becomes brittle and thin. It can rupture catastrophically, causing instant death. It can also tear and leak, which is painful and causes internal bleeding and severe weakness.

There is no conclusive test for Marfan's syndrome. Its victims have similar traits, however. They are tall and thin, with slender, tapering fingers and long arms and legs. They may have curvature of the spine and problems with their eyes that cause things to appear to be long and slender to them. Life-threatening problems can occur at an early age for someone with Marfan's syndrome, which has cropped up in later generations of our family.

Sarah began to worry about John's health on his long absences from home while at sea. She was about to suggest that he consider a different career when the Merchant Marine made the decision for him. John was discharged on August 1, 1885, for reasons of failing health. At that time, he was a fireman on the SS *Denmark* sailing from London to New York and back. He had been a mariner for fourteen years.

Sarah was grateful to have John at home, where she could look after him. John was so annoyed with his parents for not accepting his choice of a mate that he resisted asking for their assistance at this difficult time.

"John, why don't you speak to your father about starting work at the shop?" Sarah suggested.

"I hate for him to think that we need his help!" lamented John.

He did, however, eventually approach Tom Curnick about a position. Tom relented and started John in a good situation in the chandler's shop.

John didn't last long in his new mode of employment. He was admitted to Greenwich Hospital in early October with severe chest pain, internal bleeding, and horrific weakness. The Guardians of the West Ham Union began sending Sarah seven shillings per week to cover expenses while he was hospitalized. Sarah, Ann, and Tom Curnick spent as much time at the hospital with John as they could spare away from the children and the business. Sarah hoped that this family crisis would draw her closer to the senior Curnicks.

John Curnick never returned home. He died in the hospital on November 18, 1885, at the age of thirty-one. Sarah was grief stricken. She had lost the love of her life, and the children had lost their father. It took her some time to collect herself to the point of determining how she and her family might survive. She soon concluded that she needed to find work of some type.

At John's death, the Royal London Friendly Society sent her five pounds to help with expenses. The money from the Guardians of the West Ham Union was reduced upon his death to four shillings, sixpence weekly. John's parents paid his funeral expenses.

Sarah approached Tom Curnick about work in the shop. She now learned the depth of the Curnicks' dislike for her. Not only would they not offer her a position working for them, but they refused to assist their grandchildren in any way.

Sarah had a hard time coming to grips with the reality that the Curnicks were going to abandon them. When it finally sank in, she put her in-laws behind her and tried to move in another direction. She also realized that her parents, the Cookes, were not in a position to assist her and her family.

London during the last decades of the nineteenth century was a place of feast or famine. With no support from the Curnicks or the Cookes, Sarah was in dire straights. She simply could not feed, clothe, and shelter her young family. She struggled as best she could, but it was a losing battle, and she realized it after just a few months.

When Bill Curnick lost his father at age nine, he was not grief stricken. He and his father had gotten on together well enough, but John, a seafaring man, had been away during much of Bill's young life. Bill spent those periods with his mother, whom he dearly loved and admired.

Bill believed that Sarah's middle name, Patience, suited her well. She was a bright, calm, patient woman. When she lost her husband and was left with four youngsters to care for by herself, she did not panic. She was devastated when John's parents declined to provide assistance, but she was a realist and quickly turned to her own devices to care for her family. She had no formal training or much of an education, so she had a hard time finding decent-paying work. The first thing she did was to rent out all but two rooms of their house, which generated some much needed income.

She eventually was hired by a progressive obstetrician, a Dr. Harrison. The doctor trained Sarah as a practical nurse, and she cared for his patients after they had given birth. Dr. Harrison believed strongly in asepsis at a time when few obstetricians were concerned about infection.

Sarah looked after mother and child for from two weeks to two months after delivery, depending on the circumstances, to ensure that infection was avoided. She was an exceptionally warm, kind, and loving person whom her patients appreciated greatly.

The nursing job made it difficult for Sarah to spend as much time with her children as she wished. Between caring for her patients, traveling to and from their homes, and trying to properly attend to the children, she frequently felt overwhelmed.

Bill, age nine, was called upon to look after his siblings during his mother's absences. To make matters worse, Sarah was not earning enough money to make ends meet. She, Bill, and Nell frequently gave their scarce rations to little Harry and Lou. Bill was growing rapidly and began to look pale and weak. He was exceptionally thin. Nellie was ill much of the time, and Sarah herself was quite worn out.

One of Sarah's married sisters, Mary Watts, offered to take Nell. Sarah despaired at the thought of losing her and at the same time worried constantly about the child's well-being in their current situation. Finally, she agreed, and Nellie went to live with her aunt.

Dr. Harrison was concerned about Sarah and her family, but he was paying her all he could afford. He was acquainted with Dr. Thomas J. Barnardo and the good work that Barnardo's Home was accomplishing.

"Why don't you and Bill visit with Dr. Barnardo and learn more about his program? They take boys age ten and older for indenture in Canada, as I understand it," he suggested emphatically.

"Oh, I couldn't stand the thought of never seeing him again!" cried Sarah.

"I think Barnardo's arranges for you to keep in touch. They also have people in Canada to visit the children placed there to ascertain their condition and the quality of their situation," Harrison explained.

"I'll think about it," Sarah was sad. "But I really don't want to break up my family any more than it already is."

The more time that passed and the more Sarah thought about Barnardo's Home, the more she began to believe it might be her only alternative. Bill was becoming more frail with each passing day, and she believed she might be failing herself.

Sarah and Bill were very close. Finally, she decided to visit Barnardo's to discuss the possibility of Harry and Lou's moving there for foster care. Maybe she could afford to take them back by the time they were eligible for indenture at age ten. She broached the subject with Bill.

"Billy," she began anxiously, "I think we may have to place Harry and Lou into a foster home for a time. I just can't earn enough money to care for us all."

"Mother, Harry and Lou are too young and weak to survive well in a home. Those homes are full of street bullies. They'll run right over Harry and Lou. I think I should go instead," Bill offered bravely.

Tears formed in Sarah's eyes as she contemplated her eldest son's unselfishness. She knew he was probably right about the kind of children Harry and Lou would encounter. She also knew that Bill would experience the same situation. She marveled at the maturity and strength of her not quite ten-year-old son.

"Well, let's go to visit Barnardo's together and see what we learn," she finally suggested.

Sarah and Bill went to visit Dr. Barnardo and learned that the home indeed kept children until age ten, at which point they were sent to Canada as indentured servants. Bill was startled about the Canadian connection. Going to a home for destitute children was one thing. Traveling halfway around the world to live with strangers was another.

"You'll be safer on a farm in Canada than trying to find work in the mills here in London, Bill. The mills take advantage of children. And the adults who lose jobs as a result of child labor are frequently guilty of violence," advised Dr. Barnardo.

"Barnardo's has been successfully relocating boys and girls to Canada for almost twenty years. You would go to a farm in Ontario which is a Province in Canada, Bill. Your mother will always know right where you are, and you'll be able to write letters to one another whenever you like. You'll be well cared for, and you'll learn farming.

"You'll go to school for six months every winter. Barnardo's will have someone come to visit you every few months to see that you're getting good care. If you're not happy where you're placed, we'll move you until you *are* happy.

"You'll be provided with food, shelter, clothing, and a monthly allowance. If you're frugal, you may be able to save enough to visit your mother occasionally." Barnardo paused, looking at Bill inquisitively.

"I don't want to leave my mother, sir. I know she's worried about me, though, and I don't wish to be a burden. I'll do whatever she decides, sir," Bill was resolute.

"Spoken like a man!" Dr. Barnardo exclaimed. "I'll let the two of you decide then."

Sarah was depressed and felt like a failure. She despaired at the prospect of losing her eldest. She felt so helpless and despondent that she just could not bring herself to make a decision about Bill's future in that state of mind. They took a tour of the home and then headed to the train station. On the ride back, Sarah turned to Bill.

"Billy, I don't want you to have to do this! Believe me, I want you here with me, but I'm afraid for your health. I'm sorry, sweetie, so sorry! I wish I knew what would be best for you."

"It's alright, Mother, I understand. I'll be fine." But Bill was worried about the uncertainty of it all.

A few days after their visit to Barnardo's, Sarah's head cleared a bit, and she made her decision. Bill was wasting away in their current situation. She feared for his health. They had a long conversation.

"Billy, I'm fearful that you and I will have serious problems if we don't get better food. We can't keep giving ours to Harry and Lou!" said Sarah with a heavy heart.

"I know, Mother. I'm worried, too. Shall I go to Barnardo's?" Bill made it easy for his mother.

"I think so, Billy!" Sarah sobbed, and they held each other for a long time.

Sarah Curnick took her son, not yet ten years old, to Barnardo's on April 21, 1886. She packed all his belongings (mostly clothing) in a small pine wood trunk that the husband of one of her patients made for the occasion. The trunk was twenty-four inches long by fourteen inches wide by twelve inches high. It was perfectly fitted at the corners, with dovetailed mating pieces. It had a sturdy two-inch kick rail around the outside of the bottom. The handles and hinges were of forged iron. And it had a lock with a key for Bill to keep his possessions secure. It was handsomely stained and varnished a deep oak shade. It occupies a special place of honor in my home 125 years later.

Sarah had felt terrible when she sent Nell to live with her sister, Mary, but that was nothing compared to the despair she experienced upon leaving Bill at Barnardo's. Not only was he not close by with a relative, but he was going to travel halfway around the world. She had no idea when she would see him again after he left for Canada. She felt like a failure. Her heart ached for weeks, and she had trouble eating and sleeping, which exacerbated her already weakened condition.

Bill Curnick moved into the Receiving House at Barnardo's on April 21, 1886. His admissions report indicated that he was four feet, seven and a half inches tall, weighed sixty-two pounds, and had brown hair and gray eyes. His chest measured twenty-six and a half inches, his complexion was sallow, and he had two scars on his left hand at the base of his thumb. He had received his required vaccinations.

1. Bill Curnick at age ten upon admission to Barnardo's Home on April 21, 1886. Courtesy of Barnardo's.

Bill was a handsome lad. He had a round face, ears rather large for his head, a longish nose, and wide-set eyes. His hair was cut short. As one might imagine, he looked quite forlorn in his admissions photo. Upon his arrival at Barnardo's, Bill was dressed in a white turtleneck pullover and a dark wool jacket.

Bill was so weak and sickly looking that Dr. Barnardo decided to keep him in the infirmary for a time until he grew stronger. It took several days of "light duty" for Bill, who was growing like the proverbial weed, to begin to develop some energy.

Finally on May 1, when Bill felt strong enough, Barnardo moved him to Aberdeen House. There he resided with other boys who were about his age. Most had stories similar to his—they were orphans or from single-parent families that could not care for them. They shared their stories and plight and in general enjoyed one another's company.

Each boy was placed on a work detail, and these assignments rotated twice per month. In the mornings, the boys went to school taught by the house mother and father. After lunch, they went to their work site. Bill began to learn some rudimentary carpentry skills, which he enjoyed.

He was correct that Barnardo's was home to many wild boys of the street. He missed his mother severely. He was pleasantly surprised, however, with the amount of supervision at the home. The boys were divided into groups of about thirty-five at each separate house on Stepney Causeway. Each residence had house monitors (usually a young married couple) who were Barnardo's employees.

Bill was quite tall for his age, if slight of build. He decided to use his superior height to bluff an exterior gruffer than he felt. After a few days, he found that life at the home was tolerable.

The boys slept dormitory style with six or eight to an upstairs bedroom. The windows in these rooms were always open, no matter the season, in order to provide adequate ventilation. Bill imagined that it must be quite cold there in the winter. Each dormitory room (there were five or six to a house) contained three or four bunk beds. Bill was assigned a bottom bunk away from the windows. After the first couple of nights, he found that he slept tolerably well.

The mess hall where the boys ate was a chaotic place. There was much loud chatter as the group settled in for meals. They were placed at specific tables, but the assignment changed every week, which gave everyone a chance to meet all the residents of the house and tended to break up cliques. Six boys were assigned to wait tables each week, and this responsibility rotated. Bill found that there was plenty of decent food.

He was placed in a carpentry class that began to teach him enough mathematics to support that trade. He found that he enjoyed this new knowledge and looked forward to actually building something. The boys were given other responsibilities when not in classes. They cleaned their dormitory rooms, the kitchen, the dining room, and the bathrooms. There were church services on Sundays and chapel on Wednesday afternoon. There was as little leisure time as possible, no doubt for a reason.

During the second week in May, Dr. Barnardo told Bill and the boys with whom he was living, all ten years or older, that they would constitute the next group to sail for Canada and that the trip would occur in just a few weeks. They would sail to Montreal, where they would be assigned to farm families. Canada was sorely in need of English-speaking labor. Great Britain, in contrast, was in a depression, with massive unemployment and overextended welfare rolls.

Bill wrote his mother a reassuring letter in mid-May. He advised her that he was getting on well. He marveled at the quality and quantity of the wonderful food. He told her that if he kept eating there, he was certain to gain weight. He was really enjoying learning carpentry. He related how much he liked the mathematics it required and expressed how pleased he was to find that he was good at the math and with the various tools involved in the trade.

He ended his letter by reassuring Sarah that he was looking forward to his trip to Canada. The Barnardo's folks who had been there told all the children how new and beautiful it was, how clean the cities were, and how large the farms were in comparison to those in the British countryside.

Bill also asked Sarah to visit again soon. He sent his love to her and his brother and sisters.

Sarah found that his letters brought her some solace, but she still felt that she had abandoned him. Nonetheless, she was finding that she could provide care for the two little ones now. She hoped and prayed that she had made the correct decision.

Bill corresponded by mail with his mother once or twice each week. She also came to see him on Sundays when she was able. Sarah was pleased at how well Bill looked when she saw him for the first time after dropping him off. His color had improved, and he was animated, even excited she thought, about the upcoming trip. Sarah still dreaded being thousands of miles away from her eldest child. Yet she could see that he was thriving in this new environment, and he raved about the food.

"This will be our last visit for a long time, Billy!" Sarah tearfully told her son on June 6. "Dr. Barnardo says that you'll be sailing for America soon."

"I'm excited about the trip, Mother! I'll be fine, and I'll write as soon as I reach my new home." Bill put the best face he could on the upcoming adventure.

He was, indeed, excited about the trip, but apprehensive as well. Sarah brought him up to speed on the comings and goings of the rest of the family. They had dinner together, and she prepared to take her leave.

"I'm ever so proud of you, Billy! I'm also somewhat envious! You're going on a grand adventure that will change your life for the better forever." She was putting *her* best face on for him as well. "Remember that I love you very much, that I'll write often, and that we'll see each other again as soon as we can!"

Both knew that it might be a long time before that happened. They hugged one last time, and Sarah showered him with kisses.

"Bon voyage, my grown-up son!" she stammered. And she was gone at almost a run, afraid that if she did not hurry away, she would be unable to leave at all.

Bill stood with a lump in his throat and watched his mother leave. He knew he had to do as she wished in this matter. He felt almost guilty that it was he who got to leave for new opportunity. He did not see his mother again for eight long years.

3

Habeeb and the Ottoman Turks

RADIA AND HABEEB carved out a satisfactory life together, if a bit austere. Radia resented her husband's wanderlust but could not complain
about the income he provided. The tailoring business brought in plenty of
money, but there were the heavy Ottoman taxes and Habeeb's propensity
to gamble some of it away on his horses. She was left with the care of their
children—Daoud, born on January 1, 1903, and N'cola, born on February
22, 1909.

Habeeb, as a remedy for his frustration with the Ottomans, took great
pleasure in harassing them whenever he could. Early one spring morning in 1913, he and a friend raided one of the Ottoman encampments,
causing considerable embarrassment to the Turks and serious trouble for
themselves.

The whole escapade started harmlessly enough. Habeeb left home
on one of his marketing-socializing-racing ride-abouts. He packed his
saddlebags with dried dates and figs and carried a large goat skin of
water. He wandered south from Nazareth across the barren desert to Jeri-
cho and then east around the north end of the Dead Sea into what is now
Jordan.

Here the desert had hardly any vegetation. Wandering herds of camels, goats, and sheep with a single herder moved about continuously in
search of sustenance. It was a starkly beautiful place of parched dirt, clear
sunny skies, and bright moonlit nights. Habeeb spent his nights under
the stars or in the tents of a *bedou* tribe, where his stories of the outside
world were a welcome diversion. He knew the area well as a result of his
frequent travels about the region.

Habeeb had several such routes and rode large loops on each excursion. In this manner, he was able to reach all of his customers (as well as

all of his riding chums) at least once per year. He would be gone for weeks at a time.

Habeeb traveled east from the Dead Sea up Mount Nebo in today's Jordan, atop which stood one of the oldest places of worship in the world, a church established sometime after 450 CE to commemorate the death of Moses. Here it is written that God allowed Moses to see the Promised Land prior to his death. Moses is thought to have been buried by God himself somewhere on Mount Nebo. From atop the 2,600-foot summit, which was almost 4,000 feet above the surface of the Dead Sea, Habeeb could see the rooftops of Jerusalem and Bethlehem to the west of the sea, Amman to the northeast, and Madaba to the east.

From Mount Nebo he traveled east to Madaba, home to the Byzantine Church of the Map (the Church of St. George), where inlaid in the floor (and discovered in 1896) was a mosaic map of biblical lands. It was one of the most famous Arab antiquities.

Here Habeeb paused for several days at the home of his good friend Josef (Sef-Sef) ibn Haitham el Jarjoura. Habeeb and Sef-Sef were about the same age, and both were athletic and competitive.

The two old friends had on several occasions planned and carried out pranks to harass and embarrass the Ottoman Turks. The perpetrators took great glee in relating tales of their feats to the local Arab population, who relished these escapades and passed along the stories. With each telling, the tales became taller and wilder. Habeeb and Josef were folk heroes among local Arabs.

Habeeb had ridden Yallah and two other ponies to Madaba. Sef-Sef had a black stallion named Strongheart, which was as quick as Habeeb's little white filly. Competition for a bottle of arak—the potent, clear, anise-flavored Arabic liquor that turned milky when mixed with water or ice—and some side bets seemed only natural. Josef's family and friends were always interested in a horse race. Their attention peaked when they learned that Yallah and Habeeb would provide the challenge. Yallah and Strongheart were the fastest ponies in the region, and the men were two of the best riders.

Just outside Madaba was an oval approximately one-quarter mile in circumference that had been worn into the earth from years of horse racing.

The two competitors, their horses, and clan members gathered there for the fun. The usual race was four laps. Habeeb knew that Strongheart was the superior sprinter, but he believed Yallah to be the better over a longer distance.

"Let's let them run a little today," he suggested.

"Strongheart is the best over any distance," boasted Sef-Sef confidently.

"Six laps then," asserted Habeeb.

It was agreed. Yallah was small in stature. She was trim, extremely agile, and very calm for an Arabian pony. Strongheart was large for an Arabian, high strung, and nervous. His huge black eyes darted this way and that in anticipation of the competition. Both horses loved to run.

With a large crowd encircling the oval track, Sef-Sef's teenage son Raja dropped a red headdress, and the race was on. Strongheart with Sef-Sef astride him sprinted away, Yallah and Habeeb in pursuit. Habeeb held the little white filly back a bit so as not to spend her too soon. He let Sef-Sef move out to a lead of four lengths, then held fast. It was hard to hold her there. Yallah wanted to race, to be in front.

"Not yet, little one," Habeeb spoke softly into her ear, "not yet!"

Strongheart surged down the straightaway. He was very fast. Yallah was more agile, and she leaned like a greyhound on the turns. Habeeb had never ridden a horse with such great lean. And so they rode—Strongheart opening to six lengths on the straights, and Yallah closing to two on the turns.

Sef-Sef let his colt have his head. Strongheart did love to run! Sef-Sef was confident of his speed, but a mile and a half was a challenge. Still, at the end of four laps Strongheart still seemed smooth and did not slow. Sef-Sef glanced back. There were Yallah and Habeeb just two lengths behind coming out of the turn.

"Yallah, come on, little one, *now!*" Habeeb encouraged his mount.

He let out the reigns and gave the filly her head. She had never taken her eyes off the black in front. Down the straight she held him within two lengths. Through the turn she moved closer. They were one length apart down the back straightaway. She closed to Strongheart's shoulder on the next turn and held there through the front straight.

Habeeb kept her right on the black's shoulder through the next turn and the back straightaway. As they entered the last turn, he slid her back just enough to pass behind Strongheart to the inside, and then he dug in his heals, urging her onward.

Yallah swept past Sef-Sef and Strongheart, leaning way into the turn and sending them wide. Strongheart tried to rally home, but he was spent and couldn't summon the speed. Yallah pranced to the win, ahead by three lengths.

"I thought we had you!" shouted Sef-Sef in surprise. "Yallah is so tough on the turns!"

"And on the straightaway when I let her run!" grinned Habeeb.

"At a mile and a half, perhaps. Let's try five laps the next time!" came the reply.

And so they retired for food and drink with Sef-Sef's family and friends. The men sat on the floor on rugs surrounding a large brass tray filled with Arab delicacies—lamb boiled in butter, fat, and rice; olives; flat Arabic bread; hummus; squash; and incredible pastries.

One scooped up a handful of rice and lamb and rolled it into a ball between one's palms. When of the correct size and stability, the delicious mix was tossed into the mouth—a most tasty treat, if a bit greasy. There were no utensils, and because water was so scarce in the desert, the otherwise immaculately clean Arab men wiped their hands on their beards or clothing.

As usual, the after-dinner discussion turned to the Ottomans. The two friends, feeling fine after the race and with stomachs full of food and arak, thought they might try to harass the Turks once more.

Ottoman colonel Jemal Pasha was in charge of the occupying Turkish regiment in Madaba. He was a short, swarthy man quite absorbed with his personal appearance. His snug riding trousers bloused at the thigh. They fit tightly around his calf and plunged neatly into his spit-polished black knee-high riding boots. His matching brown tunic fit tightly around his ample middle. His waxed black handlebar mustache was perfectly trimmed. He looked every bit a ruthless tyrant.

The colonel's Muslim troops were bivouacked on the edge of town in tents. Their food was cooked over open fires, and the men generally lived and ate out of doors. They also availed themselves of the local arak and so after dinner were lethargic and sleepy. Their tents were small and cramped, so many left their belongings outside in the dry forgiving desert air—knives, handguns, trinkets from home, prayer rugs, and the like.

Although a guard detail was posted at all times, the guards frequently fell asleep in the wee hours of the morning, making it easy to infiltrate the camp.

At about 3:00 AM after an evening of food and drink, Habeeb and Sef-Sef saddled Yallah and Strongheart and rode quietly from Madaba to the Ottoman bivouac. They tethered the horses in a small stand of desert brush about one hundred yards outside the camp and walked stealthily toward their objective.

They moved silently through the camp of sleeping soldiers, looking for booty. They were after the Turks' personal possessions to prove to their colleagues what they had accomplished—a knife left unattended, a couple of ornately decorated mess kits with matching coffee mugs, a picture of Colonel Jemal holding the reins of his horse. All of these items made them smile with satisfaction.

When the two raiders had their arms full of treasure, they began to withdraw with care. But as they gingerly made their retreat, Sef-Sef dropped a tin coffee cup. It clattered noisily to the ground, awakening a sleeping guard. They knew that the guards would be after them momentarily, so they took off at a run for the ponies.

Strongheart was excited to pick up the scent of the returning Sef-Sef. He whinnied loudly, alerting the awakened guard as to the raiders' destination. The guard immediately shouted his comrades awake, and soon the entire camp was roused.

Habeeb and Sef-Sef sprinted to the horses, mounted, and dashed off. It took the Ottomans only minutes to organize and take up the chase. The two friends knew that if they could reach the open desert, they could easily escape. Just to be certain, they split in two directions, planning to meet atop Mount Nebo, where they would enjoy a view of their pursuers if the Turks turned out to be so tenacious.

Colonel Jemal was determined this time to make an example of the two infidels who so wantonly thumbed their noses at his authority. He quickly deployed two search parties.

The dust blew off the barren desert atop Mount Nebo. Habeeb lay on his back against the hill top and watched it swirl about him. He wore the white robe and headgear of the desert wanderer—his headgear bearing the Rizk family name embroidered in beautiful Arabic script.

Yallah shifted uneasily from hoof to hoof as he held the reins tightly to keep her head low. They had ridden hard all night, and both needed rest. He had not known the Turks to be so persistent in the past. He hoped that Sef-Sef was safe.

After a few quiet minutes, Habeeb peeked over the hilltop. His eyes searched the moonlit horizon to the east. Nothing. He breathed a sigh of relief. He waited a while longer and then decided to head west. There was no sign of Sef-Sef.

Toward dusk several days later, Habeeb made it safely back to Nazareth and the waiting Radia. He ambled slowly into town upon Yallah and tried to look nonchalant—a salesman returning after a swing through his territory. Alas, his ponies and his wares were still in Madaba!

Radia looked at him skeptically. As usual after one of these excursions, Habeeb smelled badly of sweat, dust, goats, horses, manure, and day-old arak.

"Welcome back, husband, wanderer, provider," she began with sarcasm.

"It's good to be back. I've had a successful trip and have many orders for Georges," allowed Habeeb.

He noticed Radia's gaze. She was studying him intently.

"And what of you and the children?" he queried.

"Never mind me and the children," she replied testily. "What have you and Josef been up to?"

Ah, so the story has already reached home, he thought. He wondered how the news of their escapade could have traveled so fast. Colonel Jemal would certainly not want it to leak out that his security had been breached once again.

"Oh, you know how Sef-Sef and I enjoy a good ride together! Surely you wouldn't begrudge us that!" came the nonchalant response.

"It isn't your ride together that concerns me," stated Radia. "It has been said that you raided the Turks again and that Josef was captured."

Habeeb's blood ran cold. He stared at his wife in disbelief. Surely not! Sef-Sef was as fine a horseman as he, maybe better. And Strongheart was one of the best mounts either had raised in some time. How could he have been captured?

"The local Turks are saying that Josef's horse was shot from under him and that he was injured in the fall," declared Radia. "And they say they know who was with him."

"If they come around, I will show them my orders for new clothes. They are too stupid to link me to this bit of nonsense. It will be alright, you'll see," posited Habeeb. But he worried that it would not.

Radia's heritage and education had prepared her for life with Habeeb. After twelve years of marriage, she was wise regarding the ways of relationships and productive family life. She had had two pregnancies in addition to those that produced Daoud and N'cola. One of these children came between Daoud and N'cola, the other after N'cola. Both were healthy, beautiful baby boys. Both had died in her arms before their second birthdays, victims of diphtheria.

The diphtheria menace was a scourge upon the region. Many young children succumbed to this lethal menace. Arab medicine, which a thousand years earlier had set the standard for physicians in the West for centuries, was not aware that the deadly diphtheria membrane that formed across the little tracheae of the very young could be pierced, allowing breath to be drawn.

So Radia had rocked her afflicted children in her arms as they slowly suffocated, the tears of helplessness and frustration streaking her cheeks. She was not accustomed to these feelings, nor was she willing to endure them. Exacerbating the situation were the stories she had heard about advances in medicine occurring in Europe and America.

Little N'cola had undergone the most primitive of treatments just a few weeks ago. He had run a high fever for several days, and Radia had become worried when the fever did not break, so she had reluctantly called in the village shaman to prescribe for her youngest. The shaman examined N'cola and then administered a most barbaric remedy.

He lay N'cola on his stomach and lit a fire. He heated a large cork filled with stick pins on one side. When the pins were adequately glowing with heat and sterile, he drove them into the screaming N'cola's back in four places.

His logic, he said, was that this treatment would force the fever from the child's body. N'cola bore the scars of that encounter for the rest of his life. Radia never forgave herself for subjecting her young son to such an ordeal. The fever, however, abated.

Radia loved Habeeb. He was a good man who cared deeply about his family's well-being. He had a gruff exterior but was thoughtful and dedicated to their marriage and family. He and Georges made an adequate living in the clothing business.

Habeeb was, she thought, addicted to his horses, though. She frequently felt that he lavished too much attention on them, to say nothing of the cost of their upkeep. The worst of her fears was realized all too often when Habeeb frequently gambled away his earnings betting on his ponies to win races against the horses of people he met on his ride-abouts. This problem was serious when coupled with the ever-increasing Ottoman taxes.

Now Radia had a new concern. If Josef was under arrest or worse, would Habeeb be next? Those who repeatedly crossed the Ottoman Turks often disappeared for long periods or forever.

Sef-Sef loved his friend Habeeb, the only other man he knew who was as competitive and who loved horses as much as he. He looked forward to visiting with Habeeb, to racing his horses against Habeeb's, and to sharing news and stories with his humorous friend. He also loved to provoke the Ottomans.

On their last night together, it had been Sef-Sef who had alerted the snoring guard and started the unhappy chain of events that followed. Both riders ran to their horses, mounted, and sprinted away in different directions, as was their plan if ever confronted in this manner.

Strongheart was speedy and agile. He began to open a gap between Sef-Sef and his pursuers. Sef-Sef was accustomed to the Turks shooting over his head when chased in this fashion. He knew they desired to capture, interrogate, torture, and detain him indefinitely rather than kill him. Their horses were no match for Strongheart. He was not prepared for what happened next.

Just as he felt that he and Strongheart were about to make good their escape, the colt faltered, stumbled, and then fell, all before Sef-Sef had time to react. He knew the horse was much too agile to have tripped—he had to have been shot. As Strongheart fell forward, Sef-Sef tried to leap over his head and out of his way. Instead, Strongheart somersaulted and rolled over him.

Sef-Sef lay stunned for an instant. Then he began to take stock of the situation. Something was wrong with his arms and legs. He tried to move but could only think the motions he desired his body to achieve. "Insha'Allah, God willing, I need to rise," he thought.

He couldn't. He lay in the darkness, wondering when this weird sensation would wear off. In the distance he could hear the approaching Turks' hoofbeats. "I'll just rest here for another moment," he thought. He looked up at the clear desert night sky and the bright moon, which had so grievously betrayed him. He closed his eyes. He felt peaceful. He wondered where Habeeb was and if he had made good his escape. By the time his pursuers arrived at his side, he was gone.

4

Canada

BILL AND HIS BARNARDO'S MATES sailed for Canada on June 14, 1886. He had turned ten just three weeks earlier. His pine trunk had served as his dresser at Barnardo's. Now it was packed again for the trip to Canada.

Barnardo's dressed Bill in a nice-looking wool suit, white shirt, and necktie for the departure. He had a white handkerchief in his breast pocket and a derby hat on his head. His smile was noteworthy—a distinct improvement in confidence since he had entered Barnardo's Home two months earlier.

Their ship was the SS *Lake Superior*, built in 1884 by J & G Thomson of Glasgow for the Beaver Line. She weighed 4,562 gross tons, was 400 feet long, and had a 44-foot beam, a single screw, one stack, and three masts. Her hull was iron, and she could make 11 knots. She had accommodations for 190 first-class passengers, 80 second-class, and 1,000 third-class where the boys (about 50 of them) traveled four to a cabin. Third-class passage cost the equivalent of about sixty US dollars for each boy, which Barnardo's paid. A portion of this fare was reimbursed by the receiving families in Canada.

The boys had a wonderful time racing about the ship, experiencing all of the exciting new sites at hand on the ocean liner. The summer crossing enjoyed mild weather, so they could spend a great deal of time out of doors on the main deck.

On June 24, the ship entered the mouth of the St. Lawrence River. It was so much wider and more beautiful than the Thames, Bill could hardly believe it. On both sides of the river was thick, green wilderness. Geese, deer, moose, and muskrats were visible along the shoreline. Large fish broke the surface of the water as they fed. It looked like a wild and frightening place to Bill.

2. Bill Curnick on the morning of June 14, 1886, dressed by Barnardo's Home for the voyage to Canada. Courtesy of Barnardo's.

The *Lake Superior* docked in Montreal, Quebec, on June 25. The city was the industrial hub of the newly formed confederation of Canadian provinces. The Canadian Pacific Railway was opening markets in the West for local business. Manufacturers, importers, wholesalers, and retailers had workshops, warehouses, offices, and display rooms in Montreal. Electric lighting was being installed, and ten-story skyscrapers were everywhere. The port of Montreal was second in size in North America only to the port of New York City.

The boys were met in Montreal by Alfred Owen, who was Barnardo's chief representative in Canada. It was his responsibility to house the lads temporarily until they could be sent to their permanent homes. Two days later Bill was on his way west to the Village of Iroquois, Ontario. His sponsors there, the people with whom he would live and for whom he would work, were Mr. and Mrs. Levius Serviss.

Levius Serviss was born in eastern Canada in 1828. He met and married his wife, known only as "Aunty" to our family, in 1849. The two were adventurous souls and loved traveling together. They made four trips to California during the gold rush. On the first trip, they sailed from Montreal around Cape Horn at the southern tip of South America, the entire voyage taking five months and twenty-three days. The next time they portaged overland across the Isthmus of Panama (the canal was not completed until 1914). On the third trip, they took the Santa Fe Trail. And on the fourth, they crossed the continent by rail and on the Oregon Trail in areas that yet had no rail service.

Aunty panned for gold in the California Sierra Nevada Mountains, finding a good bit, while Levius dug. They lived in tents, cooked over an open fire, and hunted their food. Aunty was one of the few women participating in this adventurous life; on more than one occasion, Levius found himself fighting to preserve her honor.

It was a rough place, and they thrived on the survival aspects of their life there. They never made a fortune but had a wonderful time on each trip, enjoying the journey as much as the prospecting experience. Uncle Levius had solid-gold cuff links made for himself and earrings for Aunty. My brother has these lovely heirlooms today.

The Servisses came back to Iroquois (near Cardinal), Ontario, to settle in 1864, purchased a farm with their gold and began to operate a small dairy business. The farm consisted of about one hundred acres, a large home, an expansive barn, and several smaller sheds. The Servisses handled the entire enterprise successfully themselves for many years.

Levius and Aunty were childless, and in 1886, when Levius was fifty-eight years old, they decided they could use some help. The farm did not produce enough to support an employee, so when Alfred Owen of Barnardo's put up posters in and around Cardinal indicating that the home was trying to place destitute British children in indentured servitude in Canada, they decided to consider this new option.

They were interviewed by Mr. Owen and deemed fit as foster parents. In May 1886, they learned that they would be assigned a ten-year-old boy named William John Thomas Curnick. They were given a copy of Bill's history as it has been presented here and agreed that he would be a good fit for their needs. Bill arrived in Iroquois on June 27.

This was the part of the journey that Bill had been dreading most. He was apprehensive about meeting his new family, so much so that he had no appetite for several days.

Bill was shocked at his first meeting with "Aunty" and "Uncle," as the Servisses suggested he call them. They were much older than his mother—more the age of his grandparents.

Bill had always lived in a large city. To say that Iroquois and the Servisses' farm were isolated is an understatement. All of it was frightening to him. He never missed his mother and brother and sisters more than those first few days in Canada.

The Servisses were sensitive to Bill's situation, recognizing that at age ten he must be filled with insecurities about his new life. They worked hard to make the transition as comfortable as possible for him. They had prepared a bedroom especially for him in their large farm home.

But having a room of his own was even more stressful for Bill. He had always shared a room with his parents or with one or more of his siblings—to say nothing about bunking with several other boys in the dormitory at Barnardo's. At night, Bill found himself alone in the dark for the first time in his life. The windows were open to the warm summer evenings. He could hear all kinds of strange sounds outside. Crickets chirped, cicadas sang loudly to one another, dogs barked, cows and horses made sounds in the dark with which he was unfamiliar. And perhaps most frightening of all, there were no reassuring city noises. The only constant in his surroundings was his pine trunk. His appetite faded even more.

But the Servisses seemed like caring people. They made no immediate demands of him, letting him follow Uncle around the farm as he performed his daily chores. Aunty was a wonderful cook but found it a challenge preparing dishes that Bill would eat. She did not know whether he was homesick or just unaccustomed to the fresh fish, chicken, turkey, lamb, and calf they enjoyed daily.

Aunty's main job was to prepare plentiful meals for Uncle Levius, whose appetite was voracious because of the strenuous work he performed on a daily basis. Her kitchen smelled wonderful and was warm and steamy almost all the time. In spite of this, Bill did not eat as much as she and Uncle thought the growing youngster needed. They worried as he became leaner and leaner.

"Do you not like the food, Bill?" Aunty tried to engage the boy in conversation regarding her concern.

"It's fine, Aunty, thank you," Bill replied politely.

"Then why don't you eat more, ahe? You're so tall and so slender! I'm worried about you!" she continued voicing her concern.

"I'm just not very hungry," the boy responded shyly.

"I know you must miss your family terribly, Bill. We're sorry you had to come so far from home. We want you to be happy here. Can you tell us how we can help you adjust?" Aunty tried to convey her caring nature to her young charge.

"I'll be all right, ma'am." Bill wasn't offering much for her to go on.

"Well, you just take your time, ahe? Uncle doesn't expect you to take on too much work till you learn some of the routine of farming. It's wonderful outdoor work, Bill. I think you'll like it when you understand it." She gave up for a time.

Bill did not adjust quickly. He missed his family terribly. He became weak and pale from lack of appetite.

On August 20, Alfred Owen from Barnardo's came to visit Bill and the Servises. At that meeting, Uncle Levius gave a poor account of Bill.

"He's so weak and frail as ta be o' na use ta me on da farm. He is, ho'ever, well manne'ed and na trouble ta have aroun'," Levius stated.

"Well, do you wish me to try to find you another youngster?" asked Owen.

"Na, no' ye'. Le's give 'im anoder trial and see if'n 'e begins ta eat be'er and grow stron'er," responded Levius.

For his part, Mr. Owen satisfied himself that Bill was in a splendid farm home with a kind, rich (relatively speaking) older couple who would do well by him if he remained there. He reported that Levius was disappointed with Bill's lack of energy for the little work he was requested to do. He also noted that, considering the boy's age, nothing was seriously amiss.

By September 1886, Uncle Levius decided it was time for Bill to learn to feed and milk the small herd of cows. The Servisses milked twice a day, at about 4:00 AM and 4:00 PM. There was no electricity on the farm, and Bill was by now accustomed to rising early with Uncle and Aunty and retiring early as well.

Uncle Levius built a milking stool especially sized for Bill. He placed the stool next to his calmest animal and sat Bill down for his first lesson.

"Lean yar head on da cow's side so's ya kin see wha' ya're doin', ahe?" He instructed. "Reach in wid bot' hands an' grab a teat wid each, be'ween yar t'umb and forefin'er knuckle. Den squeeze and pull down at da same time, ahe?"

Bill tried without success.

"It ta'es a while ta get da hang o' it," chuckled Uncle. "Jus' keep prac'icin', an' ya'll mas'er it."

"My hands are already tired, Uncle!" complained Bill after a few minutes.

"Ya, 'tis tirin', ahe? It'll be a grea' way fer ya ta begin ta buil' some strengt'." Levius smiled. "I'll move ta ole Meena here, while ya continua ta work on Rut'ie."

Bill tired quickly.

"Rest when ya're tired, and den try ag'in," instructed Uncle. "While ya're restin', wa'ch how I do i', ahe?"

By the third day, Bill was beginning to get the knack of milking. He thought it very hard work and did not imagine that he could possibly milk the entire herd (about twenty cows), as Uncle Levius did twice every day.

Feeding was also a critical part of the operation. Levius kept the herd well stocked with silage and haylage. He also kept a supply of wheat and oats mixed into a higher-protein snack for the ever hungry cows. He and Bill pitched hay and corn to the animals twice each day and gave them their protein snack once a day.

Then there was manure duty. Every other day Uncle Levius drove the manure wagon into the barn, pulled by a draft horse named Hiawatha, also harnessed for plowing in the spring. He showed Bill how to shovel the manure into the wagon from the collection trough behind where the cows stood to munch their food. Then they drove together to spread it on the fields where hay and corn feed were grown during the warm months. More hard work that Bill found taxing.

Every few days Levius would add a new experience to Bill's growing repertoire of farm tasks. His goal was not to get much work out of him, but rather to give him an overview of what it took to operate a dairy production facility. Because it was fall, no plowing or planting experience would occur until spring.

In the mornings after milking, Uncle collected the milk in a large vat, and Hiawatha and a second horse, '49er, hauled it into the pasteurization plant in Cardinal. Here he sold the milk to a processor, which, after pasteurizing it, delivered it to residents of the area and sold it to the local grocery outlets.

Between milking, removing manure, feeding the farm animals, and delivering milk to the processing plant, Bill decided that farming was at the same time fascinating and hard work. There did not seem to be enough hours in the day to accomplish it all. Aunty frequently drove the milk into Cardinal and fed the animals so that Uncle would have time to milk, haul manure, and repair the equipment that seemed to require his constant attention.

By the beginning of winter, Bill was starting to help out effectively with the daily chores. He was not a strong boy, and his endurance was not good, but he began to get the knack of things. To his benefit, Uncle Levius was patient with him.

One of the requirements of Barnardo's was that the children they placed write to them periodically to report their progress. On November 29, 1886, Bill wrote to Dr. Barnardo explaining that he had been in his new home in Canada now for almost five months. He indicated that Aunty and Uncle Serviss were very nice people and that they took good care of him. He advised that he had started school for the winter and was meeting some other children his age. He told Barnardo that he was

happy in his new circumstances and thanked him for making the experience possible.

Dr. Barnardo generally wrote back when he received such letters. He was a caring man who tried to keep up with all of the children placed by the home.

5

Radia and Habeeb's Heritage

TWO DAYS AFTER THE RAID on the Ottoman Turks, Sef-Sef's battered body was dumped not in front of his own home in Madaba, but rather in front of the house of Khouri Eassa's daughter, Radia, and her husband, Habeeb, in Nazareth. Khouri Eassa was quick to point out to his daughter that her being the scion of a priest was all that kept her husband from suffering a similar fate.

For his part, Habeeb was in a state of shock and disbelief. Not only did it never occur to him that he and his friend would be identified or caught, but it didn't seem possible that even the ruthless Colonel Jemal could cause the death of Habeeb's friend. He was filled with grief, guilt, anger, and frustration.

Radia knew her husband well. She was concerned that he would lash out in an even more dangerous way in an attempt to avenge Sef-Sef's death. She worried that he would put himself at greater risk than ever.

She knew that she and Habeeb and their children were fortunate to be part of the family of an Orthodox priest, which gave them sway in the community and some influence with the Turks. She frequently marveled that her ancestors had evolved from a band of highway thieves into the leadership of St. Gabriel's.

The founder of Radia and Habeeb's tribe in Nazareth was Khleif ibn Abdullah al Qalzi (*ibn* means "son of," and *al* means "from"). In the late seventeenth century, Abdullah had lived in Qalzi, a city in what is now Yemen. He was employed as chief aide and treasurer to the Ottoman *wali* or governor of Qalzi. Abdullah was known for his accurate bookkeeping and beautiful handwriting.

Yemen, the Khouri and Rizk families' place of origin, is in the southern portion of the Arabian Peninsula, bounded on the south by the Gulf of

Aden (part of the Indian Ocean), on the west by the Red Sea, on the north by vast sparsely populated barren desert (Saudi Arabia), and on the east by Oman.

Low country parallels the southern sea coast from east to west. Inland are arid mountains. Water for drinking and agriculture comes from occasional torrential rain, mountain snow melt, and heavy morning dew— all of which are captured in reservoirs built as long ago as five thousand years.

The Yemenis were the great transporters of goods. Yemeni pirates (a centuries-old enterprise among Arabs) controlled the narrow southern entrance to the Red Sea, preventing ships of eastern Asia from sailing up to the Mediterranean. The Yemenis held a monopoly on moving shipments from India and China on the east to Egypt, Greece, and Europe on the west.

Because the climate in the eastern Mediterranean area was much different than in India and China, the products were also quite different. Indian and Chinese merchants could ship goods west over the Indian Ocean to the Persian Gulf or Red Sea. Travel by ship up the Red Sea was dangerous owing to the existence of coral reefs and pirates, so ships tended to land in Yemen at the southern tip of the Arabian Peninsula, unload their cargo, and sell it to the Yemenis.

The Yemenis then carried the goods by caravan north up the peninsula along the east bank of the Red Sea. When they returned south, they brought products of the Byzantine and Persian empires for trade and shipment to China and India.

The *wali* for whom Radia and Habeeb's ancestor, Abdullah, worked was a typical Ottoman occupier—he cared little about the quality of life of those he subjugated. He and Abdullah worked closely, balancing the books for and managing the occupying government.

The *wali* trusted Abdullah's judgment on the business of governing the local Arabs, and he considered him and his family friends. For Abdullah's part, he knew which side his bread was buttered on. He valued his place of influence with the *wali*, his lifestyle, and the security enjoyed by his family, but he was also mindful of the subservient role he played in the scheme of things.

It so happened that both men's wives were pregnant at the same time. Abdullah's wife was very beautiful, which was not lost on the *wali*. So one day, intending to bestow a great honor, the *wali* said to Abdullah, "Abdullah, let us agree that if our children are of the opposite sex, they will eventually marry!"

Arranged marriages have long been the norm in the Middle East. Abdullah knew that to resist such an arrangement would be to incur the wrath of an offended *wali*. He reluctantly agreed, hoping that he and his wife would have a son.

He wished this because the Turks were Muslims, and their men took many wives in the course of their lives. Abdullah, a Christian, did not want such a life for a daughter of his. If, however, he had a son, the *wali*'s daughter would become part of Abdullah's Christian family.

To his dismay, Abdullah's wife gave birth to a beautiful daughter, and the *wali*'s wife gave birth to a son. Abdullah decided to renege on the arrangement, and so to avoid the *wali*'s vengeance he gathered his family in the middle of the night and secretly fled the region.

Abdullah and his family traveled north through the Arabian Peninsula in order to avoid being discovered. They journeyed a thousand miles over the years before settling in what is now the northeastern portion of Israel.

Abdullah died soon thereafter, leaving four sons in addition to his daughter. They were, from oldest to youngest, Khleif, Nimer, Mohareb, and Farah. Nimer's descendants live in Hosson, Jordan, today. They constitute the largest Christian tribe in northern Jordan.

Mohareb migrated to the Jordan River valley looking for a livelihood among the Bedouin Muslim tribes of that area. He eventually fell in love with one of their young women, converted to Islam, and married her. His descendants make up the Shamikh Bedouin tribe of Jordan. They know that their tribe was founded by a Christian, Nimer's brother, so Mohareb and Nimer's tribes get together whenever there are elections in Jordan and send two of their members to Parliament—one Muslim and one Christian. Yes, they *still* cooperate and thrive together!

The eldest and youngest sons, Khleif and Farah, immigrated to Shajara between Tiberias and Nazareth. Shajara was strategically located at the intersection of roads going east and west between Tiberias and Naza-reth as well as north and south between Mount Tabor and the Valley of Battouf. Khleif and Farah and their respective families settled at this junc-tion in their Bedouin tents and began to earn their livelihood by raiding passing caravans. Farah eventually founded the Farah Clan, one of the leading families in the Middle East. They are involved in banking and finance.

Overland caravans traveled from Yemen north up the Arabian Penin-sula through Mecca and Medina to Jerusalem, Damascus, and Baghdad in the Levant. One such route was still active through Shajara during the early part of the eighteenth century. Here Khleif collected a "tax" to assure caravans safe passage through the territory.

Most caravans were reluctant to part with a portion of their valuable wares in exchange for something they thought was their right. The trad-ers found out soon, though, that if they didn't pay the tax, Khleif and his family would quickly raid their caravans, loot everything they had, and run them out of the territory. Khleif became wealthy and notorious.

Some caravan operators accepted the threat of raids as part of the cost of doing business. Food and water along the way were essential to the suc-cess of their enterprises, so they planned accordingly. A portion of their wares was set aside for payment in exchange for these crucial commodi-ties plus safe passage.

Most, however, were reluctant to part with their hard-earned goods. They appealed to the Ottomans for protection. After all, they thought, if the Turks were indeed in control of the area, they should police it.

Khleif and his family had such a negative impact on commerce that the occupying Ottoman authorities did end up sending an armed force to intervene in their activities. They arrested Khleif in Shajara and moved the family to Nazareth, where it was suggested that they find honest work.

But the Turks, in an unusually subtle move designed to solidify their power, also indicated to Khleif, who they knew to be a Christian, that there was in Nazareth the need for an Eastern Orthodox Christian church. He was told that he and his family would be safe and unmolested if he would build an Orthodox church and become its priest. They even had a site for him to build it on. It may seem unusual for the Muslim Ottomans to promote a Christian church, but it demonstrates their shrewd approach to quelling local unrest.

It was an offer Khleif could not refuse. He became Khouri (Priest) Khleif and began to build his church in Nazareth in 1741.

Muslims, Christians, and Jews had for centuries wrestled with confrontation and accommodation as they strove to coexist in Nazareth, a city that dates from about 2200 BCE. For several centuries after the birth and teachings of Christ, Nazareth was a Judeo-Christian community.

The Muslim Ottoman Turks invaded Palestine and took control of Nazareth in 1517. They levied heavy taxes on produce—25 percent on wheat, barley, cotton, sesame, sorghum, beans, olives, goats, bees—and on *brides.*

Nazareth had a population of about three thousand at the time that Khouri Khleif began to build his church. Because it was away from the sea, not on trade routes, and had little water, the town was small. Nazareth was considered a Syrian town. About 75 percent of Nazarenes were Christian.

The basilica of the Annunciation Christian Orthodox Church in Nazareth catered to wealthier parishioners. St. Gabriel's served the common folk. Construction funds were scarce. Building materials in the region were not plentiful, and the labor was difficult and dangerous. It took Khouri Khleif fifteen years to complete his church.

The Church of St. Gabriel, completed by Khouri Khleif in 1756, still stands on the site of three predecessors. It was built over Mary's Well on the north side of Nazareth. Khleif believed the proximity to the well would provide revenue to the church and make it easier for church-goers to obtain their daily drinking water and attend liturgy at the same time. Water bubbled and gurgled in the well in the grotto beneath the church. St. Gabriel's was constructed to accommodate approximately fifty people.

A portion of the church included the walls and foundations of the first three churches built on the site, dating back to the time of Christ. Eastern Orthodox Christians believe that the site of the Church of St. Gabriel is the place where the angel Gabriel appeared before Mary and announced to her that she would conceive and bear God's son, Jesus. Upon his death, Khouri Khleif was buried in the grotto under the church he built.

Khleif's eldest son, Eassa, succeeded his father as *khouri* of St. Gabriel's. He was known as "Shammas Eassa." Khouri Khleif had another son named Rizk. Rizk's son was Ibrahim, who fathered Mansour, whose son Daoud was Habeeb's father. These ancestors and their place of origin are clearly identified in my grandfather Habeeb's name: Habeeb ibn Daoud el Rizk el Khleifi al Nasirah.

Shammas Eassa thought that he would rather remain a highwayman than become a priest. He longed for his lost sense of freedom, wealth, and independence. Family obligation and parental expectation, however, carried the day, and Eassa's destiny was sealed. He served a distinguished and lengthy leadership role at St. Gabriel's. By the time he passed the mantle of priesthood to *his* eldest son, Moussa, it was clearly understood that the eldest son in the family would always serve as *khouri* of St. Gabriel's.

Moussa was a fine horseman, as indeed were all the Khouri and Rizk men. He enjoyed raising horses and racing them against those of his colleagues. Even though the family ceased to be as mobile and as dependent on the horse for their livelihood as they had been when they were highwaymen, their fascination with and love for these beautiful and noble creatures continued to be passed from generation to generation.

Moussa's son Yacoub followed him as *khouri* of St. Gabriel's. Yacoub was studious and learned. He made education a priority for the church and in particular for his family. He made sure that his children received the best education available. From that time on, education played a major role in the preparation for life of the Khouri family. And the title *khouri,* meaning "priest," henceforth became the family name for my grandmother Radia's side of the family.

Yacoub's eldest son, Saleh, succeeded him. Saleh built the house in which Radia and Habeeb lived and that is still occupied by Khleif's descendents. Saleh was also a fine horseman. One day while on an extended ride in the desert quite far from Nazareth—all the Khouri and Rizk males loved their ride-abouts—he was bitten on the heal by a poisonous viper. Like his contemporaries, Saleh wore sandals.

Desert wanderers had to be prepared for anything, and because they frequently traveled alone for days at a time, they were self-reliant. Saleh was no exception.

With no one around for miles, he whipped out his hunting knife, sliced off the fleshy portion of his heel where the bite had occurred so the poison would flow out rather than to his heart, and limped about gathering anything that would burn. He quickly built a small fire from the sparse desert brush and heated his knife until it glowed red in the gathering dusk. When the knife was hot enough, Saleh slapped it onto his heel to cauterize the wound.

He then mounted up and rode back toward Nazareth. Like contemporary Arabs, the Khouris and Rizks were nothing if not independent and resourceful.

Saleh's son Eassa was the father of Radia and her brother, Saleh. Radia's brother was the father of George Khouri, who retired in the 1970s from a civil service position with the United Nations. George's son Rami Khouri is an internationally recognized spokesperson for reason, cooperation, progress, democratic interdependency, rule of law, and human dignity for Arab nations and their citizens. He holds bachelor's and master's degrees from Syracuse University, is executive director of the Issam Fares Institute of Public Policy and International Affairs at American University of Beirut, and serves as editor at large of the *Beirut Daily Star.* His syndicated column appears regularly.

Radia's brother, Saleh, refused to accept the priesthood of St. Gabriel's, thus ending the Khouri family dynasty there. He became a businessman, much to his father Eassa's disappointment.

Khouri and Rizk family relations live in Nazareth today. They believe that life under the Israelis' thumb is not much different than life under the Ottoman Turks' thumb.

6

Life on the St. Lawrence River

IF YOU ARE GOING TO LIVE along the St. Lawrence River, you had better like winter. The cold, bitter wind blitzes from the west across the Great Lakes like a giant razor blade, picking up speed and moisture as it goes. When this cloudy gray freight train gets east of the lakes, it dumps upward of two hundred inches of snow per year. The snow blows into huge drifts, covering whole sides of buildings. Blizzards are occasionally so bad that schools close, and no one ventures far from home.

The one-room schoolhouse in Cardinal, Ontario, attended by Bill Curnick in 1886–87 combined all grades. A large pot-belly stove heated the room. The parent/sponsor who lived closest to the school came in and built a roaring fire early every morning. By the time the school day commenced, the space was a toasty fifty-five degrees or so. The older boys in the class kept the fire stoked during the day.

Bill had learned to read, write, and calculate in Great Britain. Now he began to learn history, grammar, mathematics, and civics. He had never liked school very much but decided that it was a significant improvement over working outdoors on the farm in the winter.

He still helped with the milking before going to school and again after classes in the afternoon. The barn was almost as warm as his schoolhouse. The body heat given off by the cows and horses was enough to keep the temperature above fifty. And it smelled *wonderful* there. Bill found he did not mind his chores nearly as much when school broke up the day.

Between school and the farm, Bill was beginning to learn some useful skills. He loved the carpentry he had begun to learn at Barnardo's and was quite good at it. His mathematics from school was a big help to him here. Uncle was impressed at how quickly Bill learned the basics of good carpentry. The boy seemed a natural at it. He frequently helped Levius

47

repair portions of the barn. They built and maintained barn stalls, fences, ladders, and the like.

Bill was also learning how to maintain and repair farm machinery. His education was a good combination of the practical and the traditional.

He had never seen so much snow. Unlike the snow of a London winter, though, which quickly turned to muddy slush under foot, generally rendering the streets a soggy, cold, blackish gray ooze, the snow along the St. Lawrence River around rural Iroquois and Cardinal remained pristine and white all winter.

The river froze early in the winter season, and the sharp winds out of the west blew the snow clear of the icy surface, which was smooth and glassy. Canadian children went skating every day after school. It was not long before Bill had talked the good-hearted Levius into allowing him to try to skate for a bit before coming home in the afternoon.

Bill had no skates, so Uncle fabricated a pair for him out of a couple of old scythe blades. Ground sharp and with perpendicular shoe plates forged on, these skates strapped onto his boots. It took Bill a couple of weeks to get the hang of ice skating, but he was soon rocketing around with the other children.

Levius was pleased to see Bill finding some exercise aside from farmwork. He knew it was essential to the boy's well-being. He still worried about Bill's health, though. Bill was growing so fast that he never seemed to put any meat on his bones, and he was not very strong.

A horse-drawn sleigh provided transportation in the winter. Levius hooked up Hiawatha and '49er almost every day for the trip into Cardinal with milk. Bill, who loved these rides in the snow, learned how to place the traces on the large animals and held the reins during the journey. It was his morning ride to school. He walked the four miles home each day.

On March 20, 1887, Levius wrote (with the help of Aunty's hand) to Barnardo's Alfred Owen in Montreal. He indicated that he was writing to let Mr. Owen know how Bill Curnick was progressing with them. He advised Owen that Bill was a fine youngster, but so weak still as to be of only a small use to them on the farm. Nonetheless, Levius stated that he and Aunty had decided to continue to care for him through the upcoming growing season. If his health improved, Levius wrote, they would keep him permanently.

As much as Bill tried to work and play through the winter, he was susceptible to chronic colds and frequent bronchitis. These maladies often kept him home from school and away from his chores on the farm. The Servisses nevertheless found him to be good-natured, polite, and respectful. He tried to do whatever they asked of him, willingly attended school, and was a regular at church with them. They were developing a strong affection for the youngster.

The rich black soil of the St. Lawrence River floodplain was wet and cold and mucky in May 1887 when planting season approached. There was still a chill in the air and frost in the mornings. Bill and his classmates finished up the school year and prepared to head to the fields. He was at this point milking about five cows to Levius's fifteen.

"Time fer ya ta learn ta drive da plow team, Bill," challenged Uncle one morning.

"Yes, sir." Bill was apprehensive about his ability to handle Hiawatha and '49er with the plow.

"I'm gonna star' ya wit' jus' one hoss, ahe? Hiawat'a is more docile-like and easier ta han'le. When ya're comfor'able wid him, we'll add '49er," Levius explained.

They placed the heavy plow, which Levius had repaired and sharpened over the winter, into a hay wagon. Hiawatha pulled them out into the field. Levius showed Bill how to man-handle the plow implements without injury. They then disconnected Hiawatha from the wagon, parking it at the edge of the field.

Uncle Levius connected Hiawatha to the cumbersome plow, carefully showing Bill each step. When he finished, he unhitched the horse from the plow and asked Bill to hitch him back up.

Bill followed what he had seen Levius do. It took him twice as long as it did Uncle, but in the end he stepped back, pleased with his effort.

"Goo' job, Bill! It'll git easier each time ya do 't. Now lemme show ya how ta han'le da plow, ahe?"

Levius stepped behind Hiawatha and the plow, tipping the unwieldy implement into position so it would overturn a furrow of earth as it was pulled. When he was ready, he slapped Hiawatha's rump with the reins, clucking to him as he did so and off they slowly went.

Bill could see that even someone as strong as Levius was struggling to keep the plow on course as Hiawatha leaned heavily into his traces. He walked alongside. After going the length of the field, Uncle turned Hiawatha around and exclaimed, "Yar turn!"

Bill stepped in front of him and grabbed the two plow handles, which were more than shoulder high on him. Levius placed his hands atop Bill's and walked after him. Hiawatha started off again. Each time the plow struck a rock or heavy wet spot in the soil, it lurched to the side, pulling Bill off balance.

"This is hard!" he yelped. "How do I keep it straight?"

"It's like everyt'in' else wort' learnin', Bill. It'll become secon' nature ta ya by da en' o' plantin' season." His adoptive uncle was reassuring.

It took the better part of May just to prepare the fields for planting. Then in June came the seeding operation, which Uncle did by hand. They walked the freshly turned rows of soil, dropping hay, corn, alfalfa, and grain seeds in different fields as they went. Levius showed Bill just how much seed to apply.

"This is much more fun than plowing!" Bill allowed.

"Wait till ya see da crop comin' up. Dat's wha's *really* excitin' and fun!" laughed Levius.

It took a full week to get everything into the ground.

"Now we kin repair da plowin' machinery we damaged this spring, ahe?" chuckled Uncle.

"I'd like to learn how to fix the machinery, Uncle! That really sounds like fun," Bill replied excitedly.

So they used their nonmilking, nonfeeding, non-manure-collecting time to work on the various pieces of equipment. Meanwhile, little sprouts of plants began to show themselves. Bill thought Levius was right; it was pretty exciting to watch the fruits of their labor materialize as he completed his first year in Canada.

Between milking, feeding, collecting manure, plowing, planting, tending, harvesting, and storing silage for the winter, there was not much free time to enjoy the beauty of the St. Lawrence River and its surroundings.

But Uncle Levius, Aunty, and Bill managed a picnic at the river almost every warm Sunday after church. On these outings, Uncle brought his fishing gear and began to teach Bill the delights of catching perch, trout, bass, and—the most fun and best eating of all—great northern pike. They would cast from the shore, wade, or rent a skiff.

The river was about a mile wide where they lived. It was not terribly deep and was scattered with hundreds of small islands and with frequent and dangerous rapids. Levius was a master at shooting the rapids in a skiff. It looked to Bill that they would capsize at any moment, but Uncle always seemed to know how to direct the skiff so that it glided (very quickly sometimes) through the most treacherous portions of the river. It was an exhilarating experience.

Levius used lures as well as live bait to attract his prey. They never failed to catch enough for dinner, sometimes with great variety. Uncle taught Bill how to clean and prepare their catch. Aunty would then sauté, broil, or fry them for a delicious meal. Bill loved the fishing and boating experience. He longed to learn to handle a boat on the river as well as Levius.

Native Canadians also lived along the northern shore of the St. Lawrence. Some of the native children went to Bill's school. During the summer months when the Servisses and Bill visited the river, he watched them playing a game that he had never seen before on the wide flat floodplain.

Two teams gathered on a field with a goal at each end. Each player carried a stick with a basketlike pouch at the end. The idea was to use this basket to throw and catch a small, hard ball, keeping it away from your opponents as you tried to move it down the field and finally into the opponent's goal. There were several players on each team, and it seemed as if they ran all over the field trying to catch and evade one another. Bill thought that it looked like tremendous fun. He watched longingly from the sidelines.

Then one day while watching, he was invited to participate. Thus in the late spring of 1887 began a *long* experience on the playing field for the developing athlete.

The game with which Bill was so fascinated was lacrosse ("the stick" in French, as it was named by the settling Europeans in the seventeenth century), which was invented by Native Canadians. A player used the netted stick to pick the ball up off the ground, throw and catch the ball, and fling it into the opponent's goal. The natives frequently used the game to settle disputes in a relatively peaceful manner. As they played it, it was a rough sport.

Native Canadians and Native Americans from New York refer to lacrosse as "the Creator's Game." When employed to settle disputes, lacrosse might be played by as many as one thousand players on a side and on a field from one to fifteen miles in length. Games sometimes lasted for days. Balls were originally made of wood, deerskin, baked clay, or stone.

Bill played as often as his farm chores would permit. Levius thought his interest in lacrosse was good for him.

In August, when the crops in the fields were ready for harvest, Uncle began teaching Bill how to hitch the team to the various mowing and harvesting implements. Hiawatha or '49er would pull the implement through the fields, cutting the crop. Uncle or Bill followed, pitching the cuttings into a trailing wagon, pulled by the other horse. It was hard work, and Bill still wore out quickly.

It was hard for Bill to believe that Uncle, as old as he was, could work as hard and as long as he did. It took Bill a long time to begin to learn the techniques required to minimize the effort needed to stay at the task for long periods without becoming exhausted. Levius allowed the boy to work at his own pace, hoping that one day he would grow strong enough to handle the job.

Once the crops were harvested, they were transported to a silo next to the barn, where they were elevated to the top of the growing pile of silage stored for feed for the herd over the winter months. By the end of October, the fields were clear, and the silo was full. It was time for Bill to start back to school for the long northern winter of 1887–88.

The St. Lawrence River was usually frozen solid well before Christmas. Where there were no rapids, it froze at least a foot thick. The river, of course, continued to flow east underneath the ice.

The Iroquois played an interesting game on the ice that resembled lacrosse. In this case, they adopted the Dutch settlers' ice skates, and instead of trying to toss a ball from a net on the end of a stick, they hit a flat disc on the ice with a stick. A goal at each end of the ice provided the needed challenge to the offensive and defensive players.

The Micmac of Nova Scotia invented ice hockey in the early nineteenth century. The word *hockey* derives from the French *hoquet* (shepherd's stick). As with lacrosse, the native form of this game, their winter lacrosse, was extremely rough.

Bill, who had learned to skate the previous winter, thought the game just as exciting as its mild-weather counterpart. He joined some of his Iroquois schoolmates in this exhausting and exhilarating exercise. It wasn't easy, but he kept at it and slowly began to improve. It sure beat working on the farm!

Levius still milked the most cantankerous cows himself, leaving the more mild-mannered animals to Bill. One morning when he and Bill were milking, Witchcraft, his most obstreperous cow, stomped heavily on his right foot. Levius always thought afterward that she had done so intentionally. He knew immediately that she had crushed his little toe.

When the milking was finished, and he and Bill returned to the house for breakfast, Levius pulled off his boot to examine the damage. The toe was already badly discolored and swollen. Aunty prepared a poultice and wrapped it tightly around his foot for him. Levius was able to continue with his chores after the morning meal.

The next day his toe was even more discolored and swollen. The poultice and wrap helped, but it was very sore. Levius had no intention of letting this minor perturbation interrupt his routine. Out he went as usual.

By the end of the week, the toe hurt so badly that Levius could hardly walk. It was terribly red and warm to the touch. Aunty was quite sure that infection was setting in.

"I think you'd better consider a visit to the doctor over in Cardinal, ahe?" she urged.

"I ain't goin' ta na doc'or!" Levius stated emphatically. "I kin live wid 't!"

But the wound continued to worsen. By the end of the second week, red streaks were beginning to shoot up Levius's foot.

"Uncle, that looks really mean!" exclaimed Bill after watching Aunty treat the injury.

"Aye, it does!" agreed Aunty.

"Rubbish!" was Levius's response. But he, too, recognized that the red streaks were a danger sign.

Out he went to feed the animals, while Bill remained to help Aunty for a few minutes. In a little bit, Uncle was back, limping worse than ever.

"Wrap this again, Aunty, ahe?" he asked, pulling off his boot.

Aunty and Bill gasped!

"Where's your toe, Uncle?" Bill cried.

"Got rid o' dat mean li'l bugger!" he shot back with a strained smile.

"Oh, Levius! You're the most stubborn man *ever!*" Aunty exclaimed as she looked at the new wound with horror. At the same time, she was struck with wonder at the tough old flint she had married so long ago.

"How did you manage this?"

"Jus' pu' ma foot up on a tree stump and took ma sharpest wood chisel ta 't!" winced Levius. "Came clean off wid one blow, ahe!"

Bill was weak at the thought, but he looked at Uncle with renewed respect. How had he possibly been able to do that himself?

"You should have asked one of us to do it for you!" admonished Aunty.

"Figured it woul'n't be no easier fer you. An' I wannad ta be *cer'un;* it only too' one stroke! I's worried ya migh' not hit da chisel hard enough!" Levius chuckled. "Wrap 'er up and leave me on ma way, ahe?"

Aunty had to smile to herself. She had hitched her wagon to one heck of an adventuresome man all those years ago. Never a dull moment! She also thought this was a good experience for young Bill. Might toughen him a bit, she imagined.

Uncle's foot healed well after the trauma he had inflicted upon it. He never went to the doctor and walked with no limp thereafter. As for Bill, he learned that when the chips were down, Uncle was one tough character. He wondered if he would ever be able to live up to Levius's example. He would unfortunately learn that he could!

In March 1888, one of Dr. Barnardo's representatives, a Captain Annesly, visited Bill at the Servisses' farm. He reported that Bill was in a fine situation and receiving great care. Bill was attending school in the winter, church on a regular basis, and Sunday school. He also suggested, though, that Bill was delicate and unfit for farmwork.

Bill was almost twelve years old and approaching six feet tall. No wonder it seemed to the captain that he was so slender as to be delicate. He was growing so fast that all his weight gain went to his vertical growth, not to filling out his frame.

The spring found Bill once again helping Uncle plant the crops. He was able to make more of a contribution than in the previous year. He also found time occasionally to play lacrosse, of which he could not get enough.

Aunty and Uncle thought it good that Bill seemed to love the game. They believed that he would make more friends through this experience, that he would build his physical endurance, and that his self-confidence would benefit. Nothing like success on the athletic field for enhancing self-esteem, thought Levius.

The summer of 1888 was spent plowing, planting, weeding, harvesting, and storing the annual crops, in addition to the usual milking and tending of cows. Bill found that he enjoyed the farming cycle. There was a sense of accomplishment and completion every six months—creation of food stores for the winter taking place from May through October and utilization of these stores during the school months of November through April. And then there was the ever-steady production and sale of milk.

Bill wrote his mother almost every week, and she responded religiously. This flow of correspondence led to feelings of connectedness for both of them. Sarah was reassured that Bill was well cared for and growing and thriving in his new home, and Bill was able to keep up with his mother, brother, and sisters.

Bill also wrote occasionally to Dr. Barnardo. Correspondence with Barnardo was encouraged as a means of providing candid feedback about one's circumstances. For his part, Barnardo returned the kindness whenever he received correspondence from his boys and girls.

In May 1888, Bill received a Bronze Medal from Barnardo's in recognition of his hard work at the Servisses, his attendance at school in the winter, his regular church experience, and the Servisses' satisfaction with him. He was thrilled with this acknowledgment of his accomplishments and immediately wrote to tell his mother about the award. He also wrote a "thank you" note to Dr. Barnardo.

During the summer of 1888, Uncle bought a St. Lawrence skiff for Bill's twelfth birthday. Bill's excitement at this gift was a pleasure for Aunty and Uncle to behold.

He immediately contacted some of his Iroquois friends, and they all went to the river to try out Bill's new boat. Uncle insisted that Bill wear a life jacket when on the water because he was not yet a strong swimmer.

Bill began to learn to shoot the St. Lawrence rapids in his skiff. He thought this challenge enormously exciting and wanted to become as good at it as his native comrades. They were also superior swimmers.

The Iroquois had a rope tied to a stout tree branch overhanging the river. They grabbed the rope in the water, climbed up the bank while pulling the rope behind them, and then swung out over the river. At the apex of the rope's travel, they let go and plunged into the water.

Bill spent many hours in the long summer evenings polishing his water skills. By the end of the season, he was a competent swimmer and was beginning to get the hang of handling the skiff in the turbulent river.

He also learned how to enjoy the rope swing. It was easy to swing out and let go. The hard part was learning how to swing his legs forward and then kick them out behind him just as he let go, so he would flip over frontward and dive head first as the Iroquois did.

7

America?

DURING THE LATE NINETEENTH and early twentieth centuries, the United States was encouraging immigrants from all over the world to relocate to America. The nation's manufacturing base was expanding exponentially, and it needed a huge workforce. Good jobs that paid well were available.

It took Habeeb weeks to come to grips with the loss of his friend Sef-Sef. He felt an uneasy sense of responsibility. It had been so foolish of the two of them to provoke Colonel Jemal to the extreme.

It all had been a silly game to Sef-Sef and him. They hadn't caused the Turks any serious problems. Why had Jemal so overreacted? Why hadn't Habeeb been more cautious about risking his life and the life of his dear friend?

Habeeb was sad and repentant, on the one hand, and angry, frustrated, and vengeful, on the other. Jemal's violent act haunted him. He could not bring himself to let Sef-Sef's death pass unanswered.

He needed to get back out on the road to sell, but he couldn't muster the energy. He didn't even want to ride his ponies, let alone race them. He had retrieved them and his wares when he attended Josef's funeral in Madaba.

Georges was worried about the business, and Radia was worried about Habeeb's well-being. She was also convinced that he would do something foolish.

In twelve years of marriage, Radia had never asked for her parents' advice regarding an issue concerning Habeeb. She knew that successful relationships depended on working through difficult challenges together. She enjoyed those conversations with Habeeb, who would never admit to anyone that her opinion was so important to him. But this time she needed a sounding board, and she trusted her father to listen empathetically without judging or trying to influence her. She wanted a male perspective. Habeeb just wasn't himself, and she needed him back.

Khouri Eassa was an observant man. Radia and Habeeb had been together long enough for him to understand that Habeeb was deeply troubled by the loss of his friend and that he suffered feelings of guilt. Khouri Eassa was concerned about both his daughter and his son-in-law.

Radia had never fully recovered from the loss of two of her beloved boys, his grandchildren. Under the Turk's iron fist, it was impossible for young families to move ahead economically. As much as Khouri Eassa loved and enjoyed Habeeb, he was concerned about Habeeb's propensity to gamble hard-earned income on his ponies. So when Radia approached her father regarding the current situation, he suggested a most difficult choice for all of them to consider.

"You know, Radia, members of the Rizk family and the Kammars, the Nojaims, the Bahouths, as well as many others have gone to America. They write that things are good there. People are free to think, speak, and live as they please. The economy is strong and there are plenty of jobs. Many have started businesses of their own. And, best of all, there are no Ottomans. Perhaps you should consider such a move," he suggested with trepidation.

Radia could hardly believe her ears. She had also begun to wonder about the possibility of moving to the West as she watched Habeeb struggle with the current chain of events.

"Oh, Father, I *have* been thinking about it, but I fear that Habeeb won't consider it," she exclaimed with a mixture of enthusiasm and anxiety. "I don't know how to approach it with him."

Eassa's heart sank. He knew it was something they should consider, and he also knew that he would never see them again if they traveled halfway around the world to live. He was glad he could be so unselfish with his daughter, but he was sad at the prospect.

"So you haven't talked to Habeeb about this?" he asked, trying to cover his sadness.

"Not yet, and I think that now I must." Her anxiety was palpable.

"How do you think he'll react?" Eassa wondered.

"You know perfectly well how he'll react! He has always loved his life here. He comes and goes as he pleases. He raises, rides, and races his ponies. He loves to travel and to be the center of attention as he moves from place to place," she lamented.

"He always listens to you, Radia. One of the things I love about Habeeb is that he respects you and your opinion so much," soothed her father.

"This will really test our relationship! I need to approach him with care. And he's so moody and upset right now," worried Radia.

"And that is precisely what may help him to be receptive. I think you should discuss this with him soon, before he does something we'll all regret," urged Eassa.

"Will you discuss this with Mother, please?" begged Radia.

"I will tell her I suggested that you and Habeeb consider it. And I think that you should mention it to her soon."

"I will, Father, I just need to pose it to Habeeb first."

And so Radia set about determining her strategy for suggesting that now might be an opportune time for their family to consider immigrating to America. She and Habeeb had mourned the loss of two infant children. Both of them carried the emotional scars of these ordeals, and both had recognized that superior medical knowledge existed in the Western world. They had wondered together if their two deceased children might have survived if they lived somewhere else.

Radia was sick of Habeeb's long treks into the desert to ride and sell and race and bet and sometimes lose his earnings. And as Daoud and N'cola grew older, she knew they would need their father close by to help them develop into responsible men. She would not risk losing him to the Turks.

There were clan, tribe, and even family members living in America. They wrote that good jobs were available and that opportunities existed to establish wholly owned enterprises. The Arab families living there were already accumulating wealth. And, as her father had said, there were no Ottomans in America. Everyone lived free. Wouldn't *that* be novel?

And now Habeeb was in danger. The thought of losing him was frightening enough, but what of the boys in such a situation? She knew they would need paternal guidance more than ever during the next few years. How would she survive financially without him? She would be dependent on her father and mother—something she was unwilling to be.

Then there was her spirit of adventure. She had read much about the Western world at the Russian Orthodox convent school and in the newspapers. How exciting it would be to travel to new lands, she thought, let alone live in them and learn a new language. The prospect of a fresh start in an exciting new place thrilled her. How was she going to kindle the same kind of enthusiasm in Habeeb?

She decided to start by pointing out to him how much he loved to ride about the countryside and to suggest to him that relocating to a place where clan and family already lived would offer opportunity for the ultimate ride-about halfway around the world! She hoped he would see the adventure in such an undertaking and begin to warm to the idea.

Radia and Habeeb lived in a large multifamily home owned by the Rizk family. It was a two-story house built in the shape of a U and surrounding a flagstone courtyard that had a few trees. A number of related families lived in the building.

Radia and Habeeb had a three-room apartment on the second floor. The rooms were large and airy, and an enormous terrace overlooked the courtyard and the street outside. (The house is still inhabited by family members. Bushra Jarjoura, George Khouri's sister and Radia's niece, and her family are the current residents.)

The toilet facilities were out of doors on the terrace at the back of the building. There was a sort of outhouse structure with a bench with a hole in it. The hole dropped to a pit from which waste was occasionally removed.

One day when N'cola was three years old, Radia heard him yelling at the top of his lungs.

"Immi, Immi, Immi!" came the shrill screams.

Radia dashed outside to see what was the matter. At first, she could not find the child. She ran around the back of the veranda toward the source of the noise.

"Immi, Immi!" N'cola continued to scream.

Radia flew into the toilet room. There, hanging by his armpits and elbows was N'cola, tears of fear flowing down his contorted face as he yelled for her.

Radia scooped up her somewhat soiled youngest child and held him close as she took him inside and cleaned him up. For his part, N'cola had a clear image of the occasion for the rest of his life.

Habeeb wasn't interested in a ride-about at the moment, so Radia thought it a good time to raise the possibility of a move. She decided to wait till the boys were in bed in the evening to address the issue with him. She fixed one of his favorite meals: kibbe (ground lamb patties with pine nuts and lentils), *koosa* (stuffed squash), grape leaves stuffed with rice, tab- bouleh, and baklava and *khak* (wonderful date-filled, doughnut-shaped pastries) for dessert. A sip of arak for both before the meal to oil the con- versation, and she thought she was ready.

On the day she selected, she was very tense. She worried as she pre- pared the food and could hardly enjoy the arak and the meal, she was so preoccupied with the pending discussion. After Daoud and N'cola were asleep, she decided the time had come.

"You haven't been on a ride-about for some time, Habeeb," she observed.

"I know. I just haven't felt like getting up and going," he paused.

Habeeb wasn't in touch with his feelings. And when he did think that he knew what his issues were, he was loath to share them, even with (or, perhaps, especially with) his wife. He did not wish to seem weak or uncer- tain in her eyes. He rubbed his mustachioed face and brow.

"I know how much you love and miss Josef," Radia continued. "Do you dread going to Madaba without him there?"

She was attempting to get him to begin to talk to her about his inner- most anxieties. She knew it wouldn't be easy. There was a long pause.

"It just isn't going to be the same!" Habeeb finally blurted. "I had a hard enough time facing his family at the funeral. How can I possi- bly sit down to a meal with them and try to visit as though nothing has happened?"

"Do you think they blame you for what happened to Josef?" Radia asked.

"It doesn't matter what they think! We should never have pushed our luck so recklessly. We knew that Jemal was fed up with our mischief. We should have known he would retaliate more severely," he responded.

"So you think you should have told Josef that Jemal should not be pressed any more?" she half asked, half stated.

"I'm here, Sef-Sef isn't," came the anguished response. "There's no one else to blame!"

This was the opening Radia had been looking for. She moved to him and hugged him tightly.

"We all hate the Turks, Habeeb. No one more than Josef. We all took great pride in the fact that the two of you were so successful at badgering them. We all are responsible for Josef's death, not just you!" She saw his eyes begin to fill and his lower lip tremble ever so slightly.

"I just don't want to go out right now. I'm embarrassed that we let the Turks catch us," he croaked.

Now she knew she needed to be careful. She did not want Habeeb to think that she saw him as afraid to resume his normal activities or to face Josef's family or the Turks, for that matter. She wanted him to begin to think about starting a new life.

"Habeeb," she started, "I want us to have more children, but not if they must grow up under the thumb of the Turks. And not at the risk of losing them to disease," she paused.

She knew that if she spoke again, she would be pushing too hard. She waited.

After several long moments, Habeeb said, "I, too, wish for more children, Radia. I know you too well, woman. What are you thinking?"

He had given her the opening she needed.

"The Kawars, the Nojaims, the Kammars, and the Abdos all write how happy they are in America. They have started their own businesses. They are financially independent. They say that medicine is superior there. They are able to purchase their own homes. There are no Turks to whom they must pay exorbitant taxes. They keep most of what they earn for themselves. And they all live close to one another, so it's like having a clan all their own in America!" She put it all out there at once.

He looked at her for a long moment, his eyes widening. He had never imagined the possibility of traveling abroad, let alone *living* there. He had always relished his life here at home. He loved his family, and he loved his freedom to roam the desert he held so dear. The Turks were oppressive, but he still managed to enjoy life—at least he had until recently.

"What about my horses and my ride-abouts?" Habeeb finally managed.

"The entire adventure would be one huge ride-about, my love!" she smiled.

"Do you suppose I could have horses in America?" he wondered.

"Of course you could," she responded, although she imagined that would take time and not be an immediate priority.

"Oh, I don't know," Habeeb moaned. "I don't want to run away from difficult times."

Radia was overjoyed. She had placed the idea on the table, and Habeeb had not rejected it out of hand.

"Well, let's just ruminate on it," she suggested.

Several days passed without further discussion of Radia's proposal. She vowed to herself not to bring it up again until Habeeb did.

The following Sunday after liturgy, Radia, Habeeb, and the boys gathered for dinner at Eassa and Nasra's home. They lived in a house set in a parklike orchard on the outskirts of northeastern Nazareth. It was a beautiful old place, much in the style of a Georgian cottage. In the rear of the home was a patio shaded by a large fig tree. Cedo (Grandfather) Eassa loved to sit on the edge of the patio under the tree with his grandsons on his knees. He would reach up into the tree, pluck ripe figs, peal them, and feed them to the boys.

Eassa had shared with Nasra his conversation with their daughter on the subject of America. Neither of them was prepared for the mealtime conversation.

"Father Eassa," Habeeb began, "I have caused many people much pain. I don't know how to atone to Sef-Sef's family for his loss. I hate the Turks and wish that I could avenge his death, but I also understand the futility of that undertaking. Even if I could convince others to ride with me, I fear more would be lost," he paused.

No one spoke. Everyone at the table—Khouri Eassa, Nasra, and Radia—stared at him in silence. The boys, having eaten earlier, were playing outside. Radia knew this was a defining moment in their life. Eassa thought he knew where the conversation was going. Nasra stared in disbelief.

"Radia and I wish for more children," Habeeb continued. "Many of our clan have moved to America and seem to be enjoying life there and to be prospering. We have been discussing the possibility of a move"—he stopped again, and this time he waited.

Khouri Eassa frantically tried to determine how to engage this line of thought. He knew that he must not seem enthusiastic, and, in fact, he was not. At the same time, he wanted to support Radia's plans. He momentarily struggled with a decision about whether to speak or not.

"If I were young enough, that is what I would want to do," he finally stated matter-of-factly.

"You *would?*" Habeeb exclaimed.

"Yes. There are good jobs there. Many have opened their own businesses and are building wealth. Medicine is advanced. There are good schools and universities and no Turks to collect excessive taxes and to oppress people."

Now he pressed his point home, and Radia, who loved him deeply, would never love him more than at that moment.

"It will take great fortitude to leave that which you know and love to go to a place where you cannot even speak the language. Have you thought about these challenges and the courage it will take to face them?" Eassa asked.

Until that moment, Habeeb had viewed leaving his home as accepting defeat at the hands of the Ottomans. Not until now did he begin to see such a move as requiring courage. He had started to think more positively about a change for the better, but he still wondered how he would feel about leaving the Turks behind, which in his mind was like running away. Eassa seemed to see the potential move as requiring greater resolve than remaining to face the Turks.

"I have never in my life turned my back on adversity," Habeeb stated. "I do not wish to do so now. How do you think others in the clan would view such a plan?" he asked his father-in-law.

"Those who have immigrated to the West are seen as the daring ones, the adventurous ones, the heroes," Eassa answered. "Everyone knows the sacrifices that they and their families have made to strive for a better life for their children. You must think first of Daoud and N'cola's well-being. Where will their opportunities be better? Where can they grow up without the Ottomans' heavy hand constantly pressing them down? Where will they receive a better education? Again, I say that such a move will require all the courage and tenacity that you and Radia can muster. The truly far-sighted are not afraid of taking risks to fulfill a dream."

Eassa was not worried about Radia's resolve. Her grit and determination had always impressed him. He knew that she was equal to the challenges that would lie ahead.

It was not that Habeeb lacked the same courage. He did not. Eassa was concerned that Habeeb would miss the footloose life that he had always led in the desert. Habeeb was the closest thing to the old highwaymen like his ancestor Khleif. Eassa had to smile to himself.

Just as his ancestor Khleif had to make a choice when the handwriting was on the wall many years earlier, now Habeeb was faced with a similar decision. Stay and enjoy a romantic and adventurous life in the desert with all of the associated shortcomings and risks or leave and start anew in a strange place far from loved ones.

"You would actually leave home and travel halfway around the world?" Habeeb couldn't believe his ears.

"In the blink of an eye," answered Khouri Eassa, knowing what his daughter's move would mean for Nasra and himself.

After they returned home from Sunday dinner at her parents', Radia was overcome by Habeeb's state of mind. She had never known him to be as surprised or excited or confused. He seemed to have a hard time coming to grips with her father's thinking that the truly courageous were the ones who left the desert for a better, if uncertain, opportunity in a faraway place.

She decided to let him approach the subject first, so she went about getting the boys ready for bed. After she finished, she came to the sitting room to join him. She sat down and picked up her embroidery.

Whenever Radia sat to relax or converse, her hands were always at work on her wonderful creations. Her fingers sped with dexterity over, around, and through the fine linen thread she used. Habeeb loved to watch her fast motions and the blue-green tattoo that seemed to dance on the back of her right hand. He thought it beautiful. Not many women wore tattoos because they were quite painful to inscribe, but this tattoo was another reminder of Radia's strength of character as far as Habeeb was concerned.

"Your father is correct," he said. "Traveling halfway around the world to live is a frightening prospect."

Radia nodded thoughtfully.

"It is," she agreed. "Of course, you have always loved a new adventure."

"I do love to visit new places," he responded. "I generally can reach them on horseback, however. Half the fun of going to a new place is the journey on horseback."

Radia thought about this.

"It is true that you won't get to ride to America if we should choose to go," she said. "The trip would probably take as long as two months' time. That is about how long you usually go on your extended ride-abouts."

"I suppose," came the thoughtful response.

She knew that he was still concerned that his friends would view a move as cowardly on his part—as accepting defeat at the Ottomans' hands.

"Let's try to list the advantages and disadvantages," she suggested. "We can be comfortable about having more children, both in terms of their health and their future opportunities. Daoud and N'cola will have a better education and better business opportunities. We will have a higher standard of living and quality of life because we won't have the Turks to support. In fact, if both of us choose to work, we may quickly become financially comfortable. Maybe that is what we should consider before having more children.

"As far as disadvantages go, we will hardly ever see family. We will leave friends behind whom we may never see again. It may be some time before you are able to raise horses. Can you think of other things we should consider, Habeeb?"

"Well, there is the matter of leaving without avenging Sef-Sef's death," sighed Habeeb.

"You were correct when you told Father that you would be risking not just your own safety, but that of anyone you recruited to join you. You have said that you should not have pressed Colonel Jemal so hard, yet you still consider more risky behavior to avenge Josef? Perhaps it would be best to put the entire episode behind you.

"I believe that our friends will see us as being smart and courageous if we leave. We will preclude anymore sadness at the Turks' hands and start an exciting new adventure together. Try to think more about the future of our children and what is in their best interests," she asserted.

"I know you are correct about the children. It's just that I have always finished everything I have started. I'm having a hard time envisioning myself walking away from this," he anguished.

"Perhaps you should think of the current situation with the Ottomans as something better not continued. Why provide excuses for Colonel Jemal to become even more oppressive? Habeeb, it is time for you to focus on those things that provide you with an opportunity for success and to walk away from those that are not within your control."

She feared she might be pushing too hard, but she was getting annoyed with him for being selfish.

"If you stop to consider the boys and me, there really isn't much future for us here," she admonished.

He knew she was right. She had an uncanny ability to see to the heart of the matter.

"Maybe we could return if we generate enough wealth," he suggested hopefully.

"And pay even more taxes to the Turks? We could return if, after giving America a chance, we don't like it or are not successful," she offered.

"Where would we settle if we go to America?" asked Habeeb.

Again, Radia was *way* ahead of him.

"We have clan members in Havana, Cuba, in New York City, and in upstate New York. I think we need to go to a place where there are other Nazarenes," came her ready response. "Havana will be tropical and as warm as Nazareth, but it will not have as many opportunities. New York

City will be very exciting with many options for work, but we have never lived in a huge metropolis before. The prospect frightens me a bit. We have clan members in a place called Watertown, New York. Perhaps we should consider that," she finished with satisfaction.

Sometimes he thought that he let her influence him too much. He usually agreed with her, however, and this occasion was no exception. He knew she was right, and he could mount no meaningful argument in defense of staying. The prospect did excite him, but he would never have been able to leave had she not so thoroughly and effectively pressed the idea. He was secretly proud of being married to such a strong, competent, calm woman.

In the final analysis, Radia and Habeeb decided the prospects seemed better in upstate New York than in Havana. New York City was just too frightening a place for either of them to consider it seriously. They worried about trying to raise the boys in that hectic environment.

The clan members who were already in Watertown were enthusiastic about the quality of their lives, about jobs, about their financial well-being, and about their happiness. In an exchange of letters that took several weeks to flow back and forth, those already in America excitedly encouraged Habeeb and Radia to join them. They apparently believed that having the bright, hard-working pair in their midst would enhance the Arab American experience for them all. They also believed that Radia and Habeeb could help them start an Eastern Orthodox Church.

The Arab men in America made a special appeal to Habeeb, telling him that they had discovered a new sport almost as satisfying as horse racing: fishing. They excitedly urged him to join them, promised to teach him to fish and to prepare and cook these delicacies, and described the competition to catch the most and largest fish.

Habeeb had read some about catching and eating seafood, but because he had lived in the desert all his life, he had experienced neither. He also had a hard time believing that this new diversion could possibly compare to raising, riding, and racing horses.

Radia approached Habeeb a few days later.

"What have you decided, Habeeb?" she asked carefully.

"About what?" he queried.

"About America!" she exclaimed with no small amount of indignation.

"Well, I don't really wish to go, but at the same time I sense such excitement on your part that I fear we must. I know that such a move would be in the boys' best interests. I guess I'm willing to try it," he responded blandly.

"Have you no more enthusiasm than that?" She was exasperated.

"I'm convinced that it is the best thing for us to do," he answered. "I could not stand to attempt to avenge Sef-Sef's death and lose more friends in the process. It's just so frustrating!"

"To say nothing of risking the life of your children's father and my husband!" she scolded.

"Woman, things seem so clear to you. They are not so to me!" He wanted her to understand his disappointment and frustration at leaving without avenging Sef-Sef.

"You will be seen as an adventuresome pioneer," Radia suggested more calmly. "Many will envy us, and many will follow, I suspect."

"Leadership is a burden!" Habeeb exclaimed. "Your father was also correct in saying that such a move will require all the courage we can muster—many different kinds of courage. We will need to face the unknown together, to say good-bye, perhaps forever, to family and friends we love; our way of life will be very different, and we may even lose our culture in a new place. Remember, we Arabs have five thousand years of culture to draw upon. America has less than three hundred years!" (Habeeb was obviously thinking of culture in America only in European terms and probably didn't know anything about the native peoples and their history.) "I want the boys and our grandchildren to know and love *our* culture," he stated with resolve.

"All this is true, my love, and I wish the same for our family. Think how exciting it will be! We will establish a *new* culture for ourselves, an Arab American culture. With your love of debating and socializing, you will no doubt be at the forefront of such a movement. And remember also that no families in America—be they from Africa, Asia, Europe, or wherever—have been there very long. We will enjoy freedoms we never even envisioned before," she enthused happily.

"Perhaps, and the freedom that I will miss the most is that of riding off on my ponies to sell my robes," Habeeb sighed.

I will not miss that, thought Radia.

"There will be other adventures to pursue that we have not even thought of yet," she offered.

Habeeb sighed again. He knew his fate was sealed. He had married a strong woman. He had known this for years. The decision to go to America was the correct one. His life would never be the same, he knew. He was proud of Radia and of his choice in marrying her—in terms of both their life together and the impending move. Nevertheless, he still had his reservations.

They spent the next few weeks making preparations for the journey. Habeeb had to admit that this move would be the ultimate ride-about. He warmed to the task of packing for such an exciting adventure. Radia wanted to spend as much time as possible with her parents because she worried that it would be a long time before they would again have the opportunity.

It was not practical to attempt to take large belongings such as furniture, dishes, framed pictures, and the like. Only clothing, and not too much even of that, would go along with them. So packing was not an arduous task—saying good-bye to family and friends was more burdensome.

Radia and Habeeb had only a small amount of money with which to pay for the passage. Eassa and Nasra helped with some of their savings. Radia researched the trip. She booked them passage on a small freighter from Haifa to Marseille, France. They would travel by rail from Marseille to Le Havre, France. Then they would take a larger passenger liner from Le Havre to New York City. From New York, they would again travel by train to the upper reaches of New York State to the city of Watertown.

One of the hardest parts for Habeeb was parting with his beloved ponies. He rode Yallah to Madaba and gave all three to Josef's family. He especially wanted Sef-Sef's son, Raja, to have Yallah.

"She is the fastest, smartest, most agile mount I have ever owned, Raj," he told the boy of thirteen. "There is no one I would consider giving her to except you. Take good care of her, and she will take good care of you," he stroked the horse's neck one last time, then left near tears.

The Rizk family found themselves on the lighter in Haifa Bay on a June morning in 1913. When the small craft reached the steam freighter in the bay, the entire family boarded the little ship. They had too little money to travel in a cabin, so Radia had booked steerage—they would sleep with other travelers in the ship's hold.

When their trunks of clothing were stowed in the hold, the family gathered on the deck for the most difficult part of the voyage. Nasra, in particular, could not let go of her grandchildren. She just wanted to hug them forever. Eassa wasn't much better. Radia hugged both her parents tightly for the last time in she knew not how long.

Habeeb stood at the railing gazing to the east. He wished to cement in his memory the beautiful desert, the mild climate, the way of life he so loved, and his friends. He feared that he might never return. He could not believe, however, that he would not.

The boys were immediately intrigued with the ship. After last hugs, Daoud took N'cola and off they went to explore.

Eassa and Nasra never saw their daughter or her family again.

8

Bill's Family Comes to Canada

IN 1893, when Bill was seventeen, Aunty and Uncle decided that it was time for him to begin to build his own fortune. One evening after one of Aunty's delicious dinners, Uncle Levius approached him.

"Bill, ya've been wid us fer seven years, ahe? Ya've successfully comple'ed yar schoolin', and ya're a firs'-class farmer. Ya're also a competen' carpen'er and mechanic. What's more, Aunty and I have growed ta love ya ver' much. Ya're da son we neve' had, ahe?

"At da same time, we t'ink i's time fer ya ta become more indepen'en', ahe? We wan' ya ta know tha' ya're free ta leave an' begin ta live yar own life whenever ya wish. We also wan' ya ta know tha' we wish ya ta remain here and opera'e da farm wid us. Ya'll be foreman and earn accordingly, if'n ya decide ta stay. It's yar choice, ahe?"

Bill knew that he had worked off his seven-year indenture, and he had been expecting a conversation along these lines. He also knew that he had been incredibly fortunate to have landed with the thoughtful and caring Aunty and Uncle Serviss seven years ago. Other Barnardo's children had been less lucky. Many had bounced from one unpleasant situation to another.

Bill felt every bit a man. He knew he was a competent carpenter and mechanic, and he was confident about his farming abilities as well. It was, however, difficult to think about leaving the Servisses. He had been with them for so long that they had become his family. He loved them.

Bill, his mother, and his siblings had kept in close touch during their separation. He knew that he was fortunate regarding this closeness. Some Barnardo's children never heard from their biological families after they came to Canada. He and his mother had recently begun to think that they might be able to reunite the family. They had started planning accordingly.

"Thank you, Uncle! You and Aunty have been *so* generous to me, and I'll be forever grateful to you. I love you both. My family and I have kept in close contact over the years, as you know, and I want them to join me. My mother and I have been thinking about how we might arrange for her and my brother and sisters to move from England to Canada. I need to earn a good wage and to save as much as possible so that I can send for them. I'd like to stay on with you, if we can agree on my wages," Bill was enthusiastic.

They did, and Bill remained with the Servisses for another two years, operating the farm and taking on more and more responsibility as Aunty and Uncle grew older. These years were happy ones for Bill, who loved his outdoor life on the St. Lawrence with the fishing, the games of lacrosse and ice hockey, the rapids, and the farm.

By the summer of 1894, Bill had saved enough money from his new foreman's wages to make a trip to England to visit Sarah and his siblings. It had been eight years and hundreds of letters since he had last seen them.

Sarah was at the pier on the Thames waiting to greet him as he disembarked from the ship. Bill spotted her quickly, standing tall and still strikingly pretty in the crowd below as the ship docked. Sarah, however, had no idea who she was looking for. She had trouble imagining Bill as a man and certainly did not envision him at six foot three and 180 pounds.

Sarah waited patiently for the passengers to file off the ship. She kept straining her eyes for a sign of recognition from any of the appropriately aged young men. Bill watched her with amusement as he awaited his turn to step down the gangplank. He walked ashore and toward his mother, whose eyes were still affixed on the crowd crossing the narrow walkway above her.

"Hello, Mother!" Bill reached out his arms to her.

Sarah stared in disbelief. Before her stood the tallest, most handsome man she had ever seen. It was not until that moment that she knew she had done the right thing all those years ago when she sent him away.

"Ohhhhhh, Billy! Is it really you? Let me look at you! I just can't believe it! My little boy, grown into such a fine man! You look just *wonderful*, dear! I've missed you *so* much!" She hugged him for a long moment, her heart racing and tears of joy streaming down her face.

"I've done well, Mother! Barnardo's awarded me a Silver Medal not long ago, as I wrote you. They think I'm one of their real success stories!" smiled Bill with pride.

"I'm soooo proud of you, Billy! I'm overwhelmed!" And she was. She had to sit down and cry tears of relief for several minutes before they moved on.

"Where are Nell, Harry, and Lou, Mother?" Bill asked when he thought Sarah had regained some of her composure.

"Waiting for us at home. I wanted this moment to be just yours and mine," came the choked response.

When they arrived at Sarah's small apartment in London, Bill began to realize how accustomed he had become to the large farm homes of rural Canada, with plenty of open spaces around them. He marveled that his family could survive in such close quarters.

Sister Nellie was sixteen and as tall and beautiful as her mother. Harry was fifteen, not quite as tall as Bill and still a bit gangly. And Lou was still a girl of ten. After hugs and kisses all around, the children kept staring at Bill. They could not believe that this handsome man was their brother. For his part, Bill was astonished at these grown-up children he remembered as toddlers.

Nell, Harry, and Lou, of course, knew of their mother and big brother's plans to bring the family together in Canada. They were excited about the possibility of commencing a new life together. Times had improved in London, but not dramatically.

After dinner, Bill spoke to them.

"You all know that Mother and I have been planning for some time to arrange for you to come to Canada to live with me. I had forgotten how much squalor there is here in London. Canada is fresh and new and clean and beautiful. There is work for everyone. The trip will cost two or three hundred dollars for all of you. It will take me some time to save enough money. It may be necessary for some of you to wait longer than the rest to come. What do you think? Shall we begin to plan for all this?" he finished with uncertainty in his voice.

"Billy, we've already discussed it. We all wish to join you," Sarah reassured him. "I, for one, am anxious to see Canada!"

"We all can work to save for the trip!" exclaimed Nell.

"Yes, we can, but it still may take us several years," cautioned Bill.

After Bill's return to Canada, he began to think seriously about how he could earn more money to save toward the family's relocation. A navigation canal around the rapids in the St. Lawrence River was under construction at Cardinal. Bill asked Aunty and Uncle if he could continue to live with them and go to work on the canal. He offered to continue to assist with farm chores in the evenings. They agreed, and Bill went to work digging the Cardinal Canal by hand for fifty cents per day, which was nearly double what he earned on the farm.

The Servisses were approaching seventy years of age and had saved a great deal of money from their years of prospecting and farming. They decided to retire from the dairy business and live out their days on their farm.

It took Bill two more years to save enough money to bring some of his family to Canada. In 1896, when he was twenty, Sarah and Lou (the youngest at thirteen) were able to join him. Nell, who had been living with Sarah's sister, Mary Watts, for years, was nineteen by this time. She remained behind to care for Harry, who was much a man himself at seventeen.

Bill, Lou, and Sarah established a home together in Cardinal. Once again, all he had to move from the Servisses were his pine trunk and its contents. Sarah quickly found work as a midwife, and Lou began school. Because the Servisses were no longer farming, Bill did not need to worry about making a contribution to their well-being. He considered them to be part of his family, however, and they spent a great deal of time together.

The three Curnicks lived as frugally as they could to pay for Nell and Harry's crossing. A year later, in 1897, they had saved enough to send for them. They all were united again after a separation of more than eleven years. Nell and Harry were able to find menial work in Cardinal, and now, with everyone contributing, the family began to live more comfortably.

Now it was Bill's turn to teach his family to swim and fish and shoot the rapids in his St. Lawrence skiff. They were mightily impressed with his athleticism in lacrosse and hockey. Sarah, Nell, Harry, and Lou could see how Bill's new life had agreed with him and were anxious to become part of this wonderful adventure.

By 1898, the New York Central Railway was prospering in upstate New York. It ran as far north as Watertown, which was just across the border and south a bit from Cardinal. Well-paying railroad jobs were available. Bill thought he ought to try his hand at this exciting means of transport and its financial incentives.

The Curnicks moved to Watertown in the summer of 1898. Of course, Bill's pine trunk accompanied them. Bill became a fireman on the New York Central, and Harry got a job there as well. Sarah was in demand as a midwife; Nell worked as a cook in the city school that Lou attended.

Watertown sits about fifteen miles east of Lake Ontario's Chaumont Bay on the Black River, which empties west into Black River Bay, a part of Henderson Bay. It is near some of the world's best freshwater fishing. Watertown is also just west of and provides a gateway to the Adirondack Mountains, the nation's largest state park and a world-class recreational area.

At the turn of the twentieth century, there was a growing industrial presence in Watertown, a city of about ten thousand people. Motive power came from the fast-moving and falling Black River. The Curnicks rented a house at 419 Prospect Street. The family kept in close touch with their many friends, especially the Servisses, in and around Cardinal, where many British immigrants had settled.

9

The Rizks' Journey to America

AS RADIA PREPARED THEIR AREA of the tramp steamer's hold for the trip, Habeeb tried not to lose the boys as they galloped around the ship. Daoud wanted to see what was below decks. He led N'cola down steep steel ladder/stairs with grating that they could look right through as step treads and with shiny smooth handrails on each side. On the first deck below the main one were the quarters for the ship's officers, the kitchen and mess hall, and a meeting room. Below this deck were the quarters for the ship's crew: two large dormitory-style rooms for sleeping and a single large head with multiple showers, toilets, wash basins, and mirrors.

Finally, Daoud and N'cola, with Habeeb scrambling to keep up, came to the bottom-most deck. This deck housed the ship's boiler and engine rooms. It was a large open area with an oil-burning boiler on each side. Each boiler generated steam that was piped through a header to feed two reciprocating steam engines. The massive connecting rods on the pistons attached to a common crankshaft and flywheel (about fifteen feet in diameter), which turned a propeller shaft and the propeller outside the hull.

The boiler room also contained four tanks, each several thousand gallons in capacity, which stored the heavy number 6 fuel oil, the combustion of which fired the ship's boilers. One of the operators saw the boys and asked them if they would like to look inside a boiler. They both nodded with a bit of trepidation and much curiosity. As the operator opened the door of the negative-pressure furnace, the boys could clearly see the inferno within.

Large induced draft fans created a slight vacuum in the furnaces by pulling air at atmospheric pressure from outside the ship into and through the furnaces and then exhausting boiler flue gases up the ship's stack, so the two youngsters were safe peering into the fiery depths.

"This is the fire that boils the water inside the boiler tubes into steam, which then flows to the engines that drive the propellers," shouted the operator over the din of exploding oil, howling gas flow, and rotating machinery. Daoud and N'cola could do nothing but stare. Even Habeeb had never seen such a sight.

"When the captain signals from the bridge to begin to move the ship forward, we start to open these valves, which allow steam from the boilers to flow to the engines and begin to turn the propeller shaft. The wider we open the valves, the faster the propeller turns, and the faster the ship travels," continued the operator.

"How fast can the ship go?" asked Daoud excitedly.

"About twelve knots," was the reply.

"What's a knot?" Daoud wanted to know.

"One knot is a little more than one mile per hour," explained the operator.

"How far is it to France?" Daoud queried.

"Around two thousand miles."

"We'll *never* get there!" exclaimed Daoud in surprise.

"Well, think about this," suggested the operator. "The ship will travel all day and all night every day. That means while you're sleeping, we'll still be steaming toward France. If we're traveling at twelve knots, that means we will go about 13 miles every hour and 312 miles every day. And if we travel 312 miles every day, we'll reach France in about a week—eight days if the weather is poor."

"That's not so bad," agreed Daoud. "When will we start?"

"Just as soon as you return above decks!" joked the operator.

"Time to go, Daoud and N'cola," urged Habeeb.

He thanked the operator for explaining things to them.

Back on the main deck, Daoud wanted to see the bridge where the captain and helmsman stood watch, so up they climbed.

"Wow!" shouted Daoud. "You can see *everything* from up here!"

Indeed, the view was uninterrupted in all directions. As Daoud surveyed the harbor, he asked the captain if they could remain there as the ship moved out to sea.

"Why don't you go below for a little while, Daoud? Learn your way around the ship and check in with your mother. By the time you do that and return back here, we'll be ready to leave. You can't stay in here with us, but you may watch from the forecastle just outside. How does that sound?" asked the captain.

"*OK!*" exclaimed Daoud. He grabbed N'cola's hand, and off they raced.

Habeeb and the boys made their way to the ship's hold. There were two of these holds, and theirs was the farthest forward, which meant it would pitch the most in rough seas. The bridge and heavy boilers and steam engines were toward the rear. As they entered the hold, the noise was the first thing they noticed. They were sharing the space with twenty other families, and everyone seemed to be talking and shouting at once.

"What's *that*, Immi?" Daoud asked his mother.

"That's your hammock, Habibie," Radia replied. (*Habibie* is a term of endearment for male children, meaning "my love" or "my baby.")

"What's it for?"

"It's where you'll sleep, silly! Each of us has one. You see, we can't sleep on beds like we did at home because the ship tips from side to side during the voyage, and that might cause us to roll off onto the deck."

"I can't sleep on *that!*" Habeeb allowed.

"I guess we'll all have to learn, or it will be a long and difficult trip!" she responded.

"Immi, which one is mine?" asked N'cola with anticipation.

"This one right next to me, Habibie," she smiled.

"How do I get in it?" N'cola inquired with a concerned expression.

"Here, I'll help you," Radia lifted her youngest into his new hammock bed.

"Ooooh, Immi, it's like a swing!" N'cola was excited.

"Yes, and when you are sleeping in it, the ship will rock, and you and your hammock will hang straight. Isn't that fine?" his mother responded, trying to sell the concept to Habeeb.

"I *like* my hammock, Immi!" N'cola announced with glee.

"I don't like mine!" complained Habeeb as he tried it out. "How do you roll over or change position? I fear this *will* be a long voyage!"

"Immi," said Daoud after trying out his hammock with little difficulty, "the captain said that N'cola and I could go up near the bridge to watch him steer the ship out of the harbor. May we go now?"

"Why don't we all go?" said Radia. "That way we can wave good-bye."

When the family had gathered on the forecastle, outside the bridge, Daoud decided that he had another concern.

"Immi, the operator in the boiler room told me that this part of our trip will take seven or eight days. Where will we eat?"

"In the crew's dining room with them," she replied.

"I'm hungry! Will we eat soon?" asked her eldest.

"It's a while till lunch, but I have some dates if you like," she smiled.

"Oh, yes, please!" exclaimed Daoud, and N'cola stuck out his little hand as well.

As they munched on dates and spit the large seeds over the rail into the water, the freighter made its way carefully out of Haifa Harbor. The family clung together and waved to Khouri Eassa and Nasra on shore.

Radia's tears ran down her face, but she made no sound. She knew they would not be undertaking this adventure at all if not for her. She did not want Habeeb to know how hard it was for her to bid her parents good-bye.

They remained on the forecastle deck until lunch. The boys were able to hear the captain shouting orders down the communication tube to the engine room as they picked up speed. He also gave steering directions to the helmsman. Meanwhile, crew members moved briskly around the decks stowing gear and readying equipment for the voyage to Marseille.

The crew ate in shifts, and the Rizk family was assigned to the first one, which suited the boys just fine. So when the ship's bell signaled that it was time for the midday meal, they made their way below to the dining room.

"What are these boxes built onto the table?" questioned Daoud. The dining table was divided into squares in front of each seat. There were other squares in the middle of the table. Habeeb was glad his son had asked.

"Our plates will just fit into those squares," said Radia. "The ship may begin to pitch and roll if we encounter rough seas. The boxes will keep our plates and cups from sliding all over the table and spilling."

"Oh, fun!" shouted N'cola, hoping they would experience rough seas soon.

That doesn't sound like much fun to me, thought Habeeb.

The hammocks turned out to be surprisingly comfortable, and the four quickly learned to sleep peacefully in this new kind of bed. The crew left the cargo hatches open for ventilation because the seas were calm, and it cooled off nicely at night.

Bathing wasn't really possible. Each morning Habeeb took the boys to the head to sponge off. Radia did the same in the brief period that it was available to women. There were no women's facilities, so the few women on board kept watch for one another when the need arose. When no one else was around, Radia took N'cola with her to stand guard outside.

There were several other children on board, and Daoud and N'cola soon made new friends. They spent the next several days playing tag and hide-and-seek all over the ship. Daoud became adept at sliding down the ladder/stairs by grabbing the railings on each side and pushing up with his hands until his elbows locked and his feet were off the stairs, as he had seen the crew do. Then he slid down the railings on his hands. In this way, he could scurry away below decks before any of the other children could catch up. It was great fun—even better than the slides he had sat on at home. There was, of course, the risk of falling, but that made it all the more exciting.

The Mediterranean was quite calm on their way to Marseille. The ship made good time, and they arrived a day ahead of schedule. Radia and Habeeb decided to stay on board for one more night because they all had mastered the hammocks so well, and it was much less expensive than finding hotel accommodations while waiting for their train to make the trip across France.

The train ride from Marseille to Le Havre was a trip of about five hundred miles, taking approximately twelve hours. France had a well-developed steam rail system, as did most of western Europe and the United States at the time. The big eight-wheeled steam locomotives of the day were capable of making sixty miles per hour on a good road. The Rizks were booked on an express, with few stops between Marseille, Paris, and Le Havre.

The family boarded the train in the early morning and was west bound at high speed by 8:00 AM. Their accommodations were in coach, which meant they had four seats, two facing forward and two backward. They took turns facing the front. N'cola was too small to see out the window if he sat on the seat, so he kneeled by the window much of the time. He was doing so when Daoud shouted to him excitedly to look out the other side of the train.

N'cola never saw what his brother had wanted to show him. He was hanging onto a handrail that ran underneath the window through which he was watching. When he turned to see what Daoud was shouting about, his elbow rotated with him right through the train window! There was a crashing of shattered glass, and the conductor came running to see what had occurred.

"N'ouvrez pas la fenetre!" he shouted in French.

N'cola was terrified. He leaned away from the gapping hole, afraid that he would fall out. He was fortunate that he had not been cut. Radia hugged him tightly.

The conductor showed no concern for N'cola's well-being, only for the broken window. No one could understand him as he went on expressing his displeasure in French.

Finally, Habeeb, who had had enough of the conductor, pulled a few francs (which he had purchased at the train station) from his pocket and pushed them toward the man with a grimace. The conductor turned on his heel and left. They heard no more regarding the window incident. N'cola decided to sit for the rest of the trip.

As the train passed through Paris, the family got a glimpse of the Arc de Triomphe, the Eiffel Tower, the Louvre, the Palace of Versailles, and the River Seine, which they followed to Le Havre. Radia wished they could spend time in Paris. She had read much about France and the impact that the ancient Arabs had had on the culture. She longed to experience the ambience there, but they had no money for such frivolity.

Le Havre was located on the English Channel at the mouth of the River Seine. It was a major French port. Here they would have several days to look around before boarding the ocean liner *La Provence*, which would convey them across the Atlantic Ocean to New York City. Neither

Radia nor Habeeb had ever been in a city as large as Le Havre, which had a population of around one hundred thousand at the time.

Again, to avoid the cost of a hotel room, the family requested and was granted boarding permission on *La Provence*. Radia had booked steerage again, and this time the passenger liner had only small holds. They moved their belongings below and unpacked.

Radia, Habeeb, and the boys spent their free time wandering the streets of Le Havre and learning about the nuances of a shipping port and fishing hub. Needless to say, the experience was an eye-opener for people who had always lived in the desert.

Daoud marveled at the sheer size of the freighters loading and unloading goods. The docks reeked of the smell of fish and were consumed with the boisterousness of street vendors selling their fresh catch to the wealthy and to restaurants.

Like many large cities, Le Havre provided a people-watching extravaganza. Impeccably dressed shoppers and businesspeople stood alongside street urchins begging for handouts. N'cola hung close to his mother's skirts; Daoud danced ahead, enjoying the entertainment on every street corner.

La Provence was finally ready to sail. She was a passenger liner, unlike the freighter the family had taken across the Mediterranean. She had been built in 1906 by Chantiers de Penhote of St. Nazaire, France. At almost fourteen thousand tons and more than six hundred feet in length, she was a fairly large ship with a beam longer than sixty feet and two screws. *La Provence* accommodated 422 first-class passengers, 132 in second-class, 808 in third-class, and a few more in steerage, where the Rizks sailed.

Daoud felt superior as he tried to explain the boiler and engine rooms to other children on *La Provence*—language was never a barrier to children. Most were the children of European families that had arrived in Le Havre by rail. Daoud was the leader of a large group as he raced around the vessel, sliding down the ladder/stair railings on his hands. As the experienced sailor, he was having the time of his life. N'cola tried to keep up, but without success. Many of the other children, even the older ones, were new enough to the ship's environment that he did not get left too far behind.

La Provence was large enough to warrant a tugboat to guide her out of the harbor. The family watched with fascination as the little tug slowly maneuvered the big ship. It took all morning just to clear the sea wall and proceed west into the English Channel, heading for the Atlantic Ocean.

Once free of the harbor and under her own steam, *La Provence* was capable of cruising at more than twenty knots. Even with good weather, this meant that the crossing would take about ten days.

The Rizks did not enjoy a good-weather Atlantic crossing. Two days out of Le Havre, *La Provence* ran into the kind of North Atlantic weather more typical of late fall. Daytime temperatures were in the fifties, and at night it was in the low forties or even high thirties. The seas rolled and boiled, and *La Provence* pitched and rocked.

Many passengers became seasick and no longer turned up for meals. Children, who were less susceptible to the malady, could be observed delivering sparkling Vichy water to their parents' cabins. For some reason, none of the Rizks were so affected—even though they had never been in such a huge ship before, let alone crossed an ocean.

The boys thought it was great fun to romp about the ship as her decks tipped steeply one way and then the other while she pitched up and down from stem to stern. They made quick friends with other children on the voyage, even though none spoke a common language. Hide-and-seek, capture the flag, and games of tag were favorites understood in any language.

On one particularly windy day, Radia and Habeeb took the boys first to the bow of the ship to watch it rise up high in the air and then plunge downward into the oncoming trough between waves, which then splashed over the deck, soaking them. Habeeb held tightly to N'cola with one hand and to the railing with the other. Likewise, Radia gripped Daoud's hand in one of her own while clamping onto the railing with the other.

They then walked the length of the rolling deck to the stern and held onto the boys while they watched *La Provence*'s propellers come churning clean out of the water as the bow plunged down and the stern rose high into the air. The sight was frightening and exhilarating at the same time.

La Provence's mess hall had the same wooden boxes built onto its tables. The boys were able to see how well these actually worked in stormy weather. It was amazing how successful they were at keeping things in place. Only drinks and soups were a problem. The ship's cook soon stopped serving soup, and drinks were served late in the meal so they could be held with both hands.

The poor weather slowed their progress, and the ten-day trip turned into three weeks. The winds eased as *La Provence* neared the North American continent. At this point, the Rizks discovered that there was a company of Hungarian acrobats aboard. They were heading to Florida to join the circuses based there.

When the weather finally broke, the acrobats came abovedecks to practice their act. The boys especially enjoyed watching the athletic and skilled family toss and catch one another after spectacular spins, somersaults, and twists—all in midair.

"Can we go see them when the circus comes to where we're going to live?" asked Daoud longingly.

"If they come near to where we live, we'll try to go, Habibie," answered his mother.

Daoud thought it would be great fun to be friends with the stars of the show. He even imagined himself as one of them. Radia was glad the trip was almost over. She did not wish for Daoud to become so enamored with the performers' lives that he thought about running off with them.

Everyone on the ship was alerted early on the morning of July 13 that *La Provence* would soon be entering New York Harbor and that the Statue of Liberty could be seen off the port bow. All the passengers, including the Rizks, gathered on the main deck to take part in the excitement. N'cola saw the same kind of mist that had covered the harbor at home lying upon the estuary of the Hudson River as *La Provence* made her way toward Manhattan.

He could see land close by on both sides as the large vessel cruised through the Verrazano Narrows heading north. Then people all over the ship began to shout with joy and run to the port side! N'cola didn't understand what the ruckus was all about.

"Look, Habibie!" his mother cried. "It's the Statue of Liberty! It stands guard in New York Harbor and lets all the newcomers to America, like us, know that they have arrived safely and are welcome to this wonderful new land!"

N'cola could not understand why his mother was so excited, but he noticed that she was smiling and laughing and crying all at the same time.

"What's happening, Immi?" The child was confused.

"We're in the United States of America, N'cola! It's what you've heard your father and me call the 'New World.' We're almost to the place where we will live, Habibie!" explained his mother, her voice trembling with emotion.

Daoud looked up and saw what looked like a very large city looming in front of the ship.

"Immi, Immi!" he shouted. "What's that!" he pointed to Manhattan.

"That's New York City, Habibie! It's the biggest city in the *whole* world!" she responded excitedly.

Soon all they could see on both sides of them was city. It was an amazing sight for a family that thought that Le Havre, with its population of one hundred thousand, was large.

La Provence slipped by Bedlow Island and the Statue of Liberty and steamed up the Hudson River to a pier at Twenty-Third Street on the west side of Manhattan. Two large tugboats helped maneuver her to her birth at the pier. The ship's party then transferred to a waiting ferry boat for the ride to Ellis Island. They left their belongings aboard *La Provence*.

At Ellis Island, they would learn whether they would actually be allowed to enter their new country. Radia had been dreading this experience for weeks. Habeeb half hoped that they would be turned back.

10

Florence Elsie Belcher

UP UNTIL BILL CURNICK had brought his family to the New World, he hadn't given much thought to finding a spouse. After he and the rest of the Curnicks moved to Watertown and the New York Central Railway, he began to be more aware of his age and the young women around him. Florence Elsie Belcher was twelve years younger than Bill Curnick. She didn't enter his life until 1905. Her story was as harrowing as his and similar.

Hannah Belcher ("Annie" to her family and friends) was born on November 18, 1866, in Abingdon, Berks County, Great Britain. She was the daughter of Wellington and Mary Ann Belcher, who lived at 230 Oct Street. Wellington was a sawyer, and the Belchers were *not* people of means.

Mary Ann Belcher told her daughter that she descended from a line of wealthy landowners named Koenig (German or Dutch). The males of the family, she said, drank away the family fortune prior to 1850.

Annie was an impressionable young woman easily swayed by the desire to please. All she ever wanted out of life was for someone to take care of her. She was attractive and enjoyed many suitors. She suffered, however, from low self-esteem and was susceptible to the persuasion of those who might use her.

Annie, not yet married, became pregnant in late 1887. Florence Elsie Belcher, known to family as "Florence" and to friends as "Elsie," was born on June 28, 1888. The child never knew who her father was.

Two years later, in 1890, Annie Belcher married Eli Stimpson. He became Florence's stepfather, and he and Annie had five more children in quick succession. A daughter, Ellen, was born in 1891; a second daughter, Alice May, in 1892; a son, Charles Eli, in 1894; a third daughter, first name Elsie, in 1896; and a fourth daughter, Daisy, in 1897. The family lived in Abingdon in a rented home.

Eli Stimpson worked as foreman for G. C. Hobbs Coal Company of Didcot. Perhaps as a result of breathing coal dust much of the time, he contracted tuberculosis. He suffered a long illness and died on July 12, 1898.

Annie was left with six children, all ages ten and younger, but no way to support them. To make matters worse, little Daisy, the youngest, had contracted tuberculosis from her father. Annie was a desperate mother of six at age thirty-two.

Eli's parents, James and Ann Stimpson of 41 Edward Street, Abingdon, were also of modest means. James earned ten shillings per week as a coal carter. They could offer their daughter-in-law no support after their son died. Annie's own parents, the Belchers, were quite elderly and no better off than she financially.

Annie set about selling needlework that she produced herself. When proceeds from this work did not cover expenses, she began selling and pawning her furniture. She also took a job for two shillings per week as a shop worker at a local clothing factory. She still did not earn enough to care for the seven of them.

Annie did not know where to turn. She was not a resourceful woman and was accustomed to being cared for, first by her parents and then by her husband. She decided to consult the pastor at the church that she and her family attended. The Reverend Arnold Foster, who was minister of the Congregational Church in Abingdon, was acquainted with the Stimpsons and their plight.

"Annie, I know this will be difficult for you. I think you must consider breaking up your family," said Reverend Foster quietly and firmly after he had heard her story.

"Oh, Reverend Foster, I don't know! Isn't there some way for us to stay together?" Annie sobbed.

"Little Daisy is seriously ill! She won't last long without proper care, Annie!" the reverend admonished.

"Where can I take her?"

"I'll help get her admitted to a sanitarium. They won't charge anything to care for her, and she'll be in good hands," said Foster.

"All right, I'll consider that," said Annie. "But what about the rest of us?"

"Well, now, that will be more difficult. There is a home called Barnardo's in Barkingside that takes in destitute children. They raise them until they are ten years old, then they send them as indentured servants to Canada to start a new life," explained the preacher.

"Oh no! I could never send them across the ocean!" cried Annie. "Florence is already ten!"

"Well, why don't you go to speak with the people at Barnardo's? Maybe they will consider another arrangement for you."

Foster knew that Barnardo's would be flexible with Annie because they never turned away a needy child.

"I don't know where else to turn," stammered Annie. "I hope they'll be understanding."

Reverend Foster arranged for Daisy to go to a lovely sanitarium in the countryside in Wales, where she lived for many years and was ultimately cured of tuberculosis. He also arranged an appointment for Annie with Dr. Barnardo in London.

Annie left the other children with her parents and went to London. She found Dr. Barnardo to be sympathetic and understanding of her desire to attempt to keep her children in Great Britain. To her immense relief, she was able to negotiate an agreement whereby they could remain in one of the Barnardo houses for an indefinite period, while she tried to attain financial stability.

Annie decided that Florence and Alice May were the two strongest and most independent of her remaining five offspring. She thought that she might be able to keep and care adequately for Elsie, Charles, and Ellen.

Florence Elsie Belcher and her half-sister Alice May Stimpson were admitted to Barnardo's on November 10, 1898, in accordance with their mother's wishes and without the usual requirement that they relocate to Canada at age ten. Their papers indicated that they were Baptists and had been baptized.

Florence's admission report said that she was ten years old, had blond hair and gray eyes, was fair complexioned, stood three feet eleven inches tall, and weighed fifty-seven pounds. Her chest measured twenty-three and a half inches, and she had conjunctivitis. She had had all of her vaccinations.

Florence was a serious child who did not smile easily. She was quite attractive, with a long nose and large, wide, deep-set eyes that seemed a little hollow. Her hair was cut short for easy care. In her admissions photos, she is wearing a dark sweater under a white jumper.

Alice May was six years old, with light brown hair and gray eyes. She was three feet, three and a half inches tall and weighed thirty-eight pounds. Her complexion was fair, and her chest measured twenty inches. She, too, had had all her vaccinations. She had a bit of eczema on her cheek by her mouth.

Alice May looked nothing like her older half-sister. She had a darker complexion, a round face with large dark eyes, and a wide button nose. But her hair, too, was cut short, and she wore a similar dark sweater and white jumper.

Both girls were described as "strong and healthy." Florence was said to be "bright, intelligent, clean and willing." The Barnardo's staff evaluated her as "quite her mother's right hand with a singularly open and winning expression."

Both girls were immediately assigned to reside in the Receiving House until permanent accommodations could be arranged. On November 26, they moved together to Girls Village Home.

Florence and Alice May were placed into appropriate school grades, and Florence in particular began to learn sewing and other domestic skills. The girls enjoyed being part of the large, chaotic Barnardo's family, even though they missed their mother.

Florence had learned at an early age that Annie was not an emotionally strong parent, so Florence herself had taken on much of the responsibility for her sisters and brother, especially after her stepfather died. The fact that she had been born out of wedlock and bore her mother's maiden name rather than her stepfather's, which her siblings enjoyed, led to feelings of inferiority that were to plague her all her life.

The home's routine took over their lives, and they were continuously occupied in the structured Barnardo's environment. Florence was growing into a young woman, and Alice May was working hard in school and developing into a normal seven-year-old. Annie, their mother, was occupied trying to make ends meet and caring for Ellen, Charles,

3. Florence Elsie Belcher on the occasion of her admission to Barnardo's Home on November 10, 1898, at age ten. Courtesy of Barnardo's.

4. Alice May Stimpson pictured on her admission to Barnardo's Home on November 10, 1898, at age six. Courtesy of Barnardo's.

and Elsie. She rarely made the trip to Barkingside to see Florence and Alice May.

Just as the girls were beginning to feel comfortable and at home in their new surroundings, tragedy struck on May 14, 1900. Alice May, age eight, was running to class when she tripped and fell while carrying a slate board and pencil. The pencil punctured her left eye and entered her brain. She was rushed to Cambridge Hospital.

Barnardo's immediately tried to contact Annie, but without success, so they telegraphed her pastor, Reverend W. H. Doggett of Abingdon. Doggett wrote back that he had relayed the news to Annie and that she requested that she be kept informed of Alice May's condition. Florence never forgave her mother for not rushing to Alice May.

On May 17, Barnardo's telegraphed that Alice May's condition had worsened. The little girl died on May 18. Reverend Doggett broke the news as gently as he could to Annie, who immediately blamed herself for leaving Alice May in foster care even though she knew that she had not had much choice. The fact that she had not hurried to the child's bedside exacerbated her feelings of guilt.

Florence was heartbroken at the loss of her younger sister. She, too, blamed herself, although there was little she could have done to prevent this freak accident. Resentment for her mother had already begun to develop when Annie neglected to contact or visit them, so now, when Annie failed to respond to Alice May's crisis, Florence lost whatever respect she still had for her.

Annie was deeply saddened and embarrassed by this turn of events and made little effort to contact Florence thereafter. She was so depressed that she turned to the bottle. Florence rarely saw her mother or Ellen, Charles, and Elsie after that. Annie entered the Abingdon Workhouse for destitute adults in 1901. She lost Ellen, Charles, and Elsie to foster care.

Florence kept tabs on Daisy because she suspected that her mother would not. She knew where Daisy was and wrote to her regularly. Daisy seemed happy and contented in the sanitarium.

After losing Alice May, a sadder, lonelier Florence continued her lessons and skill-building experiences at Barnardo's. She had learned at an early age that she pretty much had to look out for herself, which hardened her in many ways, and she receded behind a thick protective demeanor few could penetrate.

Florence decided that if she did not "look out for number one," no one would. This self-absorbed shell protected her and rendered her aloof and cool toward others, even those she loved. As an unwanted child who never knew her father and whose mother deserted her after placing her in Barnardo's Home, she found it hard to see the suffering or accept the tenderness of others. She became selfish and could be quite hurtful.

She began to think of herself as a victim and never recovered from feelings of abuse at the hands of others. She believed that no one could identify with the neglect and trauma she had endured in her young life.

Florence did, however, assume her responsibilities at Barnardo's efficiently and effectively. She studied her lessons (she earned the equivalent of a middle school education), learned to cook, became a first-class baker, and was a virtuoso seamstress. She was not afraid of hard work, but she did not volunteer for anything she did not have to do.

After Alice May no longer needed her older sister's care and concern, Florence began to consider the possibility of relocating to Canada. The Barnardo's staff indicated to her that her mother expressly forbade such a possibility. The fact was, however, that Annie rarely contacted Florence, let alone came to see her. Barnardo's, in a report issued shortly after Alice May died, described Annie as "undesirable, drinks."

Florence was sensitive to her mother's concern about shipping her to another part of the world so far away. As she matured, however, her spirit became more adventurous, and she began to think it might be fun and interesting to visit a new place. There was certainly little to tie her to Great Britain.

After her sixteenth birthday in 1904, Florence decided that, having been at Barnardo's for almost six years, she could learn little else there. In fact, she had been a junior house mother to younger girls for the past two years. She began to consider striking out on her own.

Florence decided to contact her mother once more about a possible move to Canada. On July 15, 1904, she wrote Annie and asked her to come for a visit so they could discuss her future. Annie, after all these years, seemed to be unconcerned about her eldest child. She never responded to her daughter's request—the last straw for Florence. She now knew, beyond a shadow of a doubt, that she was on her own and would be for the rest of her life.

Florence had become fairly close to one of the Barnardo's staff members at the home, Mrs. Code. She decided that she would ask Mrs. Code's advice about her plans for the future.

"Mrs. Code, I've written to my mum to talk to 'er about the possibility of moving on. I'm sixteen now, and I need to make some plans for the future. My mother isn't interested in me anymore. I'm thinking of going to Canada in the indentured servants program. I want to begin a new life. My sister is gone. You've taught me all you can here. I'm bored, and I want a new experience," she persuaded.

"You know that your mother expressly requested that you *not* be sent to Canada, Florence. I'm not certain we can send you. Have you thought about staying on here as a paid member of the staff?" asked Mrs. Code.

"I like it here, Mrs. Code, really I do; and I feel safe here. I just think it would be good for me to see another part of the world and to try to get on by myself without Barnardo's to fall back on. I need to be more independent," pleaded Florence.

"Let me discuss your situation with Dr. Barnardo. I understand your desire; I just don't know how he'll feel about ignoring your mother's wishes."

"Please tell him that my mother isn't a part of my life anymore and that I need a fresh start," Florence begged.

Mrs. Code took Elsie's request to Dr. Barnardo.

"Dr. Barnardo, Florence Belcher has been with us for almost six years. She's a big help to the staff; really, she's practically a house mother. Her mother doesn't seem interested in her anymore, and, she wants to strike out on her own. I think she'd like to try servitude in Canada. That way she will be on her own and still have a safe place to live while she tries to make a new life for herself." Mrs. Code was in Florence's corner.

"But her mother emphasized that she did not wish Florence to go to Canada. How can we fly in the face of her wishes?" asked Barnardo.

"I don't think we need concern ourselves with her mother any longer. Florence has written her and requested that she come to the home to meet with her. Her mother hasn't even written her back, let alone come to meet with her. I think the girl needs a chance to be on her own," stated Mrs. Code emphatically.

Dr. Barnardo ultimately agreed, and Florence began to make her plans. Before leaving, she wrote to her now estranged mother, telling her that she was about to leave on a trip to beautiful Canada to start a new life. She indicated that this trip was in accord with her own wishes and that Annie should not worry about her. She told her that she would write to her often, a commitment she did not intend to honor.

Florence sailed from London to Montreal on the SS *Southwark* on July 21, 1904. The *Southwark*, launched in Great Britain in 1893, had been built by William Denny and Brothers of Dumbarton and was operated by

International Mercantile Marine at the time Florence sailed on her. The ship was about four hundred feet in length, with a single stack and screw and four masts.

Florence arrived in Montreal on July 31 after an uneventful summer crossing. Alfred Owen and his staff assigned her to live with Mr. and Mrs. L. H. Alexander at 214 Wentworth Street, Hamilton, Ontario. Florence moved into the Alexander household on August 3 as nanny for their three children, boys ages eight and three and a girl age six.

On August 9, Mrs. Alexander wrote to Mr. Owen that Florence had been with them for a few days now. She stated that she was a bright, mature young woman and was already doing a nice job of looking after the children. She indicated that they were well pleased with Florence.

On August 15, Florence wrote to Owen to thank him for placing her with the Alexanders. She indicated that they seemed to be very nice folks. She said that she was enjoying looking after their three children and getting on happily.

On September 1, Mrs. Owen (Alfred's wife) of Barnardo's Canadian staff, visited the Alexanders and reported that the family found Florence to be in "very good health, with beautiful hair, bright and of excellent conduct." She indicated in her written evaluation that Florence was in a good, well-kept private home with small children. The family regularly attended a Baptist church.

Mrs. Owen also found Florence to be lonely and homesick for the many friendships she had enjoyed at Barnardo's. She indicated that Florence's only companion was Minnie Wentworth, a neighbor who Mrs. Owen found to be "too full of whimsy to be of much comfort to her [Florence]."

Mrs. Owen left Florence with the names of two other local Barnardo's transfers about her age for her to contact. There were no earlier indications that Florence was unhappy, however; the report stated that Florence felt "more reconciled after the visit, and that she promised to settle down."

Florence did *not* settle down. She was lonely at the Alexanders and concluded that their three young children were ill-mannered and unruly. She was unhappy with her circumstances and asked Mrs. Alexander to write to Barnardo's staff requesting that she be placed in a different setting.

The Owens received Mrs. Alexander's letter on September 15. In it, she stated that she was sorry to report that Florence apparently was not happy there. She said that Florence had requested that she write to ask that Florence be reassigned somewhere else. She advised that Florence had given no sufficient reason to her and that this development was very inconvenient.

On September 16, the Owens received another letter from Mrs. Alexander. This one referred to her letter of the previous day and indicated that she had had a long conversation with Florence, telling her that they were already depending on her for the care of the children and that both the Owens and they would be most inconvenienced if she chose to leave. She further stated that Florence expressed regret for causing such turmoil. Florence explained that she was influenced by a girlfriend (Minnie Wentworth, according Mrs. Alexander) regarding her desire to leave. Mrs. Alexander advised that she believed that Florence had thought better of her situation and that she would remain there.

On September 17, Mrs. Owen wrote to Florence to explain the confusion she was creating for the Alexanders and the Barnardo's staff in Canada. She wanted Florence to realize how fortunate she was to land in such a desirable situation. She stated that the Alexanders had a lovely home and three beautiful children and suggested that Florence was not likely to find a better accommodation. She admonished Florence and said that she thought Florence was being ungrateful to the Alexanders and to Barnardo's. She also requested that Florence remain in her current assignment.

Florence, however, was still not happy. She believed that the Alexander children were too wild for her to handle. She wrote to Mrs. Owen on September 21, indicating that she could not stay in her present setting and requesting a move to a Mrs. Coote, a neighbor of the Alexander's.

Mrs. Coote wrote a letter to the Owens dated September 23, making an application for Florence to come to her. Mrs. Owen answered tersely the same day, requesting that Florence remain with the Alexanders, but giving permission, if she were unwilling to do so, for her to go to Mrs. Coote.

Florence was overjoyed at the news. She wrote to Mrs. Owen on September 30 indicating that she knew that she had caused confusion for everyone. She apologized but stated that she did not believe she could remain with the Alexanders. She expressed her pleasure that the Owens had agreed to let her move to Mrs. Coote.

On October 17, Florence moved to the home of Reverend Hazelwood of Catherine Street, Hamilton, remained there temporarily until Mrs. Coote could make ready for her, and then moved from the Hazelwoods' to Mrs. Coote of Hamilton in late October.

Mrs. Owen received a final letter from Mrs. Alexander on October 18. It indicated that Florence had gone to a very good home and that Mrs. Coote was a fine person. She went on to express her opinion that Florence was ungrateful, as was clear from the way she had treated all of them.

Mrs. Coote, however, found Florence to be unacceptable. She indicated in a November 4, 1904, report to Barnardo's that Florence's conduct was unsatisfactory and that she did not have good hygiene. In a second letter dated November 11, 1904, she wrote that she was most dissatisfied with Florence. She said that she did not trust her in her home. She charged that Florence was dirty and worried that if Florence could not keep herself clean, she couldn't hope to keep Mrs. Coote's home that way. She also accused Florence of being deceitful and lying to her constantly. She closed by asking that Florence be reassigned immediately.

The fact was that Florence was depressed. She missed her Barnardo's friends and the home's structure. She found herself resenting the relative affluence of the families she was serving in Canada. Why should they have so much, but she and her family so little? she wondered. This was a distressing time for her, and she desperately needed stability in her life.

Barnardo's temporarily moved Florence back to the Owens' home on November 12. Five days later she was assigned to Mrs. J. D. Browse of Iroquois, Ontario. Mrs. Browse was an elderly woman with one adult son living at home. She was crippled with rheumatism and required a great deal of care and attention throughout the day.

Florence realized that she was becoming a burden to the Barnardo's staff and the families she was leaving so quickly. She knew she needed to try to make a go of it with Mrs. Browse.

Florence was responsible for cooking and cleaning, but Mrs. Browse demanded even more. She wanted both companionship and personal care as well. Florence felt overwhelmed, but she knew she had better be successful here. On November 28, 1904, Mrs. Browse wrote to the Owens that Florence had "arrived safely and seemed happy and contented."

Florence settled in with Mrs. Browse and began a routine that consisted of rising at 6:00 AM to wash and dress for the day. She then set about preparing breakfast for her mistress. Halfway through that process, she went back upstairs to assist Mrs. Browse to rise, wash, and dress.

When Mrs. Browse was helped downstairs, Florence went back to breakfast. She cooked a full morning meal for Mrs. Browse every day. She was frequently invited to join her charge at the breakfast table. There she would eat and keep Mrs. Browse company for about an hour.

After breakfast cleanup, Florence began to thoroughly clean two rooms of the large house. She found that if she cleaned two rooms each day, she could finish the entire house once per week. This approach also provided her with a different routine every day. On Sundays, she did not clean at all.

The trouble was that Mrs. Browse frequently interrupted Florence with other requests, ranging from bringing her a glass of water to running to the store on a whimsical errand. She sometimes just wanted company because she was lonely. Florence felt pressed to stay on top of all of her chores while at the same time keeping Mrs. Browse happy. She also thought that Mrs. Browse's son, who was about twenty years old, leered at her frequently, a circumstance she did not welcome.

The Abingdon Workhouse in London was a place where destitute adults could go voluntarily to receive food, clothing, and shelter. It was like a small self-contained village. Residents wore basic uniforms.

The workhouse consisted of a laundry, bakery, sewing room for making the uniforms, shoe shop, vegetable gardens and orchards, a piggery, a sleeping dormitory, a kitchen and dining room, school rooms, a nursery, an infirmary, a chapel, and a mortuary. Those in the workhouse were "employed" in one of these places. Life was structured so there was almost no time for relaxation. Residents could leave voluntarily. Annie Belcher Stimpson had lost her other children to foster care. Now she decided that her only route to survival lay at the workhouse.

In late 1904, Annie met a man named Hanson in the workhouse where she had lived for three years. The two decided that together they could make a living "on the outside." They discharged themselves in early 1905. Annie had worked in the sewing room of the workhouse making uniforms for the inmates. Hanson did manual labor and maintenance work on the various buildings and grounds. They thought that they could get similar jobs in London.

Unbeknownst to Florence, Annie married Hanson shortly thereafter, and the Hansons went about finding and collecting Annie's three children in foster care: Ellen, Charles, and Elsie.

On April 19, 1905—ten months after Florence contacted her about going to Canada and received no reply—Annie wrote to Barnardo's indicating that she was getting back on her feet and was now married. With her new husband, she had gathered three of her other children to live with them. She stated that she also wished for her oldest daughter, Florence, to join them. She asked that Barnardo's pass along her wishes to Florence and ask her to join them.

Mrs. Code wrote to Florence asking her feelings about this development. Florence was surprised to hear from her mother. She had written off Annie long ago. She had been hurt and disappointed by Annie so many times over so many years that she could not now imagine that she could depend on her.

Florence responded adamantly that she was *not* interested in returning home. Mrs. Code wrote back to Annie and indicated that Florence was in Canada. She explained that Florence had gone there in accord with her own wishes more than a year ago, that she had contacted Florence regarding Annie's recent request, and that Florence did not wish to return.

That was the last contact of any kind between Florence and her mother. Florence was seventeen years old.

11

Ellis Island and Beyond

N'COLA WOULD ALWAYS REMEMBER CLEARLY, the chaos that was Ellis Island, even though he was only four years old at the time he experienced it. It was a bit less than thirty acres in size. Every member of every family was required to go ashore and meet with immigration officials. Radia had been dreading this part of the trip. She had heard horror stories about families who had been separated—some accepted for immigration, some sent back to their home country. Families were sometimes forced to make snap decisions about whether some would stay or all would return to their country of origin. She knew she couldn't bear the trauma of splitting up the family.

Everyone stood in a long line that snaked its way from the ferry boat wharf to the Ellis Island processing building. The building wasn't large. It was a stone and brick structure three stories high. The line of people entered on the first floor, where their names were checked off against the ship's manifest.

They then moved to another line awaiting their turn to proceed upstairs to visit with a customs agent. This line moved fairly quickly because several agents were serving in parallel work stations, much like a row of bank tellers. Nevertheless, it was late morning before the Rizk family stood before the all-powerful immigration agent.

N'cola was frightened by all the noise in the narrow hallways. Then they entered the large echoing chamber where customs agents awaited. He clung tightly to Radia's hand and buried his face in her long skirt.

Habeeb knew he was better off letting Radia handle this part of the process. Neither of them spoke English, and Habeeb knew that his general resentment of bureaucratic authority (learned so well at the Ottomans' hands) might get them into trouble.

ELLIS ISLAND AND BEYOND | 101

"Name?" queried the immigration clerk. Radia looked at him blankly.

"Appelez-vous?" the clerk tried again. This time Radia decided that he must be asking their name.

"Rizk," she pronounced carefully in Arabic.

"Rizk?" the immigration clerk tried to repeat the strange-sounding name. Radia nodded in agreement. The clerk then wrote down R-E-Z-A-K. Little did the Rizks know at the time that this clerk had officially provided their new Arab American name.

"First name?" asked the clerk, looking at Habeeb. Habeeb did not respond.

"Habeeb," stated Radia. The clerk wrote some more.

"Your first name?" came the next question, this directed at Radia.

"Radia." The clerk hesitated momentarily and then wrote again. He looked back at Radia, assessing that she was the leader here and demanded, "His name?" as he glanced at Daoud and back at her.

"Daoud," stated Radia. This time the clerk did not hesitate. He seemed to recognize this name, and he wrote down "David" to record it.

"And his name?" the clerk finally asked, looking at N'cola.

"N'cola," responded Radia. Again, the clerk nodded authoritatively and wrote down "Nicholas."

The paper upon which the immigration clerk had been writing had several layers with carbon sheets in between. He kept the bottom copy and handed Radia the rest. "Medical line," he stated, nodding toward the next long line.

The medical line did not move as fast. At first, the family could not see where it led. It soon became evident, however, that people were being given some kind of physical examination. Men and women were separated for this portion of the exercise, which caused Radia no small amount of anxiety because it meant that Habeeb and the boys would go in one direction and she in another. She worried that Habeeb might take offense at the intrusion and the probing of his children. She didn't want him to jeopardize their processing by snapping at the physicians and nurses.

Doctors spent a few minutes with each person. They listened through a stethoscope to heart and lungs. The idea was to detect and stop anyone with a contagious illness from entering the country. Tuberculosis was high on the list of undesirable maladies. If people had not been vaccinated for smallpox, that was administered. Other shots were given for tetanus, diphtheria, and the like. There was much screaming and chattering regarding these pokes. N'cola was no exception, although Daoud was much more stoic. And, finally, each person's hair was dusted with a foul-smelling delousing agent.

Radia finished first and was directed to a room with no chairs to await her men. She was confident that she had passed her physical examination and was desperate to learn how Habeeb and the boys were progressing. She really was not worried about Habeeb, but the children, especially N'cola, had had some illnesses that concerned her. N'cola had those scars on his back from the Arab shaman. She didn't know how the Ellis Island doctors would deal with this.

When it was N'cola's turn to be examined, the doctor asked Habeeb about the scars by pointing at them in a questioning manner. Habeeb tried to explain that they were part of a treatment for a fever that had long since disappeared. The doctor listened all the more carefully to N'cola's heart and lungs. Finally, he shrugged and signed them off. After their smallpox vaccination, out they went to meet the waiting Radia.

N'cola bore the scar from the smallpox vaccination for the rest of his life. He called it proof that he had come to the United States through Ellis Island.

"How did it go?" Radia asked.

"There was some concern regarding N'cola's scars," answered Habeeb. "In the end, I think we all passed."

Radia hugged him and the boys. Her sense of relief and excitement was palpable. Now she felt sure they would not be denied access. Then they were given more paper and cycled back to the ferry and eventually to *La Provence* and their belongings at the Manhattan pier.

After the new immigrants were processed and those allowed to enter the country were back on board *La Provence*, they were advised to retrieve their belongings and disembark. It was the end of a very long day, so most passengers remained on board for one more night. Before retiring for the last time, Radia, Habeeb, and the boys made their way up to the main deck to have a look at the Manhattan skyline.

As far as they could see in all directions were tall buildings—some more than forty stories high. The skyscraper was all the rage in New York City by 1913. The development of structurally superior steel as opposed to the use of plain iron in building construction, coupled with the invention of the elevator, made it possible to build higher than the previous standard of ten stories. Horse-drawn taxis paraded up and down the streets right along with motor cars.

Radia was intrigued with the city's size and mystique. None of them had ever seen such a place. She vowed to herself that she would get to know New York, with all its famous restaurants, theaters, museums, art galleries, and other points of interest. She also wanted Daoud and N'cola to be familiar with this city, which would be relatively close to their new home.

Early the next morning the Rizks—now the Rezaks—packed their belongings and disembarked from *La Provence* for the last time. They hailed one of the horse-drawn cabs lined up in the street adjacent to the pier and loaded their gear aboard.

Since none of them spoke English, Radia had purchased a map of the city from a newsstand on the pier. One of *La Provence*'s stewards had pointed out Grand Central Station on the map to Radia, so when she in turn showed it to the cab driver, he nodded and headed the buggy uptown.

The taxi ride was a great deal of fun for all of them. As in Le Havre, there was street entertainment or at least interesting people to watch all along the route. Everyone on the streets seemed to be hurrying somewhere. Daoud wondered where they all were going.

The cab conveyed them north to Forty-Second Street and west across town to Park Avenue and Grand Central Station, with its affiliated complex of office buildings. Opened just a few months earlier in February 1913, Grand Central was an ornate hall that took away the breath.

The main terminal had a huge arched ceiling, and announcements echoed throughout the building as train arrivals and departures were broadcast. Trains serving Grand Central Station were electrified once they entered the city in order to minimize coal soot pollution. The next train heading upstate to Albany, Syracuse, Rochester, and Buffalo was scheduled to depart in the early afternoon. Radia purchased four seats by pointing to Watertown on the ticket agent's map of the New York Central Railway System. (The ease with which my grandmother navigated the terrain is part of family lore, but I'm sure the first Rezaks in America encountered more difficulty than I have indicated here. My grandmother was nonetheless an impressive woman.)

"Let's walk around outside for a bit," she suggested. They placed their luggage in a locker and headed for the street. This part of the city was near the heart of uptown activity. They walked west toward the theater district.

The signage fascinated Habeeb. It seemed as though everything was designed to attract one's attention.

Mounted police officers were everywhere. Habeeb was at first concerned that these police were there to enforce an occupying government. Radia was quick to remind him that the police in America were there to protect citizens, not oppress them. But these mounted officers still looked intimidating to Habeeb.

Habeeb was enthralled with the officers' mounts. They were huge animals, much larger than the small Arabian horses he so revered. These larger versions seemed agile and well trained, though. Habeeb decided that if the police could ride horses in America, so could he.

"I wish I could ask them about their horses," he said to Radia. "I'd like to know where they keep them, how much they cost, and how to purchase one."

"In good time, Habeeb!" came the reply. "Let's get to Watertown first, all right?"

By late morning, Daoud and N'cola were getting hungry from all the walking.

"Immi, let's eat!" pleaded Daoud.

There was an interesting-looking restaurant on the corner near them. The sign, which they could not read, said, "Horn & Hardart." In they went.

"Papa, look, the food is in boxes in the wall. How do we get it?" asked Daoud.

Habeeb exchanged some French francs for US currency. They found a maitre d' and motioned to the food with a shrug. The man smiled and accompanied them to a stack of trays, silverware, and napkins. He then showed them how to place coins into the slots that released the doors of the compartments so they could reach the food. The boys thought this was grand fun. Habeeb thought it completely uncivilized.

"What a *horrible* way to eat!" he lamented.

"It's just for today!" laughed Radia. "By tomorrow, we'll be eating Arabic food with our friends!"

Habeeb wondered if all Americans ate this way. After lunch, they found their way back to Grand Central Station. At 2:00 PM on July 14, 1913, the train carrying the Rezaks to their new home in Watertown left the station heading north up Manhattan Island. Just prior to crossing the Harlem River near Spuyten Dyvel, it pulled into a yard to change from the in-town electrified engine to a high-speed steam engine.

After the change, the train picked up speed and headed north along the Hudson River. North of Manhattan, the tracks ran along the east side of the river for miles. The grade elevation on the east side of the milewide river was just a few feet above the fast-flowing surface. On the west side, high cliffs rose out of the water straight up for hundreds of feet.

"The far bank reminds me of the west bank of the Dead Sea," remarked Habeeb. "The cliffs are about the same height and look very similar, except for the vegetation. Have you ever seen such lush greenery and large, tall trees?"

"It *is* beautiful, isn't it?" replied Radia. "It's so green here! I just can't believe all the trees and plants! I like it already!"

Habeeb liked it also but was not about to verbalize that feeling yet. In about an hour and a half, they were stopping in Albany, the capital of New York State. As the train pulled into the station on the east side of the Hudson River, the family could clearly see the imposing brownstone state capitol building sitting atop a tree-covered hill about a quarter-mile from the western bank. Albany looked like a beautiful city, more the size of Le Havre. Habeeb wondered what Watertown would be like.

Upon leaving Albany, the train crossed the Hudson River and headed west along the south bank of the Mohawk River. The countryside was breathtaking to the desert inhabitants. Everywhere was deep, rich green. Dairy cows dotted the huge pastures on both sides of the river. In two hours, they were stopping again—this time in Utica. It looked like more of an industrial town to Radia. She had read about manufacturing and production in the United States. This was her first glimpse of the cities and towns and lifestyle associated with a production economy.

Just east of Utica, the train ran next to the Erie Canal. This water road and its impressively engineered series of locks had been created to enhance commerce between New York City and the western reaches of America. It was said that in building the Erie Canal in the 1820s, New York State had created Michigan. Now the railroad had displaced the packet boat.

The train was soon in Syracuse, where the family would change to a northbound local to Watertown. The tracks in Syracuse went right through the downtown area at street level and parallel to and on the south side of the Erie Canal, so the Rezaks had a good view of the city. It, too, looked like an industrial area to Radia.

"I have read that there is an excellent university located here," she said with excitement. "I want the children to get as much education as they can." America is a wonderful place, she thought. Almost anyone with the desire for an education can get one.

The ride to Watertown was as beautiful as the earlier portions of their trip. Dairy farms were everywhere on both sides of the track. At stops in the villages of Fulton and Oswego, they got a glimpse of Lake Ontario, which looked like an ocean.

"I wonder if this is the place the Kawars spoke of in their letters where they enjoy the sport of fishing," Habeeb commented. "Look at all those boats! Perhaps that is what they are doing. It doesn't appear very exciting to *me!*" He sighed and turned his attention to the boys, who were gaping out the window at this huge body of water. By the end of the day, they were in Watertown.

Radia had arranged for her family to stay with other Nazarenes who lived in Watertown. They settled temporarily into an apartment with acquaintances they had been corresponding with from home, the Kawars.

The paper-manufacturing business flourished in Watertown, and Nabeel Kawar had obtained work there in the mill. Hoda Kawar worked in the J. W. Woolworth department store, one of a chain that had been founded in Watertown.

As a tailor, Habeeb thought possibly he could find work in apparel manufacturing. He applied for a job at the Woolen Manufacturing Company, but because he could not yet function with the English language, he was given a laborer's position sweeping the plant and helping with odd jobs. He didn't much like this work but knew that he needed to start somewhere.

On the weekends, the Kawars went fishing. They invited the Rezaks to go along on one of their outings soon after the Rezaks' arrival. They rented a large rowboat on Chaumont Bay. The women stayed on shore to prepare a picnic lunch, and the men, including Dave and Nick (who were already beginning to use their new American names), got into the boat and rowed out into the bay.

Pike, bass, perch, bullheads (catfish), and salmon were plentiful. The Kawars particularly enjoyed catching and eating pike. Great northern pike grew quite large, were a game fish to catch, and were tasty eating.

The Kawar men showed the Rezak men how to use a fishing rod and reel, how to bait a hook, how to properly weight it, and how to cast. Reeling back in slowly, they enjoyed the camaraderie, the occasional bite, the catch, the beer and arak they consumed and the lovely summer weather in this part of the world. Habeeb had to admit that the countryside was very beautiful in upstate New York.

Back on land, the Kawars taught Habeeb and the boys how to clean their catch and prepare it for cooking. They then built a fire and fried their dinner. Thus began a love affair between the Rezaks and fishing.

In the evening following their first fishing experience, Habeeb declared to Radia, "That was a most enjoyable day! Fishing isn't riding, but it's loads of fun, and the catch is very tasty!"

"I'm glad you enjoyed it," she smiled. "It is beautiful here, isn't it?"

"It is," agreed Habeeb. "The desert is also beautiful," he added, not wanting her to forget his sacrifice.

Radia had the two young boys at home, so she decided against full-time employment. Instead, she began to sew and sell her gorgeous embroidery. She was a skilled creator of lace and easily produced doilies, collars, cuffs, pillowcases, and even bedspreads, which she made with very fine cotton thread and an ordinary needle. This craftwork turned out to be a lucrative enterprise, and as she marketed her wares to English-speaking people, her own English skills developed quickly and easily. She had a natural bent for languages.

Not so with Habeeb at the woolen factory. Each evening Radia (with the help of the Kawars) attempted to teach Habeeb new English words as she learned them. For his part, Habeeb learned that he could rely on a few other Arabic-speaking employees at the plant to translate for him.

He hated the sound of English and thought it uncivilized. He believed it lacked the rhythm and rhyme and flow of Arabic. The language offended his ear, so he went to great lengths to avoid using it.

In a few weeks time, Habeeb was let go by the woolen plant. He was viewed as slow because he did not seem able to pick up English as quickly as other new immigrant employees.

Radia was frustrated with Habeeb. She was enjoying her embroidery sales business and believed that, given the chance, she would learn this new American retail world and thrive in it. Habeeb did not seem to be trying. She told him so.

"I didn't like the woolen mill," stated Habeeb when Radia confronted him. "There are many farms here. I'm going to see if I can find one that raises horses as well as dairy cows. Maybe I can get work grooming and caring for horses."

Radia did not object to Habeeb's looking for the kind of work he thought he might enjoy. She did not, however, wish for him to have access to gambling on his or anyone else's ponies.

It wasn't hard to find work with horses. Many farmers still used them for plowing, but few farmers had much time for their care and upkeep. These horses were not the small, quick Arabians that Habeeb knew and loved. They were very large, very strong, and quite slow moving. Their care also paid much less than Radia was able to make selling her embroidery. Habeeb's attempt at working with American farm horses lasted only a few weeks.

Habeeb knew he was an adequate tailor, so he returned to searching for a job in that industry. He learned from talking with his Arab American friends that the apparel-manufacturing industry was based in the garment district of New York City. Both he and Radia were intimidated by the prospect of living in the city. They were especially concerned that Dave and Nick (as well as any other children they might have) would have a difficult time growing up in such a huge metropolis.

In the early fall of 1913, Habeeb purchased a copy of the *Syracuse Herald* Sunday edition. He thought that perhaps the larger city of Syracuse, about seventy miles to the south of Watertown, would have something to offer him.

It did. In downtown Syracuse, there was a custom tailor shop at 115 South Salina Street in the basement of the Onondaga Savings Bank. The owner, Joseph Greco, was looking for tailors and had placed an advertisement in the newspaper.

Habeeb told Radia that he thought he would ride the train down to Syracuse to investigate the possibilities with Greco. He asked his friend, Nabeel Kawar, to write a letter in English introducing him to Greco and advising him of his tailoring skills. Never mind that he had always sewn only Arab robes!

Habeeb rode the train down and back in the same day and was not offered a job. Greco told him that his English was not yet good enough to accomplish much in the custom tailoring arena, where one must be able to listen to and understand customers' demands. He did, however, mention that if Habeeb could improve on his language skills, he would consider him for a job in the future.

Nonetheless, Habeeb looked around while in Syracuse and decided that there were more job opportunities there than in Watertown. Radia was happy in Watertown but recognized that Habeeb needed to achieve success on his own terms, so she agreed to relocate and begin anew. In November 1913, the four of them moved to Syracuse, where they found a growing Arab American population.

Syracuse, New York, was the commercial distribution hub of the central part of the state. The Erie Canal ran east and west, and the New York Central Railroad ran both east–west and north–south through the city. Iron foundries, machine shops, automobile assembly, and the candle-making industry thrived there as well as chemical processing based on the naturally occurring salt available in the Onondaga Lake marshes and in the brine domes just south of town in the Onondaga Valley.

Syracuse University had an excellent reputation among New York State's elite private institutions of higher learning, which made the city interesting to Radia, who placed great import on her children's educational development.

Habeeb quickly found work at Brown-Lipe-Chapin Company, a manufacturer of differentials and gears for General Motors automobiles, starting again as a floor sweeper while he worked on his language skills. He was careful now to work hard on his English. He knew if he were dismissed again for this deficit, Radia would be *very* unhappy with him. He still hated the language, thought it barbaric, and refused to use it at home, but he begrudgingly spoke it as best he could at the plant.

He also worked hard in the evenings at home to learn the idiosyncrasies of tailoring Western suits, which, he quickly decided, were much more complex than sewing Arab robes. The three-dimensional aspects of suit jacket shoulders, for instance, were difficult to master. The rolled suit collars and lapels were equally challenging. Nonetheless, he practiced by ripping apart old suits obtained from the Salvation Army, laying them flat to understand how they were cut, and reassembling them.

Radia began selling her embroidery and lace and cultivating new clientele. She again met with immediate success, thanks to connections she made by marketing to the congregation of the First Methodist church that the family attended. In fact, her work was in such demand that in a very short time she was asking her family and friends back in Nazareth to ship their embroidery, lace, and linen work to America. She sold these pieces, retained a percentage of the proceeds, and sent the makers the remainder. The Turks could not tax what they did not know about!

Radia and Habeeb began to save as much of their earnings as they could, knowing that accumulation of wealth would be the key to their long-term ability to survive and enhance the quality of their lives in this new environment. They rented an apartment at 514 South West Street near the Nojaim family and other Syracuse Arab families.

Dave and Nick were taken to register at Seymour School. Dave was ten, and Nick was four. For some reason known only to the administrators at the school, both were placed in the third grade. Nick sat for a week like a good little boy, silent and well behaved and without the slightest idea of what was going on until it was discovered that he was only four. He was then sent home until the following year.

Dave was quick to learn English and begin teaching it to his father. He advanced easily at school. In order to add to the family's resources, he soon took a job selling newspapers after school on the corner of Jefferson and Salina streets, not far from their home. This corner was to be the Rezak boys' station for the next ten years.

The intersection of Jefferson (running east and west) and Salina (north and south) was the center of downtown Syracuse. Electrified street trolleys crossed there, traveling both directions. Both streets were lined with bars and restaurants, shops, department stores, five and dimes, movie theaters, and other types of businesses. A federal armory was a half-block to the west. It was a most desirable location from which to sell papers.

Dave picked up copies of the *Syracuse Herald* every afternoon from the printing facility on the north side of the Erie Canal at Clinton Street and walked south to Jefferson and Salina, hawking all the way. He usually sold half of his papers on this excursion. He then stood on the southwest corner, shouting out the day's headlines (in English, of course). Business was good, and it usually took only about an hour for him to sell out.

There was one major challenge associated with selling on this particular corner, however: every few days another boy would decide that *he* wanted to sell on the southwest corner along with or instead of Dave. Dave was sure this corner was the best in town. He did not want to share it, and he certainly did not want to lose it. So every few days he was forced to fight for the right to call the corner his own.

These fights frequently contributed to Dave's somewhat disheveled appearance at the end of the day, to say nothing of the occasional bloody nose or fat lip. Radia was very upset with him the first few times she noticed that he had been fighting, but after a while she relented. The family needed the money that Dave contributed, and as Habeeb pointed out, Dave never lost the corner.

Nick took over the corner a few years later. He never lost it, either. By then, it was an issue of family pride. Once in a while, when ten-year-old Nick first took over from sixteen-year-old Dave, and an unusually large older boy would challenge him, Nick would call Dave in as his second, which frequently settled the matter before a blow was struck.

12

Florence and Bill

ON JULY 24, 1905, eighteen-year-old Florence wrote to Mrs. Owen at Barnardo's Canada office, indicating she had been working very hard with Mrs. Browse. She indicated that she knew she needed to be successful there and that she had caused problems in her past assignments. She said that she thought that she was doing very well and "trying to keep a good name." The work was hard because Mrs. B. was crippled and required a great deal of care, she stated. Florence also enclosed money in her letter for her subscription to *Ups and Downs*. Barnardo's published the *Ups and Downs* newsletter six times a year. It was designed to provide information about the children sent to Canada so they could keep track of one another's exploits.

Florence wrote again on July 31. She said that she realized that she had just written, but that she was experiencing problems with Mrs. Browse. She believed that Mrs. Browse was too demanding of her. Not only must she nurse Mrs. Browse, but she was also required to cook and clean house for her. Florence stated that she had been there for more than nine months now and that it was time for her to move on. She asked that Mrs. Owen try to find a new assignment for her.

On August 5, 1905, a Ms. Gibbs of Barnardo's Canada office came to visit Florence. She reported that Florence was "healthy, fair and pleasant looking" and living in a comfortable farmhouse.

The stress of the relationship spilled over in this visit. Mrs. Browse complained to Mrs. Gibbs that Florence was "untruthful in character with hair so dirty that it had to be cut."

Ms. Gibbs's report indicated that Florence had been to the local Methodist church only twice since joining Mrs. Browse. It stated that Florence believed that the work was too taxing, considering that she was expected to cook, perform housework, and tend to Mrs. Browse's every personal need.

The report further indicated that Florence was quite willing to stay on provided that some arrangement was made to accommodate Mrs. Browse's personal needs. Florence believed, it also stated, that "she was scolded a good deal" and that Mrs. Browse's son made her feel uncomfortable.

On August 10, Florence wrote once again to Mrs. Owen. She advised that she still felt that she was being asked to work much too hard for Mrs. Browse. There was a woman there in Iroquois named Mrs. Stamps, and Florence indicated that Mrs. Stamps had invited her to move to her home. She requested that Mrs. Owen authorize this change.

Mrs. Owen wrote back to Florence on August 14. She expressed her disappointment that Florence wished to move again. She advised that Barnardo's would prefer that she remain with Mrs. Browse. If Florence insisted on a move, Mrs. Owen suggested that she go to Mrs. Henry Bowen of Dixon's Corners. She asked that Florence advise her regarding her wishes.

On August 21, Florence indicated that she would stay with Mrs. Browse if Mrs. Owen could arrange for her monthly allowance to be raised from four and a half to five dollars.

Mrs. Owen quickly wrote to Mrs. Browse requesting that Florence's monthly allowance be increased to *six dollars*. Mrs. Browse agreed via return letter.

After the increase in allowance, Florence redoubled her efforts to succeed at Mrs. Browse's. She worked as hard as she could to keep the house neat and clean and to prepare tasty meals. She also tried her best to keep up with Mrs. Browse's personal maintenance demands.

Florence even began attending the local Episcopal church in Iroquois. There, in the fall of 1905, she noticed a tall and handsome young man who, she learned by asking the other young women, was named Bill Curnick. Bill, she determined, lived in Watertown, New York, and had an excellent job with the New York Central Railway. She also learned that, like her, he was a Barnardo's child.

On a trip back to Cardinal to see family and friends and attend church with the Servisses, Bill met Florence Belcher for the first time. As a good-looking bachelor with an excellent set of wage-earning skills (farmer, mechanic, carpenter, railroader), Bill was an attractive catch. He was mature, and his dedication to family was noteworthy. He had been preoccupied until now with working to bring them to Canada and America. In Watertown, working on the railroad and surrounded by family, he began to notice the young women he encountered.

None caught his eye like Florence did. She was petite—four feet eleven inches, one hundred pounds—and beautiful, thought Bill, with lovely blond hair and a fair complexion. He made sure that they were introduced after church and began to try to see her whenever their work schedules and she allowed.

With a new interest in her life, Florence found working for Mrs. Browse even more burdensome. She wanted more time to be with Bill, so she indicated to Barnardo's that Mrs. Browse's son had made "improper advances" toward her.

On November 24, 1905, she left Mrs. Browse on her own volition after more than a year and went to work for Mrs. Gordon Serviss in Iroquois (no relation to Bill's Aunty and Uncle).

Florence met Bill at church on the next Sunday.

"I've left Mrs. Browse," she stated proudly. "I'm now cooking and cleaning for several women on a rotating basis. I'm living in the Montroy Hotel in Cardinal. I suspect that I'll have free time on both Saturdays and Sundays as well as evenings during the week," she finished not so coyly.

Bill was never surprised at Florence. He knew that she was compulsive and independent.

"Well, congratulations!" he exclaimed. "How about a buggy ride one evening next week? I'm not on call at the railroad after Tuesday."

"I'll pack us a wonderful picnic meal!" responded Florence excitedly. "Where shall we go?"

"Let's wait to see what the weather is like. If it's warm enough, we can go down by the river. If not, maybe we'll get some snow, and we can take the season's first sleigh ride over the fields. Sound alright to you?" he asked.

"Sounds splendid to me!" Florence replied with excitement.

So they agreed on the date and thereafter began to see each other regularly. Sometimes Bill's whole family came along, and sometimes

Florence came to Watertown to visit them. She, like everyone else, loved Bill's mother, Sarah. She wondered what it must be like to have a thoughtful, caring parent. She realized that Sarah was the glue that bound the Curnicks to one another.

Bill was not a man to act quickly, especially when it came to something as important as picking a mate. He and Florence dated regularly for over a year. All the while, she was on her best behavior. Not once did she let Bill know that she did not agree with him about everything they discussed. She was as sweet as she could be to him and all his family.

For the most part, this behavior was easy for her because the Curnicks were a relaxed, open, forthright family with little intrigue. Florence found this refreshing, even though she was sometimes skeptical of their motives—a skepticism born of years of paranoia at having her hopes dashed and her young emotions trampled upon. None of this attitude did she allow Bill Curnick to observe, however.

One evening in the late spring of 1907, just after the winter ice flow moved east off the St. Lawrence River, Bill and Florence were out for a row in his skiff.

"Florence, we've gotten to know each other pretty well at this point. I think that you're the prettiest, smartest girl I've ever met, and I love you. I'm not getting any younger! Will you marry me?" Bill managed.

Florence had been waiting for a proposal from Bill for a long time. It had come out of nowhere, and she was caught a bit off guard. She savored the moment briefly.

"Of course I will, Bill. I wasn't sure you were ever going to ask!" she responded with a demure smile.

His relief was palpable.

"You will! Oh, that's wonderful. Mother will be so pleased and excited for us! I can't wait to get back to tell them all."

Florence wished *she* had someone to tell. She sat down that night and wrote a long letter to her half-sister Daisy. Maybe now her hard life would finally ease, she thought to herself.

She wrote to Daisy that this was the best day of her life. She explained that Bill Curnick, whom she had been seeing for more than two years, had asked her to marry him. She advised Daisy that she had told him, "Yes, of course!" Florence expressed her excitement and told her half-sister that she just had to sit down and write!

Florence inquired as to Daisy's health and her life at the sanitarium. She asked if Daisy was still happy there and suggested that she must be a big help to the staff by now, working with the younger children. She indicated that she had enjoyed that part of her Barnardo's years as well.

She would be moving to Watertown in New York State in the United States of America to live with Bill and his family, she told Daisy, and was excited that she was to finally have a home of her own.

She enclosed her new address so Daisy could write to her and asked her to do so as often as she could. Then she suggested that Daisy might come to live with them at some point. She painted a lovely picture of Canada and America—much cleaner and more beautiful than London.

Florence Belcher and Bill Curnick were married on June 25, 1907, in Trinity Episcopal Church on Sherman Street in Watertown, New York. The beautiful arched timber roof, strong stone walls, and magnificent stained glass made their church the most special in Watertown, they thought.

Florence had turned nineteen the previous day; Bill had recently reached the age of thirty-one. Harry Curnick was Bill's best man; Bill's mother, Sarah, escorted Florence down the aisle; and Nell Curnick was maid of honor. Florence was thrilled but disappointed that she had no family attending.

Florence and Bill set up housekeeping at 90B Arsenal Street in Watertown, the rest of his family living with them. The house was a large one of necessity because at various times Florence, Bill, Sarah, Nell, Harry, and Lou all lived there together, and over the years new spouses joined them for a time until the couple moved out on their own. It had five bedrooms—four upstairs and one downstairs, one bathroom, two sitting rooms, a large kitchen, and an enormous dining room with an interior wall about twelve feet wide. It also had a large and lovely garden and yard that Bill loved to tend. The rent for all this was four dollars per month.

Bill had wanted Florence to have a special wedding present, so he commissioned a cabinet maker acquaintance to custom make a dining room sideboard for her. He knew he had scored a winning goal when she first saw it. And for good reason: it was a magnificent piece.

5. Florence and Bill Curnick on their wedding day, June
25, 1907, in Thompson Park, Watertown, New York.
Courtesy of the author.

The sideboard was crafted of solid walnut in a rich dark finish. It was
9 feet long, 37½ inches high, and 18 inches deep, with a lovely one-piece
top. It had been made in four pieces. A 40-by-29-inch dish cabinet stood
under each end. These two cabinets had locking doors, beautifully fitted
and hinged in cast iron, and a single shelf above the bottom storage area.

Above each cabinet were two drawers in each end of the nine-foot top.
In the middle was a 29-inch-wide drawer lined with velvet, with a hinged
draw front that folded outward, creating a desk. The back of this drawer
had small built-in storage drawers for pens, pencils, ink, and the like.

The 18-inch-wide top piece was removable, so the sideboard could be disassembled for moving. At the rear of the center section, under the desk, was a walnut back that matched the rest. The sideboard fit perfectly on the 12-foot-long dining room wall in their home.

Florence could sit with her feet and legs between the two cabinets and beneath the center of the top piece, with the drawer pulled open to write to her sister Daisy. She absolutely loved Bill's thoughtful gift! I have a specially designed knee wall in my home to accommodate this lovely heirloom, now more than one hundred years old.

Harry Curnick met and married a young woman from Watertown named Jen. They moved with the railroad to Rochester, New York. Nell met a railroad telegrapher in Watertown named Arthur Glassford. They soon married and moved to Westdale, New York, outside of Rome. Lou remained in Cardinal for a time, meeting and marrying another Barnardo's child, Frederick Spraggins. They eventually moved to Rome as well.

Florence became pregnant in the spring of 1908. Toward the end of her pregnancy in the harsh Watertown winter, she slipped and fell on the icy steps of the house. A baby girl was born prematurely and lived only a short time, having been injured in the fall. Florence and Bill were despondent. The baby, also named Florence, was buried in North Watertown Cemetery.

It took the Curnicks some time before they were willing to try again. They also could no longer bear to live in the same place where they had lost their child, so they soon moved to 158 North Meadow Street.

Try again they did. Frances Pauline Curnick, a gorgeous blond-haired little girl with a round face, beautiful smile, and large dimples was born on November 25, 1910.

Florence was attended by her mother-in-law, Sarah, and a Dr. Couch. She had a long and arduous delivery, followed by an equally difficult recovery period. Pauline, as her mother called the baby, weighed almost eight pounds, and Florence was a tiny woman. Sarah, of course, was a more than adequate caregiver.

Florence loved Pauline ("Polly" to Bill, the rest of the family, and her friends) and decided that two pregnancies were enough for her. She had suffered too much in her short life without having to endure any more pain.

Sarah was overjoyed to have a grandchild under the same roof. She lavished her warm, caring affection upon Polly. Bill loved seeing his mother so pleased to be around his daughter. The family moved to larger quarters at 413 Prospect Street, remaining within walking distance to the railyard where Bill met his trains.

The entire family loved having Sarah live with them. She was wonderfully caring, with a genuine sense of humor. She was also an extremely hard worker who helped supplement the family income by performing as a midwife.

In late 1912 in the dead of winter, Sarah contracted pneumonia. It seemed like a bad cold at first, but then Sarah began a deep, rasping cough. Bronchitis set in, followed by the accumulation of fluid in her lungs. At this point, Bill and Florence bundled her up and took her to the hospital.

The doctors steamed and sweated her to no avail. Sarah slowly weakened and slipped into a coma. She succumbed on January 14, 1913, at the age of fifty-eight with the knowledge that she had successfully shepherded her flock to a prosperous new beginning in America.

Bill eulogized his mother at her memorial service. He stated that Sarah Patience Cooke Curnick was the strongest, toughest, most determined, and loving of people. He indicated that she had borne six children and that four of them were present at the service. The other two, he explained, had died as infants.

They lost their father when he, the oldest, was nine years of age, Bill stated, but Sarah did not panic. She received no help from her parents or from their father's parents. She rented out rooms in their house and found a job as a midwife in London.

When this job did not produce enough income to care for the five of them, she made the most difficult decision a parent ever has to make. She sent their sister Nell to live with her aunt and Bill to Barnardo's Home and to Canada.

Bill indicated that he did not realize until recently what a traumatic decision that must have been for her. He explained that he didn't see his mother or brother and sisters for eight years, yet during that time she wrote every week, telling him family news and inquiring about his life in Iroquois.

When Bill was old enough, and they had saved some money, his mother came to Canada with their sister Lou. She left Nell and Harry behind for a time so she could finally be with him again.

Bill related how close he and his mother were, both during his childhood and afterward, perhaps owing to their separation. He stated that he knew now that it must have wrenched her heart to send him away. She was such a strong, pragmatic person! She did what she had to do and never looked back, only to the future. What an optimist! What a healthy attitude!

His mother's love was always obvious. It was a joy to watch her with her grandchildren, he reflected. She never took time to meet a new mate after their father died. She was way too busy working and caring for her family as best she could.

Bill closed his remarks by suggesting that Sarah had a dream that one day her family would be reunited and live together again. He stated that they all were glad that she lived long enough to see that dream come true and sad that she didn't get to enjoy it a little longer.

Sarah Patience Cooke Curnick was buried alongside her granddaughter Florence in Section L/F of North Watertown Cemetery to the left of the intersection of Row 3 Road and Frontenac Street.

Bill was grief stricken at the loss of his mother. They had a very tight bond forged through years of hardship in England, their separation and diligent correspondence, and finally their reunion. Sarah's passing was also a financial setback for the Curnicks.

Florence missed Sarah as much as Bill. Sarah was the mother she had never been able to count on and love. She had watched closely how Sarah interacted with her children and friends and grandchildren. She wanted to learn to be as good a parent and person as she believed Sarah was.

After Sarah's death, Florence began to think more about her own family relationships. She did not think that she could stand to be disappointed again by her mother, but she thought a great deal about her young half-sister Daisy, who was still in the sanitarium in Wales as far as she knew. She had kept in casual contact with Daisy since coming to Canada and America. Now she wanted to rekindle the relationship.

"Bill," said Florence emphatically after dinner one evening in the spring of 1913, "I'd like to invite my sister Daisy to come to live with us. We have room now, and you've brought your whole family over, and they're established in New York State and on their own. I'd like to give the same opportunity to Daisy."

"Why, of course!" exclaimed Bill, always willing to extend a helping hand. "I think that's a marvelous idea. She could be of considerable help to you here in the house and with Polly. How old is she now?"

"I think she's fifteen or sixteen. She's still in the sanitarium as far as I know. I think they would have contacted me if she had left. I'll write to her if you approve, Bill." Florence was as deferential as she could be.

"Yes, by all means write to her, sweetie! I think that's a grand idea."

So Florence wrote to Barnardo's in Canada (still Mr. and Mrs. Alfred Owen) and reestablished contact with the home. After several letters back and forth, Florence asked that they contact Daisy, indicating that she would like her to consider joining them in the United States.

Florence received a letter from Mrs. Owen dated April 10, 1913, stating that she had just received a letter from a Miss Kennedy of the sanitarium, enclosing a letter from Daisy, from which it appeared that Daisy did not "exactly catch on" to the idea of leaving her present place. Mrs. Owen indicated that Daisy wrote, "I am getting along fine. I think I am better here."

Mrs. Owen went on to say that Barnardo's would not think to make any change against Daisy's own desire, and "since she elects to remain where she is, I am afraid we must for the present give up the idea of her going to you." Of course, she went on, you can write to Daisy or visit her, and if she changes her mind, we are quite willing to "fall in with your plans for her, but at present I am afraid we must consider the proposal as called off."

Florence was disappointed. Her attempt at reconnecting with family seemed to be thwarted, at least for the moment.

"Daisy may change her mind once she is a little more mature," soothed Bill. "Remember how you felt about this adventure when you were younger. Why don't you try again in a year or two?"

Florence agreed, and she still felt low about Daisy's unwillingness to join them. She was used to being hurt, however, and put this latest disappointment behind her for the time being. She threw herself into a new move, this time to a large apartment at 116 Massey Street.

13

Life in Syracuse

RADIA'S WILL TO SUCCEED was enormous. She pushed herself relentlessly to be as good a mother and spouse and to sell as many of her wares as she could. She went out in all sorts of weather (which in Syracuse in the winter can be especially fierce) to contact prospects and deliver lace.

In early 1915, she contracted pneumonia and pleurisy and was hospitalized. Habeeb was at this point working long hours at Brown-Lipe-Chapin six days a week and in the evenings at the custom tailoring he was able to arrange on the side. No one was available to care for twelve-year-old Dave and six-year-old Nick.

Habeeb split what little time he had between visiting Radia in St. Joseph's Hospital and caring for the boys.

"How are Daoud and N'cola doing without me and with you here?" she stammered after she began to regain her senses.

"Well, they're pretty much on their own," Habeeb admitted.

"I feel guilty. I'm letting *everyone* down," she sobbed.

"Nonsense!" insisted Habeeb. "We're doing fine." But he, too, worried about the boys.

"Habeeb, I've heard that the Onondaga County Orphans Home takes children for short periods of family crisis. What about taking them over there for a bit?" Radia suggested through tears.

Habeeb went to the home the next day. By that evening, the boys were residing there until the family could recover from the trauma of losing Radia to illness.

The home was a large house with dormitory sleeping rooms. The children were separated by gender and age group. Dave went to an older boys' dormitory room, Nick with the smaller lads. This arrangement was very upsetting to young Nick, who had always slept in the same room

123

with Dave, if not with his parents. The nights were long, sad, and frightening for him.

During the day, the children were transported to their respective schools. This part was better for Nick, who had grown accustomed to his first-grade class. He was not able to sit with Dave for the evening meal, but he was close by. They were able to spend time together after dinner before going to bed.

This unpleasant experience made a vivid impression on little Nick. He saw Dave everyday before school in the morning for a few minutes at breakfast and again in the afternoon after Dave returned from school. He did not get to see his mother for several weeks, and his father only on Sundays. He was a *most* unhappy little boy.

Dave and Nick remained in the orphanage for three months during Radia's hospitalization and convalescence. This period was a serious setback for the family's objective of building capital.

World War I was well under way in 1916, and even though the United States was not yet a combatant, there was a gunpowder plant located just west of Syracuse in Split Rock that produced explosives for the war effort. Many immigrants worked at the plant.

Radia had a natural gift for languages and a very good ear. She polished her English as she sold her lace around town, which gave her the knowledge of three languages.

One day while returning home on the trolley to West Street from a day of selling her embroidery and linen in the university section of Syracuse, she overheard two Russian immigrants discussing something quietly in their native tongue. This was a bit unusual because most immigrants were interested in practicing their English rather than speaking in their native language. She was fluent in Russian, so she could not help overhearing the conversation.

What she heard upset her greatly. In fact, Radia could hardly believe her ears. The Russians were plotting to *blow up* the gunpowder plant! She listened more intently than ever as she continued with her ride. Sure enough, these men were scheming to destroy the plant.

That evening after the boys were in bed, Radia told Habeeb of her shocking discovery.

"Are you *certain* that you understood correctly?" Habeeb demanded.

"I'm *certain!*" she stated emphatically.

They both had worked diligently to accumulate wealth and perform well in their respective jobs. They had purposely tried not to be conspicuous as they went about their daily responsibilities. They just wanted to do a good job, be well paid, and mind their own business and that of their children. All of the sudden, it seemed impossible to ignore what was going on around them.

"Then we must tell someone in an official capacity what you heard," Habeeb asserted. "How we go about it is the question. Will an official believe you? Will they think that, as an immigrant, you might have an agenda of your own? Will they try to persecute you if they don't believe you?"

Paranoia borne of a life of oppression at the hands of the Ottoman Turks still haunted Habeeb. Finally, late in the night, Habeeb and Radia decided that she would go to the Syracuse Police Department to report what she had heard. She would tell the police that she had important information that she believed they would want to know.

Radia had become casually acquainted with the police officer who patrolled their West Street neighborhood on foot. She frequently met him as she walked to and from the trolley stop to sell her embroidery and lace.

The next day she waited for the officer to appear and approached him with her story. The officer took Radia's report and tried to decide how much import to attribute to it. She seemed credible. He could think of no motive for her to lie about such a thing. She obviously worked hard to sell her wares far across town.

The police officer submitted Radia's report to the shift sergeant, who passed it on to his supervisor. The next day the reporting officer and the sergeant came to meet Radia as she went to take the trolley to a more affluent part of town.

"Do you believe that you can identify the two Russian-speaking men?" they queried.

"Yes, I'm certain that I can," she affirmed.

The two police officers asked Radia to accompany them to the explosives plant in Split Rock. They stood off to the side and out of sight as the plant day shift left for the evening at 3:30 PM. Before long, Radia spotted the two men exiting the plant together.

"It's those two," she pointed them out quietly.

After the shift had changed, the police asked Radia to accompany them to the plant manager's office. The four of them sat there as Radia relayed the conversation she had overheard. At first, the plant manager was astonished.

"How did you learn Russian?" he demanded with skepticism.

"I studied at a Russian convent in Nazareth and learned the language there," she explained.

"And are you *positive* that you understood correctly?" he continued, still skeptical.

"I'm absolutely certain," she insisted.

In the end, he asked the officers if they would dress as workers in plain clothes on the following day and observe the two men. It did not take long for things to come to a head. The very next day the two Russians were observed pilfering gunpowder. Inspection of their lockers in the workers' dressing room turned up home-made bombs in various stages of completion. The Russians were dismissed on the spot and hauled off to jail.

The plant manager was so grateful to Radia that he hosted a reception for her at the end of the next day shift and on company time. He told the gathering of employees what she had done and how she had probably saved all of their jobs, to say nothing of many of their lives. Radia was not used to the spotlight. She was at the same time embarrassed and pleased about the recognition.

Unbeknownst to her, the plant manager also wrote a letter to President Woodrow Wilson describing Radia's heroics. He asked the chief of police and the mayor to do the same.

Several weeks later Radia received handwritten correspondence from the president himself on his personal letterhead thanking her for foiling a dangerous plot and supporting the war effort. She cherished this acknowledgment for the rest of her life.

The letter stated that she had made an enormous contribution to the safety of her fellow Syracusans and to the war effort. It thanked her for her commitment to her new country and wished her the best in her new life in Syracuse. Wilson went on to suggest that Radia and her family achieve citizenship as soon as possible. The letter became special documentation of family lore.

The Rezaks lived in the rented apartment on West Street for three years. Habeeb was doing well at Brown-Lipe-Chapin. His English became passable, and he was moved to an apprentice gear worker position. Here he settled down to a steady, well-paying job where he could continue to develop his work-related skills and his English.

For her part, Radia was making almost as much money selling her merchandise as Habeeb was at the plant. They salted away as much as they could save.

Habeeb learned to operate the mills, lathes, and other metal-shaping machinery at Brown-Lipe-Chapin. He also worked hard to learn English well enough to satisfy his employer and the customers he might later encounter in his tailoring business. He and Radia, however, believed that they would accumulate wealth faster if they operated their *own* business.

The dilemma was that neither of them had any idea of how to market his tailoring services successfully. They both had wondered about the grocery business. After all, everyone needed to eat!

There were other Arab families in the grocery business in Syracuse. It seemed like a "can't lose" enterprise to Radia and Habeeb.

In 1917, with a few hundred dollars in savings, they purchased a small grocery store at 933 South Geddes Street and rented an apartment down the street at 641. At this point, their income practically doubled. Habeeb's English had improved enough to allow him to commence custom tailoring, and the store gave him a base of operations from which to promote his tailoring services to grocery customers.

He quit Brown-Lipe-Chapin after four years and worked in the store when not sewing. Radia sold her lace and covered the store while Habeeb was sewing. Dave, now fourteen years old, went to school during the day, then sold his newspapers, and worked at the store in the evenings. Nick, eight, went to school and was stock boy at the store.

The grocery business fascinated Habeeb. He enjoyed learning how typical Americans shopped and selected food for their families. The ordering of fresh produce on a daily basis was unique and very different than anything he had experienced in the Middle East. It required a trip to the Syracuse Farmers Market early every morning to select fresh chicken, fish, beef, vegetables, and fruit. Then the produce was rushed back to the store and displayed on beds of crushed ice delivered every morning by City Ice Company.

Habeeb was equally fascinated at how ice was obtained during the warm summer months. In the winter, City Ice sent laborers to Cazenovia Lake (which had exceptionally pure water), about twenty miles southeast of Syracuse. There, using large saws, they cut huge slabs of ice from the surface where it was at least a foot thick. They removed these slabs with ice tongs, hauled them into town, and buried them in four-foot-deep pits. The ice was thus maintained for months until needed. City Ice delivered block or crushed ice to order. Habeeb was impressed.

Canned goods were acquired weekly from O'Connor-Moser Company, which delivered them by the case. The whole family pitched in to unload the supply truck and stock the provisions on display shelves at the store.

And perhaps most complex of all was the fresh meat, fish, and fowl, which needed to be kept in a cool room in the rear of the store. This room was stacked with blocks of ice every morning. Habeeb hired a butcher, who chopped the huge sides of beef, pork, and lamb and whole chickens into various cuts and pieces. The entire enterprise was a joy to Habeeb, and he relished describing his daily experiences to his family each night at dinner.

By 1918, Radia and Habeeb realized that their Geddes Street location was not the best. It was small, and there was too much competition there. They rode the bus around town to assess alternative places they could afford. With the proceeds from the sale of 933 South Geddes Street, they acquired a new grocery store property at 703 Park Street, with an apartment in the rear, and so picked up everything and moved once again.

They lived on the north side of Syracuse behind the new store for two years. Habeeb by that point had mastered the grocery business. They still had not, however, accumulated enough wealth to purchase a large building in a desirable location, which, they had come to realize, was a necessity for this kind of enterprise to be optimally successful.

Habeeb believed that his English and his ability to craft Western suits were good enough at this point to pass muster with the custom tailor Joseph Greco. So he returned to visit Mr. Greco at his shop in the Onondaga Savings Bank in downtown Syracuse. It had been five years since their first encounter. Greco agreed to hire Habeeb, and the two spent the next several years fashioning stylish suits for Syracuse's wealthy men.

Habeeb was fast and turned out high-quality work. He worked out an arrangement with Greco whereby when one of his satisfied customers returned to the shop and specifically requested that Habeeb tailor his clothing, Habeeb received a higher percentage of the garment's price.

During this period, Radia and Habeeb expanded the store at 703 Park Street into the rear apartment and rented another apartment to live in at 410 Otisco Street, on the west side. At this point, Radia operated the store during the day while Habeeb was at the tailor shop. Habeeb ran the store in the evenings so Radia could peddle her lace. And Dave and Nick worked in the store afternoons and evenings. It was a family operation from the beginning.

After Dave turned the newspaper corner over to Nick in 1919, he used some of the money he had saved for himself, after years of hustling papers, to purchase a used Harley-Davidson Silent Gray Fellow motorcycle. He had never ridden a motorcycle before, let alone owned one. He rode it home after he purchased it but did not understand how to work the brakes and clutch properly. The family had yet to own an automobile, so he did not know the first thing about motor transportation. When he got home, he could not figure out how to stop safely, so he rode in circles until the bike ran out of gas! Nick got a huge laugh at Dave's expense, an unusual opportunity for him.

The Harley Silent Gray Fellow was called "silent" because of its new efficient mufflers promoting quiet motorcycling (an oxymoron today). The bike was, of course, an austere gray color. *Fellow* suggested a reliable partnership between man and machine—a trusted companion on the road.

Dave loved that bike. He used it to go to and from school and the store and to take Nick to his newspaper pickup. It took him several weeks to master all the controls. A motorcycle is like a gyroscope: the faster it goes, the more stable it is to ride. The bike had a throttle lever, clutch, shift lever, and brakes that one had to learn to coordinate with different hands and feet, all while balancing—difficult to accomplish at low speed. Nonetheless, Dave was quite proficient by the time he had been riding for a couple of months.

For his part, Nick loved riding with his big brother. He looked forward everyday to the ride from school to the newspaper printing facility where he picked up his papers. He shouted and waved to his school pals as he and Dave went flashing by. Motorcycle helmets were nonexistent at the time.

One day as they made their way to the printing plant on North Clinton Street, Dave was sweeping through a corner as Nick turned to crane his neck toward some of his friends. Nick's movement caused Dave to wobble just enough to lose control momentarily.

They joked afterward that the elm tree Dave hit had jumped out into the street just as they were passing by. Radia was not amused. Dave sustained a broken nose and bruises, and Nick went into the tree face first, losing several teeth in the process. They looked like they had just gone ten rounds with Gene Tunney; it was a few weeks before Nick could eat comfortably, and he wore a bridge from then on. He had to hire a substitute to sell his papers for several days.

Dave's beautiful Gray Fellow was in the "motorcycle hospital" in the basement of their home for many weeks before he could afford to purchase parts and fix it. He was forbidden to give Nick a ride thereafter.

14

The Curnicks of America

BILL MADE A COMFORTABLE, if not extravagant, living working for the railroad. The Curnicks lived near the New York Central Railway yards in Watertown. Railroad workers were expected to live close by so they could be called in a hurry if needed for service. There were no telephones yet in Watertown, so workers were also expected to leave the doors of their homes unlocked at night. When someone was needed to take a position on a train, the railroad sent a "call boy" on foot or by bicycle to each worker's home. The call boy entered the house and, standing inside the front door, shouted out the worker's name.

If the worker responded, the call boy gave him instructions regarding time to report, train to be on, destination, how long to expect to be gone, and the like. It was the call boy's responsibility to see to it that the railroad man clearly understood the instructions.

If the call boy received no response to his shouting, he would enter the worker's bedroom to shake him awake and give him instructions. Florence frequently awoke to a stranger standing at Bill's side of the bed arousing him for work. It never ceased to startle her to the point that she couldn't go back to sleep.

After Nell, Harry, and Lou were married and on their own, and after Sarah died, Bill, Florence, and Polly no longer needed such a large home. They moved in 1916 to a smaller bungalow at 417 Holcomb Street. There Bill began to think about starting his own business in order to create more wealth for the family.

"Florence," he began, "I've been working for the railroad for eighteen years! It's a good living, but I'm forty years old, and I'm tired of the strenuous, dirty, dangerous work. I'm also tired of losing so many friends to gruesome accidents. And I'm constantly at the railroad's beck and call."

6. Polly Curnick at age six in 1916 in Watertown, New York. Courtesy of the author.

7. Florence Curnick at age twenty-eight in 1916 in Watertown, New York. Courtesy of the author.

"Oh Bill, Pauline and I are happy with you working on the railroad! We have enough money for both of us to wear nice dresses. We rent a lovely home. We don't want you to leave the railroad! You'll lose all your seniority! What would you *do?*" she exclaimed anxiously.

"I'd like to be in business for myself. I'm a first-rate carpenter. I'll bet I could make good money building homes. Jim Gunderson, down at the yard, and I have been considering going into business together," Bill said with excitement.

"No! Please don't do that!" Florence was emphatic. "I think its *way* too risky."

"Now, Florence, just sleep on it for a few days, and we'll talk some more," Bill cajoled.

Florence did not need to sleep on it. She was vehemently opposed to the idea. She let Bill know at every turn. She was enjoying life just fine and did not want any disruptions.

8. Bill Curnick at age forty in 1916 in Watertown, New York. Courtesy of the author.

But Bill was determined. Railroad accidents were frequent. Crew members were killed or seriously injured in the line of work. He also believed that he was so good with his hands that he could make a go of it building houses. For the first time in their life together, he flew in the face of Florence's wishes.

His timing was good. Just as he made the decision to leave the railroad, Daisy, now nineteen, decided to join them in Watertown. Florence had been writing to her regularly for the past several years, and Daisy finally *was* mature enough to see the potential benefit of the move. She came to live with the Curnicks in late 1916 when Polly was six.

Daisy had been cured of tuberculosis in the sanitarium in Wales (some went there to die, but the milder cases recovered) and had spent her entire youth there. She had received good care and learned the institution's ways. As a young teenager, she had taken on junior house mother responsibility, much as Florence had done at Barnardo's Home.

Daisy was even more petite than Florence. She stood four feet ten inches tall and was slender and very attractive in a much different way than her older half-sister. Daisy looked more like poor little Alice May. She had a round face, button nose, large oval eyes, and a darker complexion than Florence.

The sanitarium in Wales where Daisy had lived was kept exceptionally clean by its staff. This was the basic treatment for tuberculosis. The patients were taught to bathe carefully and completely every day and to washed their hands. In the final analysis, this approach worked for some, but not for others. Daisy was one of the fortunate ones.

Bill left the New York Central Railway in 1916 and formed a partnership with Jim Gunderson. They built several houses together. In 1918, the family moved to 520 Holcomb Street, and in 1920 Bill and his partner built a new home for them at 524 Holcomb Street, where they promptly moved.

Bill was a skilled carpenter and mason, and he worked efficiently. He was also so honest and good-hearted that he was forever willing to make owner-requested changes to house designs as he was building. He rarely kept track of these changes and thus frequently lost money. Florence never forgave him for relinquishing his seniority on the railroad for this frivolous enterprise. She let him hear about it at every opportunity.

Polly went to Mullin Street School in Watertown. As an only child, she enjoyed being around other children her age. Daisy worked as a domestic and helped care for Polly.

In 1917, while Bill was building homes, Aunty passed away in Iroquois at age eighty-eight. The Servisses and the Curnicks had remained close over the years. Bill thought of Uncle Levius as the father he never really had. He had taken for granted that Uncle and Aunty would always be there.

Uncle was distraught. He and Aunty had been married for sixty-seven years! Bill stayed with his beloved sponsor for several days after Aunty died. He could see how low Levius was and how much he missed his life partner, with whom he had shared so many wonderful adventures and such a long life.

"Bill, I'm na' cer'un I even wanna go on wit'oot 'er!" sobbed Levius. "We were li' two peas in a pod. We coul' finish one anot'er's t'oughts. I'm eighty-eight years old. I nee' ta go, too!"

"I know how close you two were, Uncle. That's why I was so careful about selecting a bride myself. I want Florence and me to have the same kind of relationship as you and Aunty."

Bill wished for that, but he also knew that it wasn't realistic. After ten years of marriage, he understood that Florence was stubborn, selfish, and sometimes downright mean-spirited. Still, she was Polly's mother, and he loved them both very much.

"Uncle, I don't want you to stay here by yourself with all your memories. I want you to come to live with me and my family," continued Bill.

Bill made this invitation without consulting Florence, who was not at all in favor of the idea. She believed she would have to take care of old Levius and did not at all relish the prospect while raising Polly, now seven.

This was the second time inside of two years that Bill had made a momentous family decision against Florence's wishes. He would pay ever after for doing so. Nonetheless, he knew it was the correct decision.

"I'm not going to take care of that old man!" exclaimed Florence after Bill had told her of his invitation.

"He's been like a father to me, Florence. You'll see, he'll pull his own weight. He's a wonderful gardener, and he'll be a help with Polly," Bill persuaded.

"Alright, we'll try it for a spell, but I'm warning you, Bill Curnick, I'm not going to take care of him!" came the stern response.

She sure can be ornery sometimes, thought Bill to himself. In 1917, Levius Serviss sold his farm, which had not operated in many years, and moved in with the Curnicks in Watertown. Bill was thrilled to be able to return some of the love, affection, and care that he had received from the Servisses.

Florence, however, added her displeasure at this development to her misgivings about Bill's departure from the railroad. She did not express her annoyance in front of Levius or Polly or Daisy, but she frequently vented to hapless Bill.

Levius was nothing if not cognizant of the intrusion he was making into the Curnicks' lives. He worked tirelessly to make the only contribution he could at his age. He became Polly's baby-sitter, playmate, story-teller, and companion. He taught her to play cards, and she was very good and quite competitive for the rest of her life, although she did not like to admit it.

He loved to garden, and so he and Polly planted and tended vegetables and flowers each growing season. Uncle told Polly about his and Aunty's trips to California prospecting for gold.

"I'll spin ya a yarn, if'n ya li', Polly!" Uncle would offer.

"Oh, spin me a yarn, Uncle!" Polly would respond excitedly.

"Well, I've tol' ya all aboot Aunty and me prospectin' for gold in Cali-forni'," replied Levius. "Lemme spin ya a yarn aboot the natives we met along da way when we traveled crost country, ahe? Every native Aunty and I met was frien'ly. We never encoun'ered any dat behaved like sav-ages, even d'ough we'd heard dat's what dey'd be like. All dey wanid was ta be lef' alone ta hunt buffalo and live quiet.

"When Aunty and I were in the plains country, ya coul' see buff'lo far and wide. It was like an ocean of buff'lo movin' along at a right good clip if'n they was bein' chased, ahe?"

Polly had seen pictures of buffalo in her schoolbooks. "How big were the buffalo, Uncle?" she asked, wide-eyed.

"'Boot twice the size of a cow, sweetie. Big and furry! De natives depended on 'em fer food, clothin', and shelter, ahe? Dey ate deir meat—coul' dey ever fix a tasty buff'lo steak! An' dey used deir hides ta make clot'in' and tents," came the explanation.

"I'd like to meet an Indian someday, Uncle," exclaimed Polly.

"Tell ya wha', Polly! One o' dese days, we'll all go up ta Iroquois ta meet some o' yer Daddy's frien's, ahe?" answered Levius.

"Does *Daddy* know Indians?" Polly couldn't believe her ears.

"Your Daddy was the bes' white lacrosse and hockey player dem Akwasasnee natives ever saw, pretty girl! Dey was real close frien's!" smiled Levius.

"Wow, I'd like to meet them someday soon, please, Uncle!" the excited girl responded.

Polly was a grandmother researching her genealogy long after her parents were gone before she discovered that Uncle Levius was not a blood relative!

By 1918, Bill had lived in the United States for more than ten years. The Canadian border with the United States was basically an open one, with both British (Canadian) and American citizens flowing back and forth at will.

Bill decided that he and Florence would be better off if they became citizens of their new country. All he had to do was prove that he had lived in the country for five years. That was easy, what with the railroad's payroll records. He applied on this basis and became a naturalized citizen on September 28, 1918.

Florence was also naturalized as part of his family. Polly, of course, was a citizen by virtue of being born in Watertown.

The Curnicks became active in Trinity Episcopal Church in Watertown, where Florence and Bill had been married. Polly was baptized there, Bill was active in the Men's Club and bowled with them, and Florence belonged to the Girls Friendly Society. Polly attended Sunday school and frequented Friday afternoon children's meetings. She also performed in Christmas pageants and other plays.

Down the street from the Curnick home was Grapapport's Meat Market, where Florence shopped. Mr. Grapapport always snuck Polly a piece of hot dog or a cold-cut while her mother shopped. Nearby was a fire barn with horse-drawn engines and a Dalmatian.

Levius had been a farmer for most of his life. When Bill's construction endeavors began to fail, he suggested to him that if he wished to be in business for himself, he might consider farming again.

"Bill, ya're jus' too good-hear'ed ta make a livin' buildin' houses. Ya know farmin' from A to Izard. Wha' ya don't know aboot da financial en' o' t'ings, I kin coach ya t'rough. If'n ya want ta be in bidness for yasef, why don' ya purchase a small farm?" Uncle suggested.

"Why, Bill, I think that's a marvelous idea! Let's do it!" chimed in Florence. She could see the logic in this approach, and *anything* was better than Bill continuing to lose money on his building projects. Bill was feeling defeated and had had enough of Florence's ill temper.

In late 1920, they purchased a twenty-acre farm about four and a half miles outside Watertown. It had a more than adequate house. Because there was no rural electricity there yet, the house had an acetylene gas lighting system—quite the modern convenience!

The farm had three cows, pigs, chickens, and a team of horses, which worked out well for the Curnicks. Uncle tended the large vegetable garden, and Bill operated the little farm and did some carpentry work on the side in town.

The farm had a large stand of maple trees. Every winter from about mid-February to mid-April, Bill would "sugar off" these lovely trees.

"Polly, time to sugar off," advised Bill one cold winter Saturday morning in February 1921.

"What's sugaring off, Daddy?" asked the inquisitive Polly.

"We're going to tap through the bark of our maple trees so the sap can run," explained her father.

"Can I come, too?" Polly asked again.

"Of course you can! That's why I brought it up in the first place!" laughed her father.

They made the rounds of the maple trees on the property, tapping through the bark with a small sharp metal troughlike channel in which the sap could flow. Then they hung a one-gallon bucket on the outboard end of the channel in order to collect the sap. It took about a week to fill a bucket.

The collected sap was boiled and processed into the most delicious pure maple syrup imaginable. Those who have not savored this nectar of the Northeast are missing a real treat. The liquid candy that most food markets sell in place of pure maple syrup is a far cry from the real thing. Bill and Polly also made maple sugar candy and maple syrup icicles with fresh snow—wonderful treats.

Uncle taught Polly to hitch the team of horses to the farm's buggy in the warm months and to the sleigh in the winter. She became a competent buggy driver and loved the sleigh best. There was nothing, she thought, more beautiful than an evening sleigh ride on a clear winter night with a full moon. The moonlight reflected brightly on the white snow, providing a blue-white glow all about. The air was dry and crisp. The snow crunched under the horses' hooves and the sleigh runners. It was beautiful and peaceful, Polly thought. She was a little princess with her blond curls shining under a full moon as she drove about in a winter cape, lap blanket, and furry leather gloves.

There was a fairly severe recession in the early 1920s, and Bill's small carpentry jobs dried up. There was plenty of food from the farm for the five of them to eat, but not much else. As a result, Florence and Bill discussed selling the little farm. Bill had been invited to take a job managing a larger operation with more than three hundred acres for the widow woman next door. The Curnicks decided to sell, and Bill entered a fifty-fifty partnership with the woman who owned it. Again, it was a living, not much more.

When the Curnicks sold the twenty-acre farm, they moved into a guest house on the widow's farm. Polly walked the one and a half miles each way to a country school that covered from the third grade through junior high school. There were ten to twelve pupils in the school in all grades. The teachers were always women, sometimes good, sometimes not. The students carried their lunch with them every day and used an outhouse privy behind the school, no matter the weather. The school was heated by a large wood-burning pot-belly stove. A farmer who lived nearby supplied the wood and came in to build the fire early every morning before the pupils arrived.

During the winter of 1919 on one of the Curnicks' trips to Rome to visit Nell and her family, Daisy met a local farmer named Timothy Staple. They began a brief courtship and were married that spring. Daisy moved to Lee Center, New York, where Tim owned and operated a beautiful and successful dairy farm. They subsequently had three children.

The Curnicks were living on and operating the widow woman's farm in 1923 when Harry Curnick, who by now had considerable seniority with the New York Central Railway in Rochester, came to Watertown to visit over the Independence Day holiday.

"How are things going in the farm-management business?" Harry asked.

"It's a living, Harry. That's about all we can say for it," came the reply from Florence.

Bill frowned at her. He would have put a better face on it. The fact remained, however, that her description was accurate.

"Bill, why don't you consider relocating to Rochester? There are plenty of good jobs with the railroad there. I think I can even help you get your old job back and maybe even your seniority!" suggested Harry enthusiastically.

"Oh Bill, let's think about that! Wouldn't it be fun to live in a bigger city? We lived best when you worked for the railroad before," exclaimed Florence.

Bill looked at her with a jaundiced eye. She was correct about the quality of their lives when he had worked for the railroad, but he loved farming and being his own boss.

"We'll discuss it, Harry. Thanks for suggesting it," responded Bill.

"I could go to work also," suggested Florence. "Pauline is going into the eighth grade. She's old enough to come home from school on her own while you're on the road, and Uncle will be there for her. Let's do it!"

"I said we'd talk it over," stated Bill, trying to hide his annoyance.

In the following weeks, the three of them—Bill, Florence, and Polly—discussed the possibility of a move.

"Pauline, I think you would receive a much better education in Rochester than here in Watertown," her mother offered.

"You're probably right about that, Florence," reflected Bill. "What do you think, Polly?"

"I'd miss my friends here, Daddy. I'm willing to go, though, if that's what you and Mother wish."

She is always so flexible, thought Bill. He worried that she did not put her own feelings and opinions on the table in their family conversations. He also believed that he needed Polly's opinions to help sway Florence, who often dominated their decision making.

Two incomes *were* attractive. Bill had enjoyed the railroad life, with the exception of the accidents and the fact that he functioned at the whim of someone other than himself.

One evening over dinner, he said, "Alright, Florence, let's give Rochester a try."

He had to smile at her enthusiastic response.

"Ohhhhhhhhh, that's wonderful, Bill! We'll have a terrific experience, you'll see!"

Sometimes the easiest thing was just to go along with Florence's wishes, thought Bill. It was agreed that Florence and Polly would move to Rochester over Labor Day weekend so Polly would be there in time to start the eighth grade school year. They would live with Harry's family until they found a place of their own.

Bill and Levius were left behind to pack up the house and have movers pick up their belongings for shipment to Rochester. Florence quickly found work as a film inspector at Eastman Kodak in Rochester. She soon discovered and rented a nice apartment. She and Polly moved in, living out of suitcases and sleeping on the floor as they awaited the furniture, and Polly started school. Bill shipped their belongings to them.

When the people who had purchased Bill and Florence's small twenty-acre farm a few years earlier discovered that Bill was leaving the area, they asked him to come over before he left and ignite the unused acetylene system that the Curnicks had employed for illumination. There was still no rural electricity outside Watertown, and the new owners had been utilizing kerosene lamps for light ever since they had purchased the place, so they had never learned how to use the intricate acetylene lights.

The system was supplied with acetylene piped from a pressurized canister on the edge of the lawn of the farmhouse. Bill went to the hardware store in Watertown for some carbon with which to start the system. He went through the routine he had always followed to fire it up.

Nothing happened. Bill knelt down to investigate the problem. That was the last he remembered of his actions that afternoon. The acetylene system blew up in his face!

Bill was tossed high in the air, along with metal fragments from the system. He later remembered breaking through tree branches on his way *up*.

He crashed to earth, badly injured. He was bleeding from the mouth and had numerous internal injuries, a compound fracture of his right leg, and a dislocated right shoulder. His right bicep muscle was torn from the top of his upper arm and dangled at his elbow. He was a mess at age forty-seven.

Neighbors arrived quickly to his aid, having been alerted by the thunderous explosion. They summoned a doctor, who never arrived. They then called for an ambulance, which failed to show up. Finally, after two hours of waiting, they put Bill in the back seat of a Ford touring car and drove him over rutted country roads to the hospital in Watertown.

When they wheeled him into the hospital on an emergency room gurney, the attending physician took one look at Bill and remarked, not aware that he was conscious, "You can wheel him in today, but we'll wheel him back out tomorrow."

"I'm going to fool you like hell, Doc!" Bill rasped through teeth clenched against the pain.

The hospital staff went to work on him. They relocated his shoulder and sewed up his arm as best they could. They could not set his leg until the next day. Then all the hospital could do was monitor Bill's progress and hope he was strong enough to pull through.

Florence was reached at the Kodak plant in Rochester. She left work and cancelled the rental of the apartment, losing the deposit but nothing else. That same afternoon she met the arriving moving van and arranged for their belongings to be placed into storage. Then she went to school to pick up Polly, and the two of them took the train to Watertown. Florence was tough, resourceful, and tenacious, if sometimes cold and self-focused, the result of a hard childhood that had taught her to rely on no one but herself.

Florence and Polly stayed with friends in Watertown for about ten days until it appeared certain that Bill would indeed "fool the doctor like hell!" Florence realized that she was, at least for the time being, the sole breadwinner. She decided that she had better return to her job in Rochester. Her mental toughness brought the family through this crisis. She had been through difficult times before.

Polly returned to Rochester with her mother and went back to school. The two of them moved in with a British friend whom Florence had met at Eastman Kodak. This location was close enough for her to walk to work. They commuted to Watertown on weekends to visit Bill. Levius, now ninety-five, moved in with friends of the Curnicks in Watertown.

In November, after two months, Bill was discharged from the hospital on crutches. With the help of friends, he and Levius boarded a train for Rochester to meet Florence and Polly. The Watertown Curnicks moved in with the Rochester Harry Curnicks. The house was crowded, but what are families for if not to care for one another in difficult times? These families were no strangers to hard times.

They started out well enough. After a time, though, Harry's wife, Jen, began to tire of the confusion. Bill, Florence, Polly, and Levius sensed her anxiety.

Bill's sister, Nell, came to Rochester for a visit for the Thanksgiving holiday and to celebrate Polly's thirteenth birthday. When she had assessed the situation, she insisted that the four of them move to her home in Rome, New York. Nell was much like her mother—always intent on lending a helping hand.

Another move seemed almost too much to bear. Florence would have to leave a very good job. Polly would need to change schools in the middle of the year. Poor Levius felt more and more like a fifth wheel. Nonetheless, Nell convinced them that she and her family would enjoy having them.

"After all," she stated, "didn't we all live with you after you and Mother brought us to America?"

That settled it. Florence, Bill, Polly, and Levius moved in with Nell and her family in Rome. Florence and Nell worked as cooks in the cafeteria at Rome Wire Company, and Bill kept house on crutches.

It was a lovely winter for Polly. Her family and Nell's—which consisted of Nell; her husband, Arthur Glassford; and their two children, Cecil and Violet (who were a bit older than Polly)—got on famously together. As an only child, Polly loved the constant activity that accompanied such a large group. They played games together and went to the movie theater every Saturday evening, with an ice cream sundae to follow.

Bill grew stronger and stronger. He was soon able to discard the crutches for a cane. His recovery was, no doubt, aided by all the physical activity he had experienced as an athlete and farmer-handyman earlier in his life. He began to look husky and hearty again.

In April 1924, Bill decided he could probably stand the pressures of a job once more. He applied for and was hired as caretaker for a wealthy Rome family who lived in a fashionable part of town.

They resided in a large and luxurious home at 609 North George Street, with a spacious yard and beautiful flower gardens. Bill tended the yard and gardens, performed household repairs, and maintained the automobiles. He was still limping around on his cane when he started. The Curnicks moved into an apartment upstairs over the carriage house in the alley behind 609 North George Street.

The Keeneys, for whom Bill worked, were generous, caring people. They grew to love their new caretaker, and he them. Mr. Keeney was not adept at the kinds of activities that youngsters enjoyed, and their six-year-old adopted son latched onto Bill, who taught him to fish and took him on excursions to local sporting events and the like.

The Keeneys had several cars, and Bill had the loan of a large, late-model Buick almost every weekend. It was the perfect scenario for Bill as he finished his recovery and got back on his wage-earner feet.

As soon as he received his first paycheck, Bill and Florence rented a large second-floor flat at 615 North Madison Street, about five blocks from Nell's family and within walking distance of the Keeneys as well. Their primary concern was that the place where they lived had to have at least a nine-foot wall for the treasured sideboard. Bill's pine box was also a fixture. The two Curnick families remained in close proximity and continued to enjoy one another's company.

Florence and Bill's furniture was still in storage in Rochester, so they arranged for delivery to their new home. The steep set of stairs running up to the apartment and sharp left-hand ninety-degree turn into the living room proved to be a challenge for the movers with respect to the sideboard. They eventually negotiated the turn, but not without putting some gouges on the piece, which remain on it today even though Bill quickly tried to address them.

Florence found work as house mother in a home for destitute girls, a position for which she was eminently qualified. Bill joined the Masons, one of the largest and oldest fraternal organizations in the world. Over the ensuing years, he rose to the thirty-second degree of membership. It was, after all, a way to escape the ever prickly Florence in the evenings.

In the middle of Polly's junior year in high school at Rome Free Academy in 1927, Florence decided that she would no longer provide for ninety-eight-year-old Levius to live with them.

"Bill, I can't continue to have Uncle underfoot!" she told him emphatically one evening after Levius had retired to bed. "He's just too much trouble! I'm working full-time and trying to keep house as well. I won't have him here any longer!"

"Florence, I can't put him out at his age! He's family to me, and I love him dearly. He needs us more than ever now. Besides, he's fine and is still doing our gardening for us," Bill responded.

"I don't care! I want him out!" exclaimed the bristling Florence.

Polly felt sorry for her father in these exchanges. There never seemed to be a way for him to prevail. Her mother just kept nagging and making life generally miserable until she got her way. This time was no exception. Bill finally gave in, as he had almost always done. He took Levius back to Iroquois, Ontario, to relatives there. He could hardly look the old man in the eye.

"It's awrigh', Bill. I understan'," said Levius as they parted. Bill was so overcome that he couldn't speak.

Levius Serviss died in 1928, five days before his one hundredth birthday. Bill Curnick never forgave himself. He also decided thereafter that he would spend as little time as possible at home alone with Florence. He loved Polly (they were ever so close), and Florence was tolerable with her around. But when Polly went off to college in the fall of 1928, Bill Curnick worked at the Keeney's every day, went home for dinner, and then went to the Masonic Temple *every evening* to play cards with his mates. This ritual continued for the rest of his life.

As for Florence, she preferred not to have anyone under foot or smoking cigars in the house. It just made things harder to keep clean. And she preferred her own company, anyway. That was the way she had lived most of her early life, and she was most comfortable when alone, she thought.

Polly graduated from Rome Free Academy in June 1928. She was accepted to Syracuse University, but Florence and Bill did not believe they could afford to pay her way. Bill shared this concern with his good friend and employer, Mr. Keeney, who was vice president of sales at Rome Wire Company.

"Why, Bill, why don't you let us pay Polly's tuition?" suggested Mr. Keeney excitedly.

Bill stared at him in disbelief. "Oh, I couldn't ask you to do that, Mr. Keeney! We'd never be able to repay you."

"Nonsense! I don't want you to pay us back. Polly is a lovely, bright young woman. She deserves a good education, and I'm certain that she'll put it to good use. Just call it an investment in the future of New York State on our part," laughed Keeney.

Bill was dumbfounded and could think of no response. He just gaped at his employer.

"That's settled, then. Go pack Polly for her trip to Syracuse!" demanded Keeney.

The Keeneys even lent Bill one of their new Buicks to drive Polly to Syracuse University in the fall of 1928. She arrived in grand style, if a bit embarrassed to be seen as wealthy. She decided right away to major in sociology.

Florence had worked at the Rome Wire cafeteria and then at the home for wayward girls all through Polly's high school years. In this way, she paid for the extras—four years of piano lessons for Polly, some family vacations (usually a rented cottage at one of the Adirondack lakes), and occasional dinners out.

With tuition covered by the Keeneys, Florence and Bill were able (though barely) to pay for Polly's room, board, and books. Polly also found office clerical work on campus to supplement what her parents were able to provide.

During her junior year at Syracuse University in 1930, the Great Depression hit Rome. The Keeneys lost their entire fortune as Rome Wire foundered, and Bill lost his job. Worse, the Keeneys were no longer able to pay Polly's tuition, leaving her with three semesters to complete.

Bill bounced from folding company to folding company as one after another collapsed in those Depression years. Their income was unsteady. Florence's job working with destitute girls was solid but did not pay well. Bill finally ended up as a maintenance mechanic at Revere Ware Company in Rome. He had been a Mason long enough at this point that he was able to secure a four-hundred-dollar loan from the organization to cover Polly's senior year tuition at Syracuse University.

15

Finally Another Rizk

THE YEAR 1919 was a momentous one for the Rezaks. Radia and Habeeb had been trying for quite some time to have another child. Radia was approaching forty, and they knew that her childbearing years were limited. Still, nothing developed.

Just before his tenth birthday on February 22, Nick began to complain of a stomachache. He couldn't eat and, in fact, was bringing back up everything that Radia tried to get down him. After three days of this, Radia took him to a neighborhood doctor.

At an examination on Thursday, the doctor prescribed a physic to settle Nick's stomach and sent him back home, saying to Radia that he had probably eaten too much green fruit. The physic prescribed by the doctor gravely aggravated the situation.

By Saturday, Nick was much worse. On Sunday, he began to run a fever, which increased in intensity to the point where he felt to Radia as though he would burn up. By Monday morning, Nick was in agony and afire with fever. Radia had had enough.

Habeeb had gone to work at the tailor shop, and Dave was at school. Radia did not have money to spend on taxi fare (they still did not own a car), and there was no bus route that ran easily between Otisco Street and Syracuse Memorial Hospital on Irving Avenue, so she set out with Nick on foot to walk to the hospital. She had lost two children to disease. Nick was not going to be the third. American medicine was going to cure him.

It was well over a mile to Memorial Hospital, where she was acquainted with a Dr. Mench, to whose wife she had sold some of her lace. Nick was bent double with pain and too heavy for Radia to carry. He would just have to bear up and struggle up the big hill to the hospital. Sweat poured down his face in spite of the winter cold.

Radia knew he must be getting dehydrated. On they trudged for the better part of an hour before they arrived at the hospital emergency room.

The nurses took one look at Nick and immediately stripped him and placed him in an ice bath. His temperature was higher than 105 degrees Fahrenheit. Radia told them about his horrible stomachache and the fever that would not break. Dr. Mench began to poke and probe Nick. It did not take him long to assess that he had appendicitis.

Now the concern was that his appendix may have ruptured. His blood count indicated that he had a severe infection. Dr. Mench told Radia that if Nick's appendix had ruptured (because of the prescribed physic) and filled his abdominal cavity with peritonitis, his condition would be extremely grave.

This aggressive infection had killed many who had endured the pain of appendicitis for too long before seeking treatment. Radia asked calmly what the doctor recommended. She knew that Nick was a tough little character and that, given half a chance, he would fight hard to survive.

Dr. Mench explained that the best chance of saving Nick lay in a surgical procedure to cleanse the infectious peritonitis from his abdomen. Radia agreed with the plan as long as she could be present in the operating room.

Dr. Mench called in Dr. William L. Wallace for the operation, whom was well known in Central New York for his innovative surgical procedures. Nick was in the operating room for six hours. Dr. Wallace opened his abdomen in several places, pulled his intestines outside his body, cleansed with antiseptic every part of him that he could reach, and put him back together.

There were no antibiotics with which to fight infection. Now all they could do was wait and hope that they had been successful at eliminating enough of the infection for him to begin to heal. Radia sat calmly in the operating room through the entire ordeal.

She then moved into Nick's hospital room with him. He was in a coma for twenty-three days, during which time she rarely left his side. Then little by little he seemed to get stronger. It was a very slow process and took two more surgeries to completely eliminate his infection.

Finally, in January 1920, *eleven months* after Nick had walked to the hospital with a ruptured appendix, the doctors decided that he was well enough to go home. Nick turned out to be the first case of a ruptured appendix in Central New York where the patient actually survived. Dr. Wallace, who had founded Memorial Hospital so that he could place into practice some of his forward-thinking surgical techniques, was able to publish a medical paper on the successful procedure.

Equally gratifying was the fact that during the course of Nick's recovery from appendicitis, Radia had somehow managed to conceive the child that she and Habeeb had hoped they would have in America. She went into labor and gave birth on April 26, 1920, to another son, Rizk ibn Habeeb el Rizk, thereafter known as Richard H. Rezak (Dick to the family).

Radia had secretly yearned for a daughter, surrounded by men as she was. She quickly realized that Dick was a fine, healthy baby and began to bestow upon him all the love and affection she had always lavished on her family—a good one to be born into.

Nick's illness caused a major disruption in the wealth-building agenda. Radia had not sold much in the year Nick was hospitalized, and Habeeb was stretched thin both tailoring and covering the store (not to mention any medical care expenses they may have had). Dave was still in high school during the day.

Things got so bad that Dave finally talked his parents into allowing him to quit school. He left high school and went to work as an apprentice at Franklin Manufacturing Company, a local automobile-assembly facility producing a line of air-cooled engine luxury cars. Without this sacrifice on Dave's part, it is unlikely that the family would have survived the financial crisis. Dave was never able to complete his education.

As if Nick's illness and Dick's arrival were not enough excitement for one year, Radia and Habeeb finally decided that, with Dave's help, they could afford to purchase a home of their own. In mid-1920, they bought and moved into a house at 417 Seymour Street.

They lived upstairs and rented out an apartment downstairs. The rent they collected paid for their mortgage, making the purchase possible. The five of them lived there together for the next six years.

Things smoothed out over the next year. Habeeb was making a good living at Greco's Tailor Shop; Radia resumed her retail embroidery and linen sales; Dave was progressing at Franklin; Nick got back to school in time to move up with his classmates; and Dick took all of everyone's free time. By 1922, they had bought the two-family house next door and rented it out as well.

Habeeb had always been a prankster. Part of his success in engaging and influencing people was his repertoire of jokes and humorous insults, often hurled without regard for those who might be offended. The family, especially Dave and Nick, learned quickly that the only way to survive in this atmosphere was to fight fire with fire. The two boys were always on the lookout for new ways in which to embarrass or antagonize one another, their family, and their friends.

By 1923, the newly invented electric vacuum cleaner was on the market, and Habeeb bought one as a gift for Radia, thinking that it might ease the burden of cleaning with a new baby under foot. The new device was too much for Dave, now twenty, and Nick, fourteen, to ignore.

Late one afternoon after Dave returned home from the first shift at the Franklin plant and Nick was home from school and selling his papers, they were baby-sitting three-year-old Dick while Radia managed the store. Habeeb was still at the tailor shop.

Nick was rolling a ball to Dick, who would try to catch it and roll it back. All the boys loved ball games. Dave became intrigued with the new vacuum cleaner. He was experimenting with it when a grand idea dawned upon him.

As Dick and Nick were rolling the ball back and forth, Dave stole up behind Dick, turned on the device and made as if to suck him up with the vacuum. Dick had seen his mother cleaning with this new-fangled contraption and did not like the noise it made one bit. Dave thrust the vacuum canister hose toward Dick's head and shouted that he was going to suck him inside.

Dick was terrified! He screamed loudly and tried to run away. After him charged the giggling Dave with Nick in pursuit of the fun. Dick vividly remembered the incident for the rest of his life.

Everyday after school, Nick arrived at the printing plant of the *Syracuse Herald* to pick up his newspapers for sale. He then walked along West Fayette Street toward the New York Central Railway station (the station was always a good place to sell), back east on the other side of the street, and then south along Clinton Street toward his corner at the intersection of Jefferson and Salina streets.

Just as Dave had done before him, Nick hawked his papers along this daily walk. He began to notice that a string of attractive women bought papers from him almost every day on West Fayette Street near the train station.

At age fourteen, Nick was beginning to appreciate a well-turned ankle on the opposite sex. He wondered why there were only women along this particular stretch of street. So one evening after dinner he pulled Dave aside and asked in a whisper, "Dave, did you notice the beautiful women who buy newspapers along Fayette Street when you were selling?"

"You bet!" exclaimed Dave.

"Who are they, and why are there no men living there?"

"Well, little camel rider," replied Dave with a chuckle, "maybe it's time for you to learn the ways of the world! There may be no men there *during the day* when you go by, but there are plenty of men there in the evening and overnight."

"I don't understand," Nick was confused.

"Those women are prostitutes!" Dave allowed with some excitement.

"Huh?"

"They're whores, Nick! They sell their bodies to any man who can pay the freight!" explained Dave.

"Wow! Why do they do that?" asked Nick sheepishly.

He was beginning to wish he had not approached this topic with his older brother. But Dave was in the know, and Nick was *not* going to ask his parents.

"Because they can make lots of money doing it. There are many men who don't have wives or girlfriends who just want some loving for a night. Those women give them that for a price," laughed Dave.

"Wow!" said Nick again. "I think they like me!"

"Why do you say that?" asked an amused Dave.

"Because they never stiff me!" came the proud reply.

And so it was that Nick learned about the Tenderloin District. He was too embarrassed to ask Dave if he had ever been there to visit any of the women.

Things smoothed out for the Rezaks in the early 1920s. Family wealth grew, and in 1925 Radia and Habeeb announced to the boys that they were purchasing a commercial building at 911 South Avenue on the corner of West Kennedy Street.

The building had space for a grocery store on the first floor (up until then, a bar) and a large apartment upstairs. A man named Mr. August owned the building and operated the bar. The sales transaction was closed on September 1, 1925. Mr. August always joked thereafter that the first of September was the last of August!

By the end of 1925, the Rezaks were ensconced in their new home upstairs over their place of business. They were even able to keep the two rental properties on Seymour Street. Habeeb left Joe Greco, the tailor, in order to devote full-time to the new and much larger grocery store. He took his best tailoring customers with him and continued to sew on the side.

Nick graduated from Blodgett Vocational High School in 1927, walking everyday the almost two miles back and forth to the school. He was a fairly good student, an excellent basketball player, and captain of the debate team. He had watched and heard his father argue and discuss politics and other issues with his friends over the years. Nick discovered that he also loved the mental gymnastics associated with debating. He was becoming fast on his feet—a trait that would stand him in good stead in his professional life.

Radia and Habeeb naturally assumed that Nick would join them and Dave in the store. Indeed, between 1927 and 1929, Nick clerked in the store, obtained his driver's license, and delivered groceries in the family's used Model-T Ford panel truck, their first vehicle.

He also taught himself French in order to meet the entrance requirements of Syracuse University. Vocational High School had not offered foreign-language studies, and languages were easy for Nick. After two years of working in the store, he was pretty well convinced that a career in the grocery business was not going to be his cup of tea.

With Radia's support, Nick applied and was accepted to Syracuse University in 1929. He commenced classes there that fall. He earned a position on the freshmen basketball team, and his grades were good. He joined

9. The Rezak family in 1923. *From left to right:* Nick, age fourteen; Radia, age forty-three; Dave, age twenty; Dick, age three; Habeeb, age fifty-seven; and Abe Rizik (the Ellis Island clerks spelled his name differently!), Habeeb's cousin who lived in Brooklyn, age unknown. Courtesy of the author.

the Cosmopolitan House, an international student gathering place, that fall and continued to live at home. Things were going well until the stock-market crash of 1929, followed by the Great Depression.

In the fall of 1930, Radia had to advise her middle son that not only was there no more money for his education, but that they also needed his earnings to help support the family. Habeeb's tailoring income decreased dramatically at this time, as did Radia's lace sales.

By midsemester, Nick received a letter from the university bursar's office indicating that unless he paid up, he could no longer attend classes. He stayed home with a heavy heart. A week later, though, one of his class-mates and friends, Delbert Smith, contacted him.

"Nick, why have you been cutting classes? Professor Manwell has been asking about you," inquired the concerned Del.

"The bursar said that I couldn't attend class anymore. I don't have enough money to pay the tuition I owe," Nick explained sadly.

The next day Professor Reginald Manwell contacted Nick and asked him to come by his office for a visit.

"Nick," he offered, "you're too good a student to drop out. I think I can arrange an extension on your tuition bill if you're interested."

"Of course, I'm interested!" exclaimed the excited Nick.

He was subsequently able to obtain an interest-free loan from the First Methodist Church, which the family had attended until they were able to assist in the establishment of an Eastern Orthodox Church. This loan plus his earnings got him through Syracuse University.

During the summer of 1930, Nick worked as a contractor's helper, which paid more than working in the store. He mixed concrete, dug basements by hand, and, most notably, carried sixty-seven-pound concrete blocks up two flights of ladders. The latter turned him into a strapping six-foot two-hundred-pounder.

When Dave left high school in 1919, he began working at the Franklin plant. He worked there for six years, until the family purchased the 911 South Avenue property, at which point he moved to full-time partnership with Habeeb in the new store. Dave's contribution to the family's wealth during those years was a major reason they were able to buy the store property as early as they did.

The same year that the family moved into the apartment above the store, 1925, Dave met the love of his life. He and Habeeb and some Arab American friends took some bootleg beer and arak (remember, 1925 was smack in the middle of Prohibition) and went fishing early one summer morning on Lake Ontario in Chaumont Bay not far from Watertown.

By midafternoon, the fish were biting, and the men had run out of arak. Dave, the youngest, was asked to go ashore to visit a Lebanese family in Watertown (the Habeebs) in search of more. The group dropped Dave off on land and went back to fishing while he drove his father's delivery truck to the Habeebs.

When Dave found the house, the most beautiful young woman he had ever seen was sweeping the sidewalk in front. He climbed out of the panel truck and introduced himself to Mary Habeeb. Mary had long, black hair, huge black eyes, and a lovely smile.

"I've been sent to get more arak for my fishing party," Dave explained as he smiled at Mary.

"Why did you come here for arak?" asked the confused Mary.

"Why, because your family distills the best bootleg arak in the state!" Dave exclaimed.

"We do no such *thing!*" stated Mary emphatically.

Dave was baffled. He knew that he was at the house to which his father had sent him. Finally, he said to Mary, "May I speak to your father, please?"

"If you must! But I can assure you, we do *not* have any arak!" she responded dismissively and with no little annoyance.

Dave went inside and soon returned with his quest fulfilled. "It was very nice to meet you, Miss Mary!" smiled Dave as he left.

Mary looked up from her sweeping to see him carrying a package under his arm. She watched him leave, then went inside and confronted her father, who, after some meager attempts at mollifying her, owned up to the fact that part of the family's business was supplying bootleg arak to upstate Arab American clientele. Thus came Mary's introduction into part of her family's business and to Dave Rezak.

Dave returned to the fishing party with the arak. "I've met the woman I'm going to marry," he exclaimed.

His father looked at him with astonishment.

"Who?" was all he could manage.

"Mary Habeeb!" responded Dave with pride and excitement.

He was right. They were married on May 26, 1929, after a long Arab-style courtship. Radia and Habeeb shared their spacious apartment above the store at 911 South Avenue with the newlyweds.

Dave and Mary started the next generation of Rezaks with the birth of their first daughter, Laurice, on November 30, 1930. A second daughter, Helen, was born there on April 24, 1932. She was followed over the years by Robert (Bob) on March 2, 1934; John (Jack) on June 12, 1935; Louis on October 22, 1940; and Barbara on August 16, 1950. It was a home of much love, fun, and constant activity.

Radia and Habeeb were social people, so in addition to their own growing family there was a good-size crowd in their apartment almost every evening. It was so boisterous that Nick had to study at the Syracuse University library.

Habeeb was a world-class backgammon player—one who could roll his dice as soon as you have rolled yours and finish his play as you are finishing yours. He was also skilled at whist (the predecessor of bridge) and pinochle. Almost every night two or three card tables of these games were going on in the apartment.

In the early 1920s, Dave had put together a crystal-set radio, which brought in music very faintly using ear phones. By the time they moved to South Avenue, the family had acquired a Magnavox radio that, amid many screeches and howls, brought in stations from as far away as Schenectady and Pittsburgh. The programming was primarily music with some skimpy news.

Habeeb thought the radio the eighth wonder of the world and listened to it for hours at a time. He never learned to read or write English, so he listened to radio news and subscribed to several Arabic printed newspapers published in New York City. He also had a considerable library of Arabic books.

The year 1926 saw the entire Rezak family become citizens, except for Dick, who was already a citizen by virtue of being born in the United States. Habeeb had studied all the citizenship requirements and US history and government, which Dave or Nick read to him.

Habeeb passed the oral citizenship examination easily. He was well versed in current affairs because he read the Arabic newspapers distributed from New York City and listened to the radio on a daily basis.

On the day that Habeeb was to become a citizen, he invited the whole family to accompany him to the federal courthouse in Syracuse where the swearing-in would occur. Each person to be sworn in was called individually before a federal judge. The judge had a brief conversation with each and then the swearing-in took place. It was a nice ceremony.

When it came Habeeb's turn to appear before the judge, he rose and approached the bench. The judge had a few more questions for him, which he handled with ease. Then the judge picked up the morning's *Syracuse Post-Standard* and said to Habeeb, "Can you read this?"

Habeeb looked at him blankly. There was a long pause during which Radia's heart leaped to her throat. Then Habeeb pulled a folded copy of the day's Arabic newspaper from his suit jacket pocket, handed it to the judge, and replied, "No, Your Honor, can you read this?"

Radia's heart stopped. Habeeb always pushed the envelope. Had he gone too far this time? Then the judge grinned broadly and broke into a hearty laugh.

"Good thing he has a sense of humor!" she sighed. Habeeb received his US citizenship, and the rest of the family became naturalized citizens.

After the purchase of the property at 911 South Avenue, Habeeb determined that in order to make the most of business opportunities in his adopted community, he had better become active in local politics. He began to support Republican Party causes and to develop strong relationships with Twelfth Ward politicians.

In the fall of 1930, Nick was a sophomore at Syracuse University, thanks to Professor Reginald Manwell, Syracuse University, and First Methodist Church. With help from Habeeb's political cronies, Nick was able to obtain a patronage job six nights a week driving trash-collection trucks for the City of Syracuse. Landing this job was incredibly fortunate, considering that there was 20 percent unemployment in the city because of the Depression.

Nick's route, with his two helpers, was to pick up boxes of trash from behind the businesses along Bank Alley in the downtown area starting at 7:00 PM. They then hauled the trash to the city incinerator on Hiawatha Boulevard. The crew normally finished the job in about two hours, which meant they were finished work at about 9:00 PM. They were paid for four hours work even if the task took only two hours.

They frequently pulled the truck out of site into Bank Alley between Washington and Jefferson streets, parked, and played poker for a while before trucking to the incinerator and clocking out at 11:00 PM.

Nick became an excellent poker player in the process. He earned the princely sum of seventy-five cents an hour on this job, and his helpers earned fifty cents. The two helpers were married men supporting families on this wage during the Depression.

During the fall months, Nick worked additional hours on a full night shift driving his heavy garbage truck as crews of workers shoveled fallen leaves from the streets. His favorite assignment was at the city dump. At least once every night, a light two-ton truck dumping its load would slide down the face of the dump site on the wet leaves. They were then not heavy enough to haul themselves out. Nick's job was to attach a chain to the stricken truck and pull it out of the dump with his heavier five-ton truck. For the rest of the night, though, he would stretch out on the seat and catch up on his sleep.

In the winter months, with the heavy snowstorms three or four times each month, Nick was drafted as a snowplow driver and sometimes worked straight through the night, finishing about 7:00 AM.

Sometimes he drove the open, unheated cab trucks in subzero temperatures all night. He would then dash home, shower, and head to class at Syracuse University. Needless to say, he was not bright-eyed and bushy-tailed on these occasions.

16

Polly and Nick

BOTH THE CURNICKS AND THE REZAKS understood that education was the pathway to a better life. During her senior year at Syracuse, Polly was active in the Sociology Club, which brought in speakers with special expertise for occasional lectures, provided students with access to professionals practicing in the field, and was a source of social contact between students.

In the fall of Nick's junior year at Syracuse in 1931, he attended a Sociology Club tea in the Hall of Languages basement. There he met the pretty, fair-skinned blond with a million-dollar smile whom he had noticed in one of his classes. He was eighteen months her elder and a year behind her at the university. She, it seems, had for some time admired from afar the dark-complexioned Arab.

After meeting him at the tea and observing him sleep through class on a couple of occasions after working all night, she offered to share her lecture notes with him. Thus began a five-year courtship and sixty-five year romance between Polly Curnick and Nick Rezak.

All his work, his classes, and his studies left no time for sports for Nick. He was unable to play basketball after his freshman year. His social life was also limited. It was hard to find time to date Polly around his work schedule, to say nothing of the rather Victorian rules relating to female students at the time. He attended one University Club dance, escorting Polly, who was "the belle of the ball and the light of my eye," he later commented.

College, combined with his work schedule, was no bed of roses for Nick, and he was glad to get it behind him. He graduated with a bachelor's degree in social science in 1933, a year after Polly.

Polly hoped to continue her education with a master's degree after graduation in 1932 but had no money to pay for such an undertaking. It just so happened that William Allan Neilson, president of Smith College, came to Syracuse University to speak in the spring of Polly's senior year. He was an acquaintance of Polly's sociology professors, Elizabeth and Reginald Manwell. The latter arranged for Polly to have an interview with Dr. Neilson during his visit. He was late arriving, however, and had to rush right back to the station to catch a train to another engagement.

As Dr. Neilson was dashing to his taxicab for the return trip to the train station, Dr. Manwell grabbed Polly's arm and shoved her into the car with him, saying, "Dr. Neilson, this is Polly Curnick, one of our very best students. She needs a scholarship to attend Smith next year. I think you should give her one."

Polly was mortified. She was not prepared for such an abrupt encounter and was fearful that Dr. Neilson would not wish her to be forced upon him in this way. Nonetheless, she and Neilson visited as he rode to the train station.

A few weeks later Polly received a letter from the graduate admissions office at Smith College inviting her to attend that fall in their master's sociology program with a full scholarship. She had never even applied!

Polly and Nick loved the Manwells and remained in touch with them for the rest of their lives. Everyone who has ever accomplished anything has benefited from the support of others, and so it was for Polly and Nick.

In the summer of 1932, off to the prestigious Smith College School of Social Work in Northampton, Massachusetts, went Polly to earn her master's degree. She was also given room and board at Worcester State Hospital in Worcester. She attended classes for two months on the Smith campus and then worked a nine-month internship in the Social Service Department of Worcester State Hospital under the direction of a Smith faculty member. After the internship, it was back to Smith for two more months of classes and preparation of her thesis.

She graduated with her master's degree in August 1933, shortly after Nick finished his undergraduate work at Syracuse. The only time the two saw each other that entire year was at spring break, when Nick drove his ancient Essex coupe (complete with rumble seat) to Worcester for a few days.

In the summer of 1933, after graduating from Syracuse, Nick took a job with the City of Syracuse Department of Welfare (this time a nonpolitical appointment). Polly accepted a position with the City of Rochester Department of Social Services. Now that they were only seventy-five miles apart, Nick's Essex wore out tires making the trip to Rochester. Polly had never learned to drive and so could travel only by train.

In the spring of 1934, Nick decided to apply to the New York School of Social Work (now part of Columbia University) in New York City for a master's degree. He received a fellowship from New York State that paid thirty dollars per week plus tuition for three semesters. By June 1935, Nick had finished the coursework for the program.

In order to be near Nick, Polly accepted a job with the American Red Cross in New York City in the fall of 1934 and remained with this organization for three years. She and Nick had a wonderful year together in the city. They took long walks in Central Park and had lovely luncheons at the Tavern on the Green. They rode the horse-drawn carriages around the city. They were regulars at Broadway (and off-Broadway) shows. They enjoyed the jazz scene in Harlem, and they frequented the opera. During their year in New York, they began to speak of marriage. Nick was twenty-six and Polly twenty-five.

After finishing his coursework at the New York School of Social Work and prior to completion of his thesis, Nick took a position with the City of Syracuse Department of Social Services as intake supervisor. During the winter of 1935–36, he commuted to the city every weekend that the New York Central Railway ran an excursion train.

To Florence and Bill Curnick, Nick was a foreigner (never mind their own backgrounds). He was not from a western European, English-speaking family. Their expectation was that Polly would eventually marry an Anglo-Saxon. Radia and Habeeb assumed that Nick would marry a Middle Eastern woman, as had Dave. Neither set of parents was prepared for a Polly and Nick partnership.

In December, Nick traveled to New York City to be with Polly for the holidays. They decided to give themselves a Christmas present by eloping.

They were married at Union Theological Seminary at Riverside Church on Riverside Drive on December 28, 1935. Delbert Smith, their friend from Syracuse University, was best man; Helen Denson, Polly's college roommate, was maid of honor; and Eleanor Smith, Del's wife, was the only witness.

When Polly and Nick obtained their marriage license (a public document) on the morning of their marriage, the license bureau issued a report on the wire to the Watertown and Syracuse newspapers. The Curnicks were living in Rome, and so Watertown friends called to congratulate them on their daughter's marriage. Polly and Nick's honeymoon was not a peaceful one!

Florence threw an absolute hissy fit. She screamed and yelled at both Polly and Nick. They both sat quietly and patiently while she ranted and raved about how ungrateful Polly was and how irresponsible Nick was. In the end, she spent herself, as they knew she eventually would, and sent them away.

Bill was wounded but accepting. He loved his daughter very much and trusted her judgment. Florence never forgave either one of them and never fully accepted Nick into her family.

Radia and Habeeb, in Polly's words, "were amazing." Radia, as we have said, was a remarkably intelligent woman with great strength and much human understanding. Polly grew to love her deeply. Radia always told Polly that she could accomplish whatever she set her mind to, something she had never heard from her own mother. As Radia and Polly grew closer through their new relationship, they learned that their thinking and values were much alike.

Habeeb always spoke Arabic at home, even though his English was by now more than adequate, so it was harder for Polly to get to know him. He was, however, kind and generous to her, even teaching her backgammon and putting up with her relatively slow play (his was lightening fast).

Dave Rezak, in Polly's words, "was kindness and helpfulness itself." This characterization would surprise no one who knew him. Dave had developed into a shrewd businessman as he helped found the Silver Star Supermarket chain in Syracuse and as he quietly bought up apartment house after apartment house as rental property on the south side of town.

Despite Dave's able and no-nonsense business mind, he had a heart of gold. He carried grocery customers on credit until they could pay. His customers so loved him that they continued to trade at Rezak's Silver Star even if they moved across town.

Dave's younger brother's new wife was his new sister as far as he was concerned. The two became the closest of friends. Mary took Polly under her wing and made certain that she was introduced around the Arabic community in Syracuse and included in the many women's activities.

Polly and Nick started married life with her working at Red Cross in New York City and him working back in Syracuse and living with Radia and Habeeb. Polly lived at Chistadora Settlement House, and Nick commuted on weekends.

In the early spring of 1936, there was serious flooding in the northeastern United States. Nick took a short-term assignment with the American Red Cross managing disaster relief in Rumford, Maine. Polly visited him there once during his three-month stint. Married life so far was not of the "together" variety for them.

After Maine, the newlyweds sublet an apartment on St. Marks Place in the Lower East Side New York City Bowery area. Polly worked at the Red Cross, and Nick finished his marathon thesis and earned his master's degree from the New York School of Social Work at the end of the summer of 1936.

In the fall, married life began in earnest as Nick took a job in the Intake and Certification Section of the Works Progress Administration in the city. They moved to a one-bedroom apartment in Spuyten Dyvel on 214th Street. The two began to think in terms of a family. Both wanted children, especially after enjoying Mary and Dave's growing brood.

Polly became pregnant in early 1938, but things did not go well. She miscarried in the spring of that year. She was terribly low, and she and Nick spent long hours in each other's arms as they recovered from this setback.

The New York World's Fair was in progress in the spring of 1939, so Polly and Nick had a steady stream of friends and relations staying with them in their small abode, which helped both of them keep their minds off their recent loss.

Nick was soon appointed chief of the Intake and Certification Section—he was on his way up. Not far, however. He quickly ran into policy differences with the administrator of the New York City program, Colonel

Breton Somervell (later lieutenant general and army chief of supply during World War II). Nick was right (according to him), but Somervell was the boss.

After being "fired with enthusiasm," Nick started job hunting again in the fall of 1939. It was a good lesson in diplomacy for the argumentative debater. He accepted a job with the New York State Department of Social Welfare in Rochester. Polly left the job she loved at Red Cross and began working for Child and Family Service of Monroe County in Rochester. They rented a second-floor two bedroom flat on Werner Park.

Nick soon left the Department of Social Welfare and accepted a position with State Charities Aid Association, where he did community organization work in Allegany, Livingston, and Seneca counties south of Rochester. He traveled these three predominantly rural counties promoting child- and public-welfare services.

Western New York is a beautiful part of the country, winter aside. The two enjoyed playing at Lake Ontario and Irondequoit Bay in the warm weather. They hiked Letchworth State Park, the "Grand Canyon of the East," year around. Niagara Falls was a frequent destination.

Nick enjoyed prowling around his rural territory. The hilly vistas just south of Dansville were spectacularly beautiful to him. The spacious old mansions built by nineteenth-century oil barons on Main Street in Wellsville were lovely. The hillside upon which the Geneseo State Teachers College was perched overlooked the Genesee River valley. He never tired of his drives through the region.

In late 1939, Polly became pregnant for a second time. This time the pregnancy was normal, and I, William David Rezak (after my grandfather Bill Curnick and my uncle Dave Rezak), was born on August 30, 1940.

My father was at a work-related conference in New York City when I decided to arrive. I had been due for more than two weeks. Florence came to Rochester to care for Polly and me. She called Nick and announced the birth, pleased that it was she who got to see me first.

Nick skipped out of the meeting to which he had driven. He hopped into his 1935 Dodge Coupe and sped north up US-9 and west across US-20 to Rochester. He drove all night and dashed into Strong Memorial Hospital to meet me.

10. Nick and Billy in 1941. I'm one, he's thirty-two. Courtesy of the author.

11. Polly in 1943 at age thirty-two. Courtesy of the author.

I was fair like my mother, with the same dimples. Polly and Nick told me that some of their happiest memories were of those months after I was born as they "watched [my] development and . . . beautiful grin."

World War II started in Europe that year, and the economy was expanding as the United States headed into manufacturing and supplying equipment and munitions for the European allies. Polly and Nick were in the car with me taking a Sunday drive on December 7, 1941, when they heard on the radio the fateful news that the Japanese had bombed Pearl Harbor. They realized immediately that their involvement was inevitable.

Soon after the first of the year, Nick took a job with the federal Office of Civil Defense in New York. Back to the city they moved, this time with a child. They rented a two-bedroom apartment near Columbia University's Baker Field football stadium at the northern tip of Manhattan. Polly remained at home at this point, caring for me.

Within a year, Nick, now age thirty-three, was promoted to assistant to the deputy director of the Office of Civil Defense. This step up required that we move to hot, humid, un-air-conditioned Washington, DC. We found a place to live—after some intervention by Nick's boss because housing was in very short supply—in McLean Gardens, an apartment complex being built in McLean, Virginia, for people working on the war effort in Washington.

In mid-1943, Nick moved to the US Department of State, Office of Foreign Relief, where he was appointed chief personnel officer. He, Polly, and I continued to live in McLean.

Nick helped to put together the administrative plans for the United Nations Relief and Rehabilitation Administration (UNRRA), which is today the United Nations Children's Fund (UNICEF). He became an employee of that organization when it was formed by the United Nations in January 1944 and was always pleased and proud to have played a role in the formation of an organization that has had such a positive impact on the world. The fact that Nick was fluent in English and Arabic was not lost on UNRRA.

In the meantime, although he was now thirty-four years of age, Nick was classified 1-A in the military draft. He was offered a commission in the navy and turned that down. The US State Department indicated to the draft board that Nick was essential to their war effort, which took care of the potential draft obligation.

St. Elias Church and the Other Rezaks

RADIA AND HABEEB had been in America for thirteen years before an opportunity to establish an Arabic Eastern Orthodox Christian church where they lived presented itself. For years, they had attended the occasional celebration of the Eastern Orthodox liturgy by circuit priests visiting from the New York City area. Once in a while they attended Russian liturgy. The rest of the time they attended First Methodist Church.

This situation was far from satisfactory for a couple whose religion had always been a large part of their lives. Both longed for a more regular spiritual experience along the lines of their old-country tradition.

The Ketaily family from Acre, Palestine, came to Syracuse early in the twentieth century and lived on Oswego Street, near the Rezaks. They assisted others from the Levant to make the transition to American life and had begun to form the nucleus of an Antiochian Eastern Orthodox church.

Radia and Habeeb joined with the Ketailys and other Arabic nationals working toward establishment of such a church. Radia was instrumental in this endeavor, for which she was well suited because of her long family tradition. Habeeb, as the family patriarch, took the more visible leadership role. He and a small group of men formally chartered St. Elias Syrian Orthodox Church of Syracuse on November 10, 1929. Habeeb was elected the first president of the church council. A certificate of incorporation was filed with Onondaga County on March 15, 1930.

The first order of business for the council was to find a permanent home for the new church, which was a challenge because the congregation had no funds. Habeeb researched local church properties that were for sale. One in particular drew his attention: the Lafayette Methodist Church at 241 West Lafayette Street.

Financing became the next challenge. Habeeb and his colleagues were able to negotiate a contract with the current owner for one thousand dollars down (which they raised from the congregation) and an eight-thousand-dollar mortgage. The congregation was amazed that the council had so skillfully purchased the property for a mere nine thousand dollars.

Next came the task of finding a permanent pastor. Appropriately enough, the Reverend Father John Khoury was assigned.

The early years of St. Elias were not easy. Organizational and financial problems plagued the congregation during the Depression years, and in 1936 a fire caused extensive damage. In the struggle to recover and flourish after the fire, the council initiated what would become an annual festival, the Mahrajan, in celebration of Christian Arab American heritage. The festival was hugely popular among the Arab Americans of central New York. Delicious Arabic food was plentiful, as was Arabic music, dancing, and, of course, the obligatory arak. This annual event turned out to be the church's financial salvation.

As funding stabilized for the church, a resident pastor was affordable. In 1939, the Very Reverend Father George Karim began his illustrious twenty-year tenure at St. Elias. He and his family were housed in rented space on Midland Avenue until a rectory was acquired on West Lafayette Street.

Dick, who was seventeen years younger than Dave and eleven years younger than Nick, continued to live with Radia and Habeeb after his older brothers married and started families. Mary became a second mother to him.

Dick attended Seymour School and then Syracuse Central High School, where he graduated in 1938. He went right on to study geology at Syracuse University. He was halfway through his junior year when on December 7, 1941, the Japanese bombed Pearl Harbor. Dick had become enamored with flying at an early age. While a freshman at Syracuse, he had taken flying lessons in the Civilian Pilots Training Program, a federally funded flight-training program initiated by President Franklin D.

Roosevelt in 1938 to begin to prepare for national defense. He soloed and became qualified in a Piper J-3 Cub. He also signed up for an acrobatic flying program and became proficient as a stunt flyer, training that served him well as the war unfolded.

As a licensed pilot, Dick knew that he would stand a good chance of qualifying early as a military aviator. In February 1942, after the United States entered the war, he left college and joined the navy. He wanted to be part of the action that was sure to follow.

Dick postponed telling Radia and Habeeb about his plans until after he had enlisted. He approached Dave and Mary for help with this difficult conversation (Nick and Polly were living in Virginia by this time).

"Dave, would you and Mary please come with me when I tell Mother and Father my plans?" a nervous Dick enlisted the aid of his eldest brother.

For his part, Dave was not certain that he liked the idea of his little brother going off to war, but he remembered how hard it had been to convince his parents that he should leave school and go to work to help support the family more than twenty years earlier.

"All right," grumbled Dave quietly. "They're not going to be happy about this!"

"I know," worried Dick. "That's why I need your help."

Dick waited till Sunday dinner when the whole family gathered. "Mother and Father, I've joined the navy. I'm going to leave school for a while and learn to fly some *real* airplanes. I think my chances of becoming a naval aviator are good, what with my experience already," he blurted out before pausing.

Radia and Habeeb stared at him in disbelief. Finally, Habeeb said, "You've enlisted already, without consulting your mother and me?"

"I know I should have, Ba, but I was afraid that you'd try to talk me out of it, and I know this is what I want to do," apologized Dick.

"What about college?" Radia managed.

"I'll finish after the war. You know how much I've always wanted to fly. This way I'll get first-class instruction. I'll be fine, you'll see," Dick explained excitedly.

"When will you have to go? Why not finish college first?" asked Habeeb.

"The good flying assignments will go to those who sign up early, Ba. I'm waiting for assignment now."

"It will take your mother and me some time to get used to this idea, Rizk. Don't expect us to warm to it anytime soon!" warned his father in Arabic.

After dinner, Dave took his younger brother aside. "That wasn't too bad, was it?" he smiled.

"Well, no! I guess after you quit school to go to work and Nick eloped with a non-Arab woman and left town, they resolved to deal with whatever we decide to do," Dick agreed with relief.

"Yes, you owe Nick and me a huge debt of gratitude, little brother! And don't forget that Mother and Father also have fond memories of their own youth," suggested Dave.

In early 1940, Mary was pregnant for a fifth time. In the wee hours of the morning of October 22, 1940, she became uncomfortable. At 5:00 AM, she was experiencing the by now familiar pains that signaled the birth would be soon.

Having already delivered two daughters and two sons, she knew that it was time to go to the hospital. Dave was equally experienced and was anxious to take Mary to Syracuse General Hospital on State Street, where he would gladly turn her over to the doctors and nurses.

Dave pulled the store panel truck up to the hospital emergency entrance, parked, and helped Mary out, reaching behind the seat to grab the small suitcase that she had packed days ago to be ready. As they walked into the hospital, Dave was surprised to see his sister-in-law, Emily (Habeeb) Kammar, waiting for them. Mary, of course, was not, for she had called her sister an hour earlier and told her she would be going soon. A charge nurse came to escort Mary away, leaving Dave and Emily to sit in the small waiting area.

After a few minutes, Emily suggested, "Dave, this is probably going to take some time. Why don't you go get some work done?"

Dave was hoping for something like this. "If you think there's time, I could run to the farmers market and pick up produce." This was why he drove the truck instead of the used 1936 Packard sedan he had purchased not long ago.

"Go," Emily smiled, "It makes no sense to sit around here for several hours. Go and come back in a couple of hours. I'll call if anything happens."

Dave knew he could go to the market, return to the store to help his father open, and then get back to the hospital in two hours, so he eagerly agreed. He was thinking that after the store opened, Habeeb could manage things with the help of Pat Carney in the meat market. Harold Mendenhall would also be there, and he could call Bill Robitou to unload the truck. Dave could drive the Packard back to the hospital.

The Syracuse Regional Farmers Market was on the north side of the city at the intersection of North Salina Street and Hiawatha Boulevard. It was a large collection of sheds and consignment houses where all manner of produce was bought and sold.

It was a fascinating place. Men were rushing hither and yon pushing two-wheeled carts piled high with crates and sacks of produce; trucks arrived loaded with poultry; horse-drawn wagons were being loaded with various fruits and vegetables. The aromas were strong and diverse—hay, fresh-cut melons, burlap, baked goods, and manure. The sounds were equally enjoyable—chickens clucking, horns blowing, horses snorting, and people haggling over price in different languages, Italian being prominent.

Dave went to the market almost every morning. If you had to describe Dave in one word, it would be *responsible*. At thirty-seven, he was responsible for the financial support of his youngest brother, for the grocery business, for his own family (Mary and four children), and for his parents (Habeeb was now seventy-four). The store was his obsession, and its success his personal mission.

Rezak's Silver Star Supermarket had been recently renovated and enlarged (the first of many such expansions), which included removing the steps in front on South Avenue, enlarging the basement, putting brick facing on the front (west) and south (West Kennedy Street) sides, and adding several adjacent shops, including a meat market, a tailor shop, and a barber shop, all with two fine new apartments upstairs. The family lived in one and rented the other.

Dave pulled into the market around 6:00 AM and went to the farmers shed area first. This late in the year, home-grown produce in upstate New York was almost finished for the season, but farmers were still there selling corn, potatoes, pumpkins, and large Hubbard squash.

He parked the old panel truck by a shed and walked through the dark parking area to a few farmers with their produce displayed on the back of their farm trucks and on the ground. Bare bulbs hanging loosely from wires lighted the area.

He ran his fingers through a bushel of green beans, shaking his head as if the beans were inferior while thinking how good they would taste when Immi slow-cooked them with ground lamb and tomato sauce. He glanced up at the farmer and wordlessly arched an eyebrow. The farmer showed three fingers to indicate three dollars. Dave's face was pained, as if to say, "Are you crazy?" and he raised his index finger for "one dollar." The farmer spat over his shoulder and shook his head while straightening his goods.

Dave shrugged his shoulders and started toward the next farmer, who had some nice-looking *koosa* (squash) on the back of his truck. Before Dave had gone three steps, the first farmer touched his arm and held up two fingers. Dave nodded and pulled the store money pouch out of his right-hand coat pocket and counted out two dollar bills. He handed the money over and jerked his head toward his truck. The farmer would carry the bushel over and put it in the back, having done so countless times before.

Dave continued through the shed, buying and at the same time watching to make sure the beans he looked at actually went to the truck and not some old produce the farmer might try to substitute. After half an hour of looking and buying, often wordlessly as before because of the language barrier, Dave pulled the truck up to the Caruso Produce Consignment House. As he walked up the five concrete steps to the loading dock, Joe Grazziola was pushing a two-wheeled handcart of oranges to be loaded onto a truck.

"'Allo, Dave," Joe called in heavily accented English. He flashed a big smile that displayed his brownish teeth, then spat a long stream of tobacco juice in the general direction of the edge of the dock, some of it falling on the front of his jacket, some on his chin. "I gotta mosta you stuffa done," he said. "Maka sure you looka red grapes, justa come in."

Dave had called the previous afternoon with a list of produce he would need, but there was always fresh fruit to be sampled and things to add. Don, one of the salesmen, saw Dave come in and called out, "Hello, Dave! I've got tageter most of da t'ings ya calt in. Just gotta get da bananas. While ya're waitin', try some o' dem red grapes, dey're fine. And we jus' got in a skid o' Californi' figs. Dey ain't cheap, but Habeeb would give a camel and four goats fer one," he joked.

Dave tried the grapes and nodded to Joe, who grabbed a crate and put it on Dave's pile of produce, calling over to Don to "adda boxa grape to Dave."

He decided to pass on the figs, for although they looked delicious and his father would indeed love them, they were too expensive. The family was not poor—they were in fact quite prosperous by local standards—but paying the mortgage each month, servicing the loan for the store renovation, plus keeping clothes and shoes on four (soon to be five) children didn't leave much left over. What little there was always went into new equipment or stock for the store.

Dave was respected on the Southside as an honest, hard-working businessman who ran a clean, well-stocked store. With this respect came the friendship of many established neighbors, one of whom was Charlie Ryan. Charlie was a realtor with close ties to city hall and the heartbeat of the Syracuse real estate market. He would come into the store and tell Dave about a piece of property that could be "bought right." In many cases, Dave never even looked at the property but would act on Charlie's recommendation. He would then resell at a profit or rent and then sell to the occupants. These funds helped in making ends meet and financing the store's growth.

Joe finished loading the truck while Dave was paying inside. They exchanged good-byes on the dock, Joe again spitting a stream of tobacco juice in the general direction of the road, this time hitting his shoe.

Dave had one more stop to make before returning to the store—the poultry shed. Although chickens were available now through local poultry houses and were delivered to the store processed and on ice, Habeeb would not eat a chicken unless he killed it himself, guaranteeing its freshness, quality, and cleanliness.

Insha'Allah, Dave thought, shaking his head. He loved his parents and would never disobey or disrespect them.

With the old truck groaning and creaking under the heavy load, Dave drove back to the store, the trussed live chicken on the seat beside him. It was now fully light at 7:00 AM, and he would have to hurry to be back to open the store and then go back to the hospital. He hoped Mary was doing alright.

He drove south from Hiawatha Boulevard on Salina Street as he always did. Traveling along Salina, he looked up at the "little house" on top of the Penfield Manufacturing Company building. Then he motored through the center of downtown, past Sears & Roebuck to West Kennedy Street. Traffic did not get heavy until after 9:00 AM, when the big stores opened—E. W. Edwards, Dey Brothers, W. T. Grant's, Kresge's, Flah's, Wilson's, and so on. Syracuse wasn't New York City, but it was Dave's city, and he was proud of being a successful part of it.

Five movie houses had been built downtown: the Eckel on West Fayette Street, the Lowe's State across the street from his old newspaper corner at Salina and Jefferson, the Paramount and RKO Keiths clustered in the middle of downtown, and the Strand at the southern end of downtown.

The Strand was special because the management had entered into an arrangement with some local businessmen and St. Elias Church to show films in Arabic on Sunday afternoons once or twice a year. They were religious, drama, or travelogue features and were always well attended.

Dave finally arrived at the store and backed over the curb to the front door to unload. Habeeb was waiting anxiously outside for him, dressed as always in white shirt, necktie, trousers, and vest. He wore a pocket watch on a gold chain in his vest pocket and the ever-present black Christian Orthodox skullcap perched on the back of his head. He had made his own clothes for years.

"Daoud, where have you been for so long?" he asked anxiously in Arabic. Habeeb would only speak "Englizzi" at gunpoint or to customers. "Emily has called twice looking for you. I hope nothing has gone wrong!"

Just then the phone rang again. Dave rushed by, handing his father the chicken on his way inside. Habeeb held the chicken by the legs with his left hand and reached for some grapes with his right, following Dave into the store. It was Emily again, congratulating Dave on the arrival of a new son.

"I'll be right there!" Dave shouted and hung up.

No assignment came for Dick for several months. He remained in Syracuse for the first portion of 1942 and took a job chrome-plating automobile bumper guards at Brown-Lipe-Chapin while he waited. During this period, he kept his hand in flying by practicing every time he could with the Civilian Pilots Training Program in Amboy, New York. There he flew the Stearman PT Trainer.

In May, Dick was sent to E-base (E for "elimination") in New Orleans. He quickly passed primary training and was accepted for further instruction. From New Orleans, he shipped to Pensacola, Florida, in August 1942 for basic training, which was followed immediately by instrument training, completing the latter in October while still in Pensacola.

Dick then undertook advanced training in Pensacola. This was a longer experience as he qualified in the Consolidated Catalina sea plane. He earned his Navy Wings in Pensacola in February 1943 and was assigned to an Advanced Training Squadron--Multiengine Patrol Boat. The *Catalina* was a slow, lumbering sea-going patrol bomber. Dick longed for the days of his acrobatics training in small, fast, maneuverable planes.

Because he had so much flying experience and was good at what he did (especially flying on instruments), he had a leg up on his fellow trainees. The navy selected him to instruct other pilots. In March 1943, he was shipped to Corpus Christi, Texas, as an instrument flight instructor. Here, he flew the North American T-6 Texan, a high-powered two-seat aircraft. The instructor sat in front, and the student behind. The student was blindfolded to everything except his instruments. He had to rely only on what those instruments told him.

In May 1943, Dick was reassigned to Beeville, Texas, still as instrument instructor. He remained there until October 1944, when he was finally able to talk his way into fighter training.

Dick returned to Corpus Christi for preoperational fighter training for a month until November 1944. Then he shipped to Daytona Beach, Florida, for three months of operational fighter training. There, he fell in love with the Grumman F6F Hellcat, a 2,000-pound aircraft with a 2,000-horsepower Pratt & Whitney reciprocating engine and six 50-caliber machine guns. This maneuverable little fighter plane was capable of 375 miles per hour, and Dick loved every minute of his time with it.

The plane was so powerful that Dick was able to execute "Immelmans" with her. An Immelman is performed on takeoff by attaining vertical attitude as quickly as possible. The stick is held back through the vertical until the plane completes a half-loop and is inverted. At the top of the half loop, the aircraft is rolled back to the upright position, flying 180 degrees in the opposite direction of takeoff. It is an evasive combat maneuver first accomplished by Max Immelman, a World War I German flying ace.

Dick's experience with the Hellcat culminated with his qualification for flight off of aircraft carriers. Training consisted of takeoffs and landings on land with a jeep (small escort) aircraft carrier deck painted on the runway.

The plane was catapulted off the deck and caught the tailhook on landings. For takeoff, the pilot wound up the 2,000 horses to maximum revolutions per minute and signaled to the deck chief, who authorized catapult actuation. The catapult, together with the plane's power, thrust the aircraft into the air with a small dip just off the end of the carrier deck.

Catching the tailhook on landing was dicier. Here, the pilot came in with nose in the air and eyes on the deck chief. The deck chief signaled the pilot down. The pilot had to back off the throttle at the precise instant to drop down and catch the cable with the plane's tailhook.

Dick was the first in his flight to try a landing on an actual carrier at sea. The pilots took off from the Daytona Beach base and flew out to the carrier. Dick located the carrier landing deck without incident. When painted on the runway at the land base, it was no bigger than a postage stamp. In the vast ocean, it appeared smaller than ever.

As he descended, he located the deck chief with the signal flags he would follow down. He lined up and put the nose down. As he approached, he leveled off and then raised the nose. At the last moment, he cut power to drop to the deck when signaled by the deck chief. He slammed down and caught the tailhook. The plane decelerated from about ninety miles per hour to a dead stop in the space of about one hundred feet. Dick pitched forward as the safety straps bit into his shoulders.

Then the deck chief guided him to park the plane out of the way of more incoming aircraft. The deck chief kept signaling Dick closer and closer to the edge of the carrier. All Dick could see from his upward facing cockpit vantage point was ocean. Still the deck chief signaled him farther toward the water. It took him forever to park the plane, for fear he would end up in the drink.

After six successful carrier landings, Dick qualified for active-duty day-fighter flying from aircraft carriers. In February 1945, he shipped to Vero Beach, Florida, for night-fighter training, still in the Hellcat. Night-fighter Hellcats were equipped with a radar dome on the starboard wing. The radar picked up potential targets in the night sky.

One dark night as Dick broke off from attacking the last target and was vectoring back home, he spotted a white light. He approached it thinking it was his land base. He radioed in his identification and requested permission to land.

"We don't have you on radar," came the response from the base.

"Well, what's that light I'm flying toward?" Dick inquired anxiously.

"Must be a ship or a navigation beacon!" the base tower advised.

With his altimeter reading about one hundred feet, Dick realized that the light indeed *wasn't* the base. Up he roared in the Hellcat, grateful for the power, and scurried back to find his way home in the dark. Night-fighter training took another three months.

In May 1945, Dick was sent to Charlestown, Rhode Island, to participate in forming night-fighter squadrons for service in the war in the Pacific. He and his squadron practiced intercepting enemy aircraft after dark over the ocean. One evening off Nantucket Island, Dick was returning from an intercept exercise when he encountered antiaircraft tracers off his wing.

"Who's shooting tracers out here?" Dick shouted into his radio.

"No one!" came the surprised response.

"Well, then there's a German U-boat below," screamed Dick. He and his squadron searched the area thoroughly, but with no luck.

After night-fighter intercept exercises, Dick had one more bit of training prior to being shipped to the Pacific: learning to find and land on a jeep carrier at night—no easy proposition.

He was in the midst of this training in August 1945 when the war ended. At that point of the conflict in the Pacific, the navy was losing about 50 percent of the pilots who flew off of carriers. Dick was given the option of remaining in the navy as an officer. He elected to return home to finish his education. He mustered out in New York City in September 1945 at the rank of lieutenant. A few years later, in January 1949, he joined the US Navy Reserve and served until his retirement at the rank of commander in September 1964.

Mary and Dave named their fifth child Louis—in Arabic, Illyas (Elias or Elijah), after their church patron saint: Louis Rezak (Illyas Ibn Daoud el Rizk). Louis's crib was in the front bedroom of the large apartment over the 911 South Avenue store, just off the dining room near the front door and the stairs down to the street.

In the front by the windows that overlooked South Avenue was a phonograph player, with a large horn on top where the music came out and a crank on the side to wind it up. Dave played Arabic records that were purchased from Malko Brothers Importing in Brooklyn, which made Mary and him happy and Radia and Habeeb *very* happy.

In the back part of the front room was a brick-faced fireplace. In the winter, Dave built fires using orange crates from the store for fuel. The apartment had working gas lights on the walls, but because electricity was now available, they were not used. And there was also Habeeb's Magnavox radio set. It was a large wooden floor model, and when the news came on, no one spoke or made a sound: Habeeb was *listening* to it.

By 1943, America was immersed in World War II. Dave, now forty years old, was a civil defense neighborhood warden. He wore a special hat when there were air-raid drills. During drills, the Rezaks turned out most of the lights and pulled heavy drapes over the windows to keep light from showing. Louis thought they would be bombed, so he always sat in Cedo (Grandfather) Habeeb's lap when this happened. Cedo was *his!*

Dave, Mary, and the five children lived together over the store with Radia and Habeeb. Dick also lived with them until he left for the navy in 1942. Dick was Louis's and my hero!

Daytime found Dave and Mary's older children in school and the adults downstairs working in the store, so Louis had the run of the house. Taita—Grandmother Radia—spent the day cooking and baking. Cedo would work for a while in the morning and then come upstairs for a nap, as he pleased. He was the undisputed ruler of the family—that is, *when Taita allowed.*

Cedo often held court on the second-floor screened back porch, where he could see all that was happening down Kennedy Street to the east and South Avenue to the south. If he observed something that displeased him, the offender would be cursed—in Arabic, of course. Depending on the seriousness of the infraction, Cedo had the ability to curse someone regarding the degeneracy of the transgressor's ancestry going back several generations without ever taking a breath.

Taita was tolerant and had the patience of a saint, but if Louis did something *very* bad, such as peeking under the paper sheet she used to cover bread dough as it was rising, causing the sheet to fall on the floor, where it would get stepped on, she would yell, "Ya ghusic!" as she came after him. This translates to "my darling," but that is *not* what she was thinking. By the time Taita caught up with him, Louis would be safely in Cedo's lap. Cedo, as already noted, was his sanctuary.

In the 1940s, work horses were still common. The milk man and his horse-drawn wagon would come down West Kennedy Street, and he would step off to go to a house, open the little milk-delivery door, put in full bottles and take the empties, then go back to the waiting wagon, the horse knowing when to stop and when to go.

The rag man also clopped down the street behind his horse-drawn wagon, singing his monotone song, "Srags, srags." Louis was afraid of him because he was old and dirty and couldn't speak English.

Because horses were still in use, the city maintained watering troughs located adjacent to main intersections. There was one on West Kennedy Street near South Avenue between the road and the sidewalk next to the store. It was made of cast iron, about three feet high, four feet long, and oval shaped. It always had a green coating of moss growing on the sides and bottom, and it refilled itself with an automatic float valve as the level dropped. What a great place to get a cool drink on a hot summer day!

In late 1943, Radia and Habeeb visited Polly, Nick, and me in Virginia. Habeeb had pretty much retired from the store, turning it over to Dave. Nick thought his father looked tired and weak.

"Immi, Baba looks like he's failing. Is he alright?" Nick inquired with concern.

"He's been a bit tired," his mother responded. "I think he'll be OK."

But Habeeb was not "OK." He was, of course, fourteen years Radia's senior. She was a spry sixty-three, and he a weakening seventy-seven. He frequently found himself wondering where the time had gone. A mere thirty years ago, he and Radia had set forth on a new experience in a strange land. His father-in-law, Eassa, had been correct. It had required all the courage the two of them could muster to undertake the adventure.

It had also taken all their energy over a long period of time to be successful in their new land. While they were working so hard to succeed, the boys had grown up under their noses.

Dave had been running the store for many years now, and he was a successful real estate investor. Nick had college behind him, and his career seemed to be taking off, what with the war effort. Dick was an aspiring fighter pilot, having interrupted college to enlist.

Dave and Nick had married lovely, thoughtful women, and Radia and Habeeb were enjoying their grandchildren. Dick was not yet married, but he was dating a beautiful Lebanese woman. Life was good, and it seemed to Habeeb to have flown by while he was busy trying to secure the family's foothold in this exciting new country.

Secure it he and Radia had. They had raised determined, caring, contributing, thoughtful men—men who would be responsible to and for their families and who would make meaningful contributions to society.

Habeeb was proud of his family. Sometimes he could not believe the good fortune they had enjoyed.

"Insha'Allah," he said to himself. "God willing and with a lot of hard work!"

A few weeks later in early 1944 Habeeb died quietly. The old equestrian never got a chance to own horses in America. With him died the last of the old-world Rizk "mustache Petes." The desert wanderer had gone on the ultimate ride-about in bringing his family to America. He is buried on a lovely knoll in Morningside Cemetery on Colvin Street in Syracuse.

Louis was especially distraught. His Cedo, with whom he had been so close, took part of his heart with him when he went.

18

Nick Overseas

AS MENTIONED EARLIER, UNRRA had recognized the fact that Nick was fluent in Arabic and English. He had spent his time in Washington helping to organize UNRRA. It was now time to contribute where the rubber met the road.

Nick's UNRRA travel authorization dispatching him to Cairo, Egypt, came through on May 8, 1944. On June 13, shortly after the D-Day invasion of Europe (June 6), Nick received Invitational Travel Orders from the War Department Adjutant General's Office and directed to the commanding general, Air Transport Command.

He was instructed to have all prescribed immunizations. A Certificate of Identity of Noncombatant arrived for Nick dated June 17 from the adjutant general in Miami. He was designated district director for UNRRA and attached to the US Army. In case of capture by the enemy, he was assigned the rank of lieutenant colonel. This document was sealed by the War Department's Air Transport Command and included Nick's right-hand fingerprints. He was thirty-five years old.

Nick left Washington for Cairo to begin rehabilitation of North African war refugees. He was an obvious choice for this assignment because of his Arabic-language skills—he spoke it fluently but could neither read nor write it. Little did he, Polly, or I know that it would be eighteen long months before he would get back for a visit and longer before we would be permanently reunited.

Nick traveled to Cairo by air because that office had requested that he be sent by the quickest possible route. Owing to war transportation priorities, however, it took him a *month* to make the trip.

He flew via Puerto Rico, British Guinea, Brazil, Ascension Island, and the Gold Coast and finally landed in Cairo. In some of these places, he was forced to wait for six or seven days to catch an empty seat on a military transport plane, the C-47s and B-24s. He did, however, put his time to good use and arrived in Cairo with twelve hundred dollars (a veritable fortune in those days) in poker winnings, which he promptly sent home to Polly.

Meanwhile, she and I could no longer live in the McLean, Virginia, apartment because it was reserved for those working in Washington on the war effort. The two of us moved to a ground-floor apartment at 306 West Court Street in Rome, New York, to be near my grandparents Florence and Bill Curnick and to sit out the war. The Curnicks lived at 615 Madison Street, about six blocks away. Polly knew that she could not move in with her parents. Her mother was simply too overbearing.

Nick began a series of warm, loving letters to the son he would not see for so long. They started from the Gold Coast in western Africa in early July 1944, a few weeks before my fourth birthday. Nick described to me some of the different customs and clothes. He said that the women there did all the work, while the men relaxed in the shade all day. The flowers and animals were very different from those in the United States. The houses and furniture were made of heavy, attractive mahogany.

Nick was stuck in the Gold Coast for almost a week waiting for an empty seat on a plane to Cairo. He closed this first letter by telling Polly and me how much he loved us both and how fiercely he missed us, even though he had been gone less than a month.

Those war years in Rome were bonding time for Bill Curnick and his namesake. Every Sunday morning my grandfather and I walked hand in hand to Gorman's Cigar Shop on Washington Street to purchase the newspaper and a week's worth of cigars. With pride, Bill introduced me to his friends.

After returning home with the newspaper, Bill lit a cigar, pulled me up on his knee, and read me the funny papers, much to both his and my enjoyment. Florence and Polly fixed a delicious Sunday meal of turkey or pork or rib roast.

On weekdays after the evening meal, Bill took me with him to the Masonic Temple. There we escaped Florence's biting tongue, and Bill played cards and introduced me around.

Bill was still an avid fisherman, and he frequently took me to Delta Reservoir to "drop a line in the water." The two of us sat on the bank and fished quietly together. It was peaceful and lovely.

When Nick finally arrived in Cairo in mid-July 1944, he worked as budget analyst for the UNRRA Mid-East Mission. He was also asked to build staff organization tables for the Italian, Yugoslav, and Greek missions. His salary authorization from the UNRRA chief accountant was dated July 31, 1944, and amounted to $1,050 per month, an excellent salary in those days.

American, Australian, British, French, Greek, New Zealander, and Polish troops swarmed over Cairo. They filled the souks (markets) shopping for souvenirs. The most striking feature of the local culture was the enormous disparity between the wealthy, who were fabulously rich, and the poor, who were destitute.

The rich lived in huge villas surrounded by expansive gardens. The poor lived in dilapidated slums. The living conditions of the poor, in Nick's words, were "appalling and beyond description." He observed men who for only a few pennies per day labored their entire lives turning the screw of an Archimedes wheel raising Nile River water a couple of feet in elevation to the height of irrigation ditches.

On July 20, 1944, Nick wrote to us for the first time from his UNRRA post in Cairo. He described seeing a boy there who was a little older than I. The youngster was selling watermelons. He had one under each arm (they were small watermelons) and, as if that were not enough, another balanced on his head. The boy walked down the street shouting, "Buteekh!" which meant "Watermelons over here!"

Nick described a large water buffalo with enormous horns that he had seen right in the city. The animal was being led to a dairy to be milked. Nick allowed how the beast was huge, with a bellow like "six ocean-liners playing tag in the fog."

The man leading the water buffalo was also interesting. He wore a long white robe that looked like a nightgown. Nick explained that the robe was called a *kumbaz*. The man also wore a red fez on his head but no shoes on his feet. Nick sent me a red fez of my own.

He also described seeing a crowd of native Muslim *fallahin*, farmer women who looked from a distance like a number of large tents moving down the street. Their gowns consisted of many layers of flowing black cloth. They were without shoes, and each wore a silver anklet to indicate that she was married.

The most interesting thing to Nick about these women were the small, black veils that covered their faces from just below their eyes to below their chins. Nick did not find these women very fetching, and he wrote to me that he was glad that "your Mommy was so beautiful."

Nick described seeing a man with a dancing bear. The man was playing a long reed pipe recorder instrument. As he did so, the bear got up on his hind legs and danced from one foot to the other. Nick wished that I had been able to see this spectacle with him.

There were hundreds of outdoor cinemas in Cairo. They were not like the drive-in movies in America—just large screens, people sitting on the ground in front of them. They could depend on clear, mild, cloudless evenings to watch movies together because it so seldom rained in the Egyptian desert.

Nick wrote of attending a cricket match with a friend and colleague named Brownbridge. He thought cricket quite boring when compared to baseball. He did, however, enjoy the camaraderie of lying around on comfortable, shaded, wicker lounges and sipping a tall, cool drink with friends, servants hovering about to see to his every need.

Nick closed his long letter by sending "all my love to you dear boy and [to] your mother. I miss you so much more than I can say, and love you both very dearly." He did not yet realize how long it would be before we saw each other again.

Nick's Arabic was good enough to allow him to wander freely around Cairo and up and down the Nile Valley. He was in constant demand by mission personnel to go shopping with them and to act as interpreter.

The shopkeepers in the souks began to recognize him and to call him *ibn il balad*, "son of the city." They would insist that he sit with them in the rear of their stalls and drink thick, black, sweet Turkish coffee and tell them about America.

On August 4, Nick wrote to tell me about the thousands of donkeys in Cairo. These little beasts of burden were everywhere in the city hauling all manner of things from place to place. They pulled carts full of bricks (buildings were constructed of bricks and cement because there was little wood available in the desert) or huge sacks of grain with the owner perched on top. The poor donkeys looked insignificant under their great loads.

Nick described long caravans of camels walking single file through the city, carrying huge packs on their backs. He wrote the following verse to me.

> The camel is an ornery beast.
> He looks as though he'd like to feast
> on Billy.
> But, when you come to see this city,
> The camel won't recall this ditty.
> So, you can ride up on his back,
> And be tossed about like a pig in a sack.

Nick was assigned to inspect refugee camps in the Sahara Desert and along the Mediterranean Coast. Conditions were at best primitive, and the refugees were a sorry lot. Most had had no choice but to leave their homes for fear of their lives. They were essentially marking time in the camps, waiting for liberation.

Nick was slated to go to Greece as one of several UNRRA regional directors in that country but was disenchanted with the man chosen to head that mission, so he elected to join the Yugoslav Mission in the same capacity. In early September 1944, after Allied troops had invaded Italy, the nucleus of the Yugoslav Mission, six of them, sailed from Alexandria in Egypt to Bari, Italy. Nick's North African stint was a short one—so much for his Arabic-language skills.

From Bari, Nick's team went immediately up the east coast of Italy to the tiny fishing village of Santo Spirito. There they lived in one of scores of beautiful, unheated, unfurnished summer villas. The setting was lovely, if cool and damp in the southern Italian fall. They slept on army cots and used their wooden travel trunks as tables and chairs.

They were billeted with a British army unit headed by a stuffy colonel, and after a few weeks of eating incredibly bad food at the British evening mess, Nick made arrangements with the US Army Quartermaster Corps to draw rations there for the American personnel at the Italian Mission and suggested to the British colonel that they merge the fresh meat and vegetables from the American army into a joint mess. The British colonel drew himself up to his full five feet six inches (Nick, remember, was six feet tall) and allowed that they were eating better than the home folks in London and would not accept additional rations.

Nick was the junior of the two in terms of rank and could not force the issue, so he set up a separate mess for the Americans at the mission. They were soon joined by all the civilian personnel from the other countries, including Great Britain. They had far better meals, but they did have one regret: they lost the monthly liquor issue of one quart of Scotch whiskey and one quart of top-drawer sherry that the British army gave to each of its officers.

Nick and his colleagues moved into a different villa with a large garden featuring a grape arbor and fig, pomegranate, and almond trees. After lunch each day, he picked his dessert from the trees. This villa was right on the sea. Their office was close by on a peninsula called Island Site because it was surrounded by water on three sides. Each day before lunch the group went for a refreshing swim, which worked off some of the rich, plentiful food they were now eating.

On September 29, Nick wrote to say that he was doing some Christmas shopping. He advised, "Tell Mommy not to get me anything for Christmas, except perhaps a new pipe—straight stem, natural wood (no varnish), and [with] a fairly decent sized bowl." Nick was nothing if not particular about the large collection of pipes that he smoked incessantly. A lit pipe smoking with exotic tobacco was a fixture with him.

He related that he had received Polly's shipments of tea, undershirts, tobacco, and pictures of the two of us. "Mommy looks swell doesn't she? And you kinda look nice yourself!"

But Nick was particularly disturbed by one of the sights he encountered in his travels about Italy.

I thought so much of you last week when I visited some refugee camps. Some of the children there looked so forlorn, and some had been so starved and had grown so thin that they were too weak to stand up. One poor little boy who was brought out (evacuated from the war zone) two months ago (just your age) just sits and stares into space. I was so terribly glad that you were in the United States with your Mommy to take care of you.

Imagining me in these circumstances was a frightful thought for Nick. He was grateful to be able to begin to ease the suffering of those so negatively impacted by the war.

Southern Italy was now a huge supply dump for eastern Europe. Allied countries were shipping in tanks, armored cars, trucks, ammunition, troops, and their supplies—all moving north to the fast-retreating German front.

Back home I apparently got angry and depressed wondering where Daddy was and if he would ever come home again. Nick wrote on October 12.

Mommy tells me you miss me and sometimes wonder where I am and if I'll ever come back. Well, I'm in Italy and I think Mommy knows the name of the city near where I'm living; so, why don't you have her show it to you on the map? [The whereabouts of UNRRA operations was classified information. Nick was not allowed to write it in letters for fear the mail would fall into enemy hands.] And, as for coming back to you, you know that I will 'cause I love my Billy and I love my Polly and want nothing else as much as to come back home and live with you both again. You see, Bill, Daddy has some work to do and where this work is, you and Mommy cannot come. So Daddy had to come here alone, far, far away from the people he loves. But, when Daddy finishes his work, I'll come home; or, better still, maybe you and Mommy could come part of the way to meet me. That would be nice, wouldn't it, dear? And then we would be together again and much happier, all of us.

It was stressful for everyone in families of Allied forces disrupted by German and Japanese aggression, to say nothing of the poor refugees.

Nick, as socially liberal as they came, had little sympathy for the consequences suffered by the Axis powers. He was even vengeful in his conversations about them. This vengefulness was no doubt a result of the horrendous atrocities at the Germans' hands that he witnessed.

He and his colleagues, whose ultimate destination was Yugoslavia, waited in Santo Spirito for Yugoslav leader Josip Broz Tito to complete negotiations for interaction with the Allied forces. Tito, it seems, wanted no American or British troops on Yugoslav soil.

They used this time to tour southern Italy and to drive to Rome after it was liberated. While there, Nick requested and was granted an audience with Pope Pius XII—an important and exciting encounter for him. He explained the role of UNNRA to His Eminence, along with the plans for rehabilitation of the war-weary nations. The pope asked many questions about Nick and his teammates. He seemed pleased that Nick had taken the time to brief him and also fascinated at the extent of resources being brought to bear on the challenge of returning Europe and its peoples to normalcy.

Nick and his crew moved to new quarters. He wrote on November 28 and described the house in which they were now living. Fourteen men were residing together in five rooms. There was one bathroom, and no hot water. Nick traveled from Santo Spirito to Naples once a week for a hot bath. He slept on a short, narrow US Army cot.

Nick told me that when he was very busy at work, he did not miss us quite so much, but when things were slower, he missed us ever so terribly. He asked us to send him tea, coffee, jam, pudding mix, fruitcake, and pancake flour. He said not to bother with tobacco anymore because he had found a good source. Indeed, he imported Syrian Latakia pipe tobacco for the rest of his life (I can attest that it was absolutely *awful* stuff).

Nick wrote on Christmas Day 1944, a particularly lonely time. He put the best face on things and described the holiday festivities that he and his colleagues had arranged. Nick was social chairman for the group, and they did their best to brighten up their time away from their families. Nick, with the help of some local Italians, found a fifteen-foot tree in an evergreen grove, which he was able to "requisition" for Christmas with the help of the US Army.

The group decorated the tree with anything and everything they could find—crepe paper from the Red Cross and stars, balls, moons, and candlesticks made of pressed board and enlivened with red, white, and green paint. They made icicles for the tree from the small aluminum sticks that the army deployed to fool enemy radar.

On Christmas Eve, they sang carols and had a Santa Claus dressed in red cloth scrounged from the British army and trimmed with bits of white sheet. Everyone procured or made a gift for one other person (identified by drawing names from a hat) and wrote a little jingle about the gift and the recipient.

Then they enjoyed a Christmas dinner with provisions they had begun collecting at the beginning of December. There was a turkey for every six people. The British army provided prewar sherry, and everyone drank and ate too much.

Nick's Christmas letter was full of loneliness and longing as he coped with his separation from his family. He had not seen us in six months. Another year would pass before we had the briefest of visits.

Nick wrote again on January 11, 1945, still in Italy. Progress driving the Nazis north toward Germany was slow. He continued to express his sense of loneliness for his family. He and his colleagues were responsible for planning the repatriation of Yugoslavia. They were not as directly involved in efforts to provide relief to Italy. They helped out as support personnel but had too much time on their hands in which to miss loved ones at home. They took excursions around the countryside, sightseeing and exploring.

Nick promised that we would not be apart for another Christmas—a promise he was just barely able to keep. He described what an incredible learning experience he was having. He was learning not only about Italian and Balkan culture, but also about the logistics of providing food, clothing, and medicine in massive quantities.

He related a humorous incident in his letter. He had requisitioned a command car—a large army sedan with a folding desk in the back seat—to drive from Santo Spirito to Naples to purchase some provisions. After shopping at the PX (US Army post exchange) and having lunch at the Army Officers' Mess, he hopped into the car to head back home.

Just as he started the engine, a towering army military policeman, MP, came up and tapped on the window, demanding that Nick get out of the car. He did so, wondering what was up, whereupon the officer informed him that he was driving a stolen vehicle!

Nick and the MP went to the police station, where he learned that the car he was driving had been reported stolen from Naples. Then Nick remembered that one of his colleagues had driven a car to Naples about two weeks earlier and had reported it stolen. It was recovered the next day and returned to Santo Spirito, but no one had remembered to notify the Naples police. Nick was able to explain things to the authorities' satisfaction and set off back to Santo Spirito. So much for his career boosting cars!

In a letter addressed to his "little can of baked beans" dated January 24, 1945, Nick described a hunting trip that he and his mates took close to Polignano, Italy, which is near Monopoly. The Italians furnished the hunting rifles and dogs. They shot and roasted a few woodchucks, which they thought were a delicious addition to their diet.

He also expressed how much he missed us both.

> Billy honey, before too long your Daddy may be going on another trip, and it may be some time before my letters reach you. But, if I don't write; or, if the letters don't arrive, I want you to know that I am thinking of you and Mommy all the time, and that I love you both very, very dearly. I miss you both so much, Bill, and I don't know how much longer I can stand being away from you. But, it is such a nice thought to know all the time that I have such a nice family to come back to some day. I wish I were with you right now to go out to play in the snow and slide on your sled.

As I have said, the slow periods were the worst for Nick. Tito and the Allies finally reached a compromise, and about fifty American and British personnel, including Nick's team, were allowed to enter Yugoslavia. They sailed from Bari east across the Adriatic Sea starting early in the morning on February 6, 1945, on a Landing Craft Infantry.

They were aboard for thirty long hours in a violent sea. All but five (of which Nick was one) were utterly seasick. There was no food aboard save K and X rations.

They landed in Split, Yugoslavia, about midday on February 7. Behind and above Split rose the five-thousand-foot-high Mosor Planina, their stark rock formations looking blue in the morning sun, an effect caused by a reflection off the indescribably blue Adriatic Sea. There the team waited for the first supply ship to arrive. While they waited, they rode around the countryside—at least that portion in Allied hands—assessing needs.

Nick found the mountainous Yugoslav Dalmatian Coast and especially the city of Dubrovnik incredibly beautiful. The people there, however, were suffering from years of war and devastation. When Nick and his team landed, they were immediately informed that there was no food up and down the coast. Although the coast had been liberated, the interior just a few miles inland was still in German hands.

Needless to say, he and his colleagues were welcomed with open arms. The UNRRA contingent shared its rations with the natives for two weeks until they were able to arrange for the first shipment of grain to arrive. They were treated like heroes when the food began to flow regularly into the port of Split.

As the weeks went by and the Germans withdrew to the north, Nick traveled inland to the small towns and villages to check on food and medical needs and arrange for distribution. His team would then follow, delivering provisions behind him.

He literally stalked the Nazi retreat and made certain that supplies flowed to areas where needed. One of his team members was killed by a land mine on a road that Nick himself had traveled just a few days earlier on one of his scouting expeditions. He withheld this story from us until we were together again.

With a Jeep and a loaded trailer, Nick drove to Sarajevo, Yugoslavia, just two days after its liberation from the Germans. He was to be regional director for Bosnia-Herzegovina, and because Sarajevo was the capital of the federated Republic of Yugoslavia, he wanted to get in as soon as possible.

He drove a circuitous route to make certain that he avoided the retreating Nazis. In places, the road he followed was barely a track across the mountains. The direct route through Mostar and the Neretva River valley was still in German hands, and they were mining it as they retreated.

The Yugoslav *commando grada* in Sarajevo advised Nick upon his arrival that the area had less than a two-day provision of food and no medical supplies. Nick reported this information right away to the mission base in Italy, and within two days emergency supplies began arriving by air. He then met with local authorities to assess long-term needs and arranged with mission headquarters for regular shipments of essentials.

After the liberation of Belgrade, a Russian, Mikhail Sergeichic, was appointed chief of mission for all of Yugoslavia. Nick wrote him a report based on his experience in the country to date and detailed recommendations of how he believed the regional offices should operate in relation to local authorities. As a result of this report, Sergeichic invited him to Belgrade and offered him the position of director of field operations for the Yugoslav Mission. Now all of the seven regional offices in Yugoslavia reported to Nick.

On February 9, 1945, Nick sent me (this time to his "little cherry lollipop") a letter from his new billet in Yugoslavia. He described some of the heaviest fighting of the war, which had occurred in the region where he now resided. So many things were destroyed in the fighting that the people had very little left with which to make a living. Nick explained that he was there with many other men to help the Yugoslavs put their country to rights "so they can live the same kind of life we all do when Daddy is home."

Nick's job was to travel the countryside to assess conditions and then obtain everything from food to medicine to trucks to bridges to railroad trains for the struggling region. He described the incredibly beautiful mountains with the lovely villages between them and the unbelievably blue Adriatic Sea.

Nick mentioned that his letters might be infrequent for a while. The American army mail service had been handling his letters in Italy, but it had no postal facilities in Yugoslavia. So the mail awaited boats, planes, trucks, and sometimes mules for transport back to Italy. It sometimes took weeks for mail to be picked up or delivered.

Nick wrote to his "little pepper pot" on February 12 from Split, where he awaited a supply ship bringing goods for distribution to war refugees. It would also bring much anticipated mail. While waiting several days for the ship, Nick went mountain climbing up a steep 2,200-foot "pile of grey limestone" overlooking the Split Harbor on the Dalmatian Coast. He thought it the most beautiful scenery he had ever experienced. He could see for fifty miles up and down the coast. Nick and his colleagues also went fishing the day he wrote this letter. It was their last leisure time for a while because the ship arrived the next day.

The Yugoslav winter on the Dalmatian Coast was quite cool. There was no heat in the bedrooms of the quarters where Nick resided. He slept on a small army cot with three layers of canvas underneath him for comfort and warmth. On top were three army blankets and a quilt he had scrounged locally, and he wore wool pajamas that the Curnicks had sent him for Christmas—even Florence appreciated the contribution he was making.

Nick closed this letter with the following cryptic note: "Honey, there is something else I want to ask you to do. If you have outgrown any shoes or clothes, I wish you would give them to us so we can give them to all the children here who have nothing to wear. So many of them run around in t-shirts and no shoes."

The hardest thing for Nick to swallow was seeing children my age who were in need. His "little piece of Roquefort cheese" next received a letter dated February 19. Nick was still in Split, which had been in the grips of a cold winter wind called "the Boar." It swept down from the mountains and felt like "a cold icicle rubbing your skin."

In the evenings in the Split city square, crowds of natives gathered to listen to postwar political speakers and sing and dance the Kola until the 9:00 PM curfew. The Kola is a circular line dance in which the participants hold hands and dance complicated steps around and around while singing.

Only Allied officers (which included Nick) were allowed out after curfew and then only until 11:00 PM. Guards were authorized to shoot anyone in the street after curfew. These orders were in place to prevent German stragglers from looting or hiding in bombed houses.

Nick wrote on March 5 about his new billet in Split. It was located at the water's edge across a small bay from the main harbor. The house was about 350 years old. Nick's room overlooked the water and the mountains beyond. The most spectacular aspect of the place was his bed, which actually had inner springs and a mattress—the first real bed he had slept on in months.

Split also had a convalescence center for Yugoslav partisans wounded in the war. Some had horrible injuries—loss of limbs, loss of eyesight, and other mutilation. Nick was constantly amazed at the cheerfulness these people exuded despite their injuries.

Unlike France, Belgium, the Netherlands, Poland, Austria, and Hungary, the Yugoslavs had never surrendered to the Axis powers; indeed, they had fought them "underground" for four years. Their spirit was unconquerable, and they were filled with the exuberance of building a new nation and a new life. They were extremely proud of their accomplishments and were ready to do more for their country and themselves, no matter how severe their injuries.

On March 7, Nick wrote again, this time from deep in the Yugoslav mountains at a desk that less than a week earlier had been occupied by a German officer. This was a fascinating time for him. He was accompanied by American army captain Joe Rachlin. The two felt like the most popular people in the world. As they walked the streets of an unnamed village (the army censored any locations mentioned in letters), the locals stopped them and patted them on the arms and shoulders, saying, "Americonski!" They beamed as they mouthed the word, a synonym for freedom. "Dobro, dobro!" (Good, good!). The men and women continued to praise the two Americans until in their embarrassment the men broke away, only to be stopped by another group a few steps farther on.

The Yugoslavs had been under the Nazis' heel since 1941 and had suffered as much or more from German brutality as any group in Europe. Nick and his colleagues listened to the tales of German and Italian fiendishness—entire villages burned to the ground, execution of all the men in the villages, mass graves for the dead. Their guide informed them that the Croatian Roman Catholic fundamentalist group the Ustashi, who had joined the Nazis and were charged by them with ruling Croatia, had buried a thousand bodies in a field nearby.

The natives did not accept their fate at the hands of their oppressors. The roads were lined with the burned-out skeletons of German trucks, tanks, half-tracks, and armored cars—all stripped by the canny partisans.

These pieces of equipment were the victims of the local guerrillas' effective hit-and-run tactics.

"Here, we killed 150 Germans," beamed Nick and Joe's interpreter with pride. "It was three months ago—they never knew what hit them! We had two heavy machine guns, and a squad of men with hand grenades was assigned to deal with each vehicle. We did!"

Nick spoke with the president of Bosnia-Herzegovina, Novak Mastilovic, whom he described as a "scholarly looking man with finely chiseled features and a square cut goatee." He was a Christian Orthodox priest. Nick told him that his grandfather was also a priest, which created instant rapport. Nick and Joe came away assured that the Yugoslav administrators were a sincere, capable group.

Nick's "dish of apple dumpling" then received a letter dated March 8. Nick had been traveling inland for almost a month and was finally back in Split on the coast. He simply could not get over the beauty of this Adriatic paradise. He wrote about it in almost every letter. It was still not warm enough for his much-anticipated swim.

Nick expressed his desire to show me this beautiful part of the world and to teach me to swim in the gorgeous Adriatic Sea. He had taught his younger brother, Dick, to swim fifteen years earlier and looked forward to the same experience with me.

Nick was always moved when he encountered refugee children about my age. While out walking one afternoon, he observed a sweet little girl who made him think that she would be a great playmate for me. Her mother was a Yugoslav soldier who was wounded in combat and was recuperating in the hospital next door to his billet. Her father was also a soldier away fighting the Germans and Italians.

While her parents were fighting, this little girl had resided in a refugee camp in Italy. She had recently come to Split to be near her mother during her recovery. Because she had been in the care of relative strangers and away from her mother and father for so long, the little girl was at ease around strangers, and she offered everyone a lovely smile. She had not seen her father in four years.

Nick thought about his comparatively brief separation (about eight months at this point) from his family. He wondered how these people had endured; again, he felt relieved that his family was safe and sound in America with warm clothes and plenty to eat. This sense of gratitude made it easier for him to deal with the loneliness he felt. The work he was doing now was far and away, he believed, the most meaningful of his life.

Nick's admiration for the Yugoslavs grew each time he encountered a returning partisan fighter. These brave people had no armaments other than their prewar hunting weapons. They had no trucks and no supply lines. They captured enemy weapons and learned to use them. They hauled captured cannons and supplies by donkey through the rugged mountain terrain. They froze and starved in the brutal mountain winters, but they never gave up and never became the impotent slaves of their barbaric occupiers.

The Yugoslavs were so proud and happy that they had held out and survived that even those most severely injured were joyous. Nick drew much inspiration from them.

He described some of his travels through the beautiful Oblasni Mountains of Herzegovina in a letter dated March 9, 1945. The mountains towered thousands of feet above the dirt roads, which hung precariously along the edges of deep precipices. He drove slowly and cautiously.

At one point, he came upon a river bridge blown up by the Germans in their retreat. There he met a Yugoslav partisan general. The bridge had been the only link between the shipping ports on the coast and a large portion of the interior. No food, clothing, or medicine would reach the needy in the region without it.

The Yugoslavs were equal to the challenge that the missing bridge posed. They built a scow made of forty-four-gallon steel oil barrels that was just large enough to hold a truck. They then fastened the scow to a heavy cable on block and tackle and stretched across the river. With ropes attached to both ends of the scow, thirty men on each shore pulled it ever so slowly across the river. The current was fast, and the men were thoroughly taxed. Nonetheless, they knew the importance of their labor and never complained or shirked. Nick's challenge was to obtain material for a new bridge.

While he was jotting down details in order to procure appropriate material for the bridge, a war supply truck came across the river on the scow to move its supplies to the fighting front, about ten miles to the north. It ran out of gas while there. With the truck was US Army Major General Shegert. Nick siphoned four gallons of gas from his Jeep to the stricken vehicle, which made him feel as though he were "taking a crack at Gerry."

That problem dealt with, he turned back to the bridge issue. He ended up ordering a Bailey bridge, which was delivered and installed within twelve weeks. (A Bailey bridge was a portable bridge composed of component structural steel panels and floor grating that were shipped to the site via rail or truck. These panels of structural steel and the floor grating were then assembled on site and quickly erected. The bridges were designed to US Army specifications and had been developed during the war.)

Nick wrote to "his little package of popcorn" on March 24. He had just returned from traveling deep into the Yugoslav mountains through the Neretva River valley. On this trip, he encountered the remains of a German motorized column. It had been ambushed in late January as it retreated north. The scene, including the frozen bodies of dead Germans, had been preserved by the mountain cold and snow, which was now melting. While there, Nick spotted and picked up some photos of the German soldiers and their families. The partisans had already scavenged everything useful. He was careful not to leave the road because the Nazis had a habit of booby-trapping their disabled gear.

The road Nick drove wound precariously through the mountains, going up and up and up. He finally reached the ridgeline at about six thousand feet. The snow was deep and heavy starting at about two thousand feet. Great drifts fifty to one hundred feet deep filled the ravines. The roads were narrow, and Nick "felt like a fly walking around the rim of a tall chimney."

Four-wheel-drive Jeeps with tractor gear were the only vehicles suited to the challenge. Nick said that you could go through anything in them. He also thought them fun to drive, even if they were a bit stiff to ride.

From Dubrovnik to Mostar to Konjic and the Evone Pass, Nick encountered death and destruction everywhere—dead animals and Germans and an incredible stink. In a twelve-mile stretch of road, he experienced forty obstructions—blown tunnels, bridges, and culverts.

Nick passed Korilla Jama (Korilla's Leap). Way up on the side of a deep mountain valley was a great, almost bottomless cleft. In attempts to explore the cleft, people had descended it with lights on ropes down to a depth of five hundred, but never sighted the bottom. In 1941, when the war had first broken out in Yugoslavia, the Ustashi began to persecute the Serbian Muslim minority living along the Dalmatian Coast and in Bosnia-Herzegovina. One night the Ustashi rounded up 950 Muslim men and pushed them into this deep pit. Nick knew the Yugoslavs to be a just people. He also knew that if these Ustashi were not already dead, they soon would be. The gutsy partisans did not easily forget acts of terror and barbarism.

I (this time Nick's "little green pea") then received a letter dated April 16, 1945, telling me that it looked like the war in Europe would end soon and that then we could join him in Yugoslavia. He had just returned from a trip to Sarajevo five days after the Allied forces liberated it from the Germans.

This city of seventy-five thousand people before the war had swollen to two hundred thousand with the influx of refugees. There was a great deal of tension in Sarajevo as the partisans searched for, found, tried, and executed Ustashi and Nazi sympathizers. The retreating enemy had murdered hundreds of suspected partisans during the last days of the occupation.

There was little or no food in Sarajevo. The Germans had taken it all with them when they left. The local peasant farmers had been supplying what food they grew to the Yugoslav partisan warriors. Nick's task was to get supplies to the starving city. Here is a dramatic excerpt from a letter he wrote to a colleague in the chain of command in Great Britain on April 14, 1945.

> The city of Sarajevo escaped major damage from the war. Most public buildings and houses escaped destruction. However, because of the overcrowding, serious outbreak of either typhus or typhoid is feared. The power station and water supply are undamaged. The railroad yards and repair shop, however, are a shambles.
>
> The villages between Mostar and Sarajevo, particularly Jablanica, Konjic and Tarcin, show evidence of hard fighting. In Konjic, particularly, there is hardly a building in tact. The railroad between Dredjaznica and Jablanica is, I think, one of the most vivid news stories in the country and someone with a camera should record its present condition for a

"before and after" story. Bridges and tunnels are blown and the whole reconstruction effort looks hopeless. Yet, the Yugoslav authorities have hopes that before the winter sets in, they will have the line in operation.

Driving along the road north of Konjic (Evan Pass), one is continuously impressed with the severity of fighting that must have taken place. The area is honeycombed with slit trenches, gun emplacements and dugouts; but, the most noticeable is the permeating odor of death and decay. Men in shallow graves, horses and other animals (probably humans too) in ditches and ravines send out an odor that hangs over the country for miles. (The danger to public health of this kind of thing should be brought to the attention of the proper authorities.) The whole area is mined so that clearing it will present a major problem.

Speaking of death, I was forced (largely by pride) to see the disinterred remains of more than 100 victims of Ustashi terror—men and women who, two or three days before the liberation, had been rounded up by the Ustashi and killed. Many had been horribly tortured and mutilated. The most touching and poignant thing to see was the relatives looking over the bodies for identification. (. . . [M]any hundreds had been imprisoned during the last few days of occupation and only a few hundred bodies have, as yet, been found.) One very old man, whose face was terrible in its tearless grief, had just identified the bodies of his three sons. It was a completely horrible example of sadism, and while it may come under the heading of "interesting experiences," I shall never be able to wipe the ghastly picture from my mind.

We were told that the month before liberation was literal hell for the people of Sarajevo, with arrests and disappearances occurring right and left. Hundreds of people are missing and their whereabouts are unknown.

Nick wrote about these experiences both to make certain that there was a record of them and to ensure that he never forgot them. He next wrote to his "little baked bean" on May 26. The Germans had finally surrendered on May 8, 1945. On May 21, Nick moved to Belgrade and joined his new Russian boss, Mikhail Sergeichic, who was UNRRA chief of Yugoslav Mission and for whom he would work for another two years. He thought Sergeichic bright and capable.

Nick spent as much time as he could studying the Serbo-Croatian language and touring Belgrade, which he found unattractive after his

12. Nick in Sarajevo, Yugoslavia, at age thirty-six in 1945.
Courtesy of the author.

seacoast and mountain experiences of late. He did enjoy the scenery at the confluence of the Danube and Sava rivers in the city.

The Danube seemed dead to Nick. It was wide and deep and sluggish, unlike the swift, shallow streams of upstate New York. For centuries, the Danube had carried commerce and militias between Asia and Europe. During peacetime, it was alive with traffic; now there were no ships or barges save an old side-wheeler chugging along. The other craft had been destroyed by bombs or mines that the Germans had floated down the river. The flotsam of war traveled down the river, much of it unhealthy. No swimming was allowed, and drinking water was filtered and chlorinated.

Nick visited Sarajevo again. On his return trip to Belgrade, he caught a ride on a Yugoslav transport plane piloted by a Russian. He related that he was certain that he had never flown with a better pilot. The Russian flew the lumbering cargo aircraft as though it were a fighter. Nick said it was "like riding a roller coaster."

The Sarajevo airport was located in a deep valley. The pilot started the twin engines and immediately rolled out for take-off with no warm-up. Planes taking off from Sarajevo typically circled the valley two or three times as they climbed out. Not the Russian! He raced down the run-way, pulled the stick straight back, and headed for a narrow saddle in the mountains. As they drew closer, Nick could see that this pass was just about twice as wide as the plane's wingspan. He was sure that they cleared by only about five feet!

They bumped along uneventfully until it was time to land in Belgrade. Nick was sitting on a long bench that ran down one side of the transport. As they banked to land, Nick found himself sitting on the top side of the plane looking straight down and out the windows on the opposite side. There was the Danube about twenty feet below the wing tip! His letter said in dramatic understatement, "All in all it was quite a ride."

The countryside around Belgrade was very different than anything Nick had seen in Yugoslavia thus far. No hills or valleys, only a wide, flat plain that was as fertile as any he had seen in the United States.

He wrote on June 6 and expressed boredom and frustration with the Yugoslav administration, which was desperately attempting to secure its borders, roads, and bridges, which led to travel restrictions on Nick and his colleagues for a period of time. He had been cooling his heals in Belgrade for a couple of weeks while the government went about issu-ing passes for travel. He hated bureaucracy and idleness and was getting quite antsy, to say nothing of how he missed his family when not busy.

While he waited for his travel pass, Nick continued work on his Serbo-Croatian language skills, which were coming along nicely. He also went to the US embassy in Belgrade to inquire about the State Depart-ment's attitude regarding wives and children joining their husbands at their various posts now that the hostilities were over. He was informed that the status of families coming over was still "on the shelf." US State

Department personnel wanted to bring their families over as well, but the official position was "not just yet."

Nick expressed concern for us. He had not received a letter in more than a month owing to the mail issues in Yugoslavia. He worried about his family when unable to correspond with them.

He wrote on June 11. He and his colleagues were desperate to have their families join them, but the State Department and the Yugoslav government were not yet ready to deem it safe. Nick declared his intention to visit us in the fall of the year and again at Christmas.

On June 19, he wrote to "his little jar of maple sugar." He had not heard from us for weeks until the previous day, when he had received two letters. He learned that I had developed a hernia and had been wearing a truss. Hernias ran in the Rezak family, and Nick assumed that I would need surgery. This possibility was worrisome for him, and he wrote: "Do have Mommy write as soon as possible and let me know how you are, 'cause it's perfectly terrible to be away and have something happen to someone you love."

Nick was still impatient about getting down to work in Belgrade. The Yugoslav bureaucracy was slowly beginning to allow his UNRRA team to function. He had been attending meetings designed to plan establishment of their mission. He was anxious to get to work on it and to be able to bring some relief to the local people. He closed his June 19 letter as follows: "I guess that's all now Billy, honey. I wish I could be with you right this minute to see how you are—and to pick you up and toss you in the air as I still think I can do, even though you are a year older. Tell Mommy that I love her and that I am looking forward to being with you this fall, if it is at all possible. Goodbye now and take care of my own little boy."

Nick's loneliness was evident, as was his anxiety about my surgery. It had been a year since he had seen us. Another six months would pass before we were together again. It really troubled Nick not to be able to be with us during this stressful time.

On June 19, Nick received some back mail. He sat right down and wrote a second letter on that date. This one, to his "little Juniper berry," expressed concern regarding my hernia surgery, and he wondered if I was home from the hospital yet.

At the time of Nick's letter, and as a result of the Germans being driven from their land, the Yugoslavs were trying to decide for themselves what type of country they desired. An election was to be scheduled to determine whether a kingdom, a democracy, or a Communist state would evolve. Nick thought that a planned economy along the lines of communism was most likely.

He wrote to his "little tough turnip" on July 15 after learning that my hernia surgery had gone uneventfully. Polly cabled him that all was well. Nick had been away from Belgrade for a while and was fearful that word might not reach him right away if there were any kind of problem with the surgery.

Nick and Dave Leff had moved into a villa in Dedjinje, a suburb of Belgrade. They shared it with the owners, a Yugoslav family named Nedic. The Nedic home at 4 Milenka Vesnica was lovely. The family lived on the first floor, and Nick and Dave lived upstairs. The second-floor living room had an L-shaped terrace on two sides. The terrace overlooked the former king's palace and the Sava River. The view was beautiful, and Nick liked to sit there as he wrote home.

We received a letter dated July 24, this one referring to me as "Daddy's little toughy." Nick wrote that he just realized that it had been thirteen long months since he had seen his family and that I would be starting school soon. He hated to be so far away as such milestones occurred without him.

Nick wrote to me on my fifth birthday, August 30, 1945. The letter waxed a bit philosophical.

Dear Son,

Today is your birthday and I want to wish you many happy returns of the day. I hope that you will think of me a wee bit today as I am very lonesome for you and for Mommy. I think that Mommy planned a party for you and I know it will be a good one for Mommy does those things so well, doesn't she? This birthday of yours is a very important one, for when a little boy reaches the age of five, he ceases to be a baby officially and becomes a boy. I know you have really been a boy for quite a long time. In fact, you were already quite a little boy before I left home. By this time, you must be well on your way to being a big fellow.

Aside from the fact that you are now officially a boy, you will this year begin your school work. That is such a big event in a boy's life for now you will learn to read and to count up numbers and find out about geography and all the interesting places that there are in the world. Going to school is a great adventure for it is the best way of starting to find out all of the things that will make your life rich and meaningful for yourself and all the people who know you. I hope that you will like school for it is such fun when you do like it. I hope that when I come home late this fall, you will have a great deal to tell me about your experiences at school. I am looking forward, of course, to seeing you and talking a great deal about other things, but I will especially look forward to discussing school with you.

Another reason that this birthday of yours is so important is that it comes at a time when the wars all over the world have ended. [The war in the Pacific had ended in early August 1945.] Now men will go to work on the vastly more important and more difficult job of building a world that will be a fit place for you and all the other little five year olds to live. I hope that they will succeed in doing so; but, you and all the other children who, this year, are five will be the judges of how well they do so. You will read about the things that they have done in school and you will be able to see the mistakes that they have made in retrospect and when you take over your place in the world of men, you will be able to say this is the right way and this is the wrong, for I watched these things when I was a boy.

I do hope you will have real teachers in your school who will give you a real insight into why it is that we make little boys sit at a desk for hours on end going over material that should be most interesting but can be so boring unless it has in it some of the breath of real life. It is very stimulating to me to see you growing up this way, for just as you want to be the kind of little boy that Mommy and I can be proud of, I want to be the kind of man that my little boy can, with pride, call Daddy. I hope that I will never do anything that will make you sorry that I am your daddy. And, I hope that nothing ever happens that will stop you from telling me anything about the things that may be troubling you.

I wish that I could be with you today for I want that so much. I am extremely busy for I am getting some increased responsibility and some increase in salary, I think. That is good, you see, for it means that I can give you and Mommy more of the things that make life more comfortable and gracious. That is all now, Sonny—again, my love on your birthday.

Nick was a thoughtful man with a terrific value system. He was to become a well-read humanitarian. He could discuss anything at all with ease and loved to argue arcane issues. His sentimental side shows in these letters. This side was not as obvious to me as I grew up, although Nick's love and support were never in question.

On September 10, Nick wrote his monthly report to the chief of the Yugoslav Mission Mikhail Sergeichic. In it, he described several challenges facing his operations. First, he was concerned that enough supplies and materials be delivered throughout the country prior to winter and the then impassable mountain roads. Food was scarce because the partisans were away fighting the Nazis rather than staying home farming. There was also a severe drought, which exacerbated the food shortage. The population was wholly dependent on foodstuffs from UNRRA, and Nick was concerned about getting it distributed before winter set in.

I received a letter addressed to Nick's "little cow hand" dated September 21—a letter to Nick had just arrived in Belgrade describing my fifth birthday party and containing a picture of me in a new cowboy suit. Nick's response indicated his loneliness and the impact that his work was having on him.

There is a great deal to be said about how fortunate we are to live in America, for over here, in many parts of the country, little boys are lucky to get something to eat on their birthdays. And instead of going to school as you are now, many little five year old boys must spend their days minding sheep out in the wind and the rain and the cold. You must always be aware, Honey, that there are people in the world who are not as fortunate as you and who will never be able to have even a small portion of what you now enjoy, unless you are willing to help them. Not so much by giving them things, but in sympathy and seeing to it that they are able to make their countries as pleasant to live in as you find the United States today.

Nick also wrote that he knew I was in school by now, and he wondered how I liked it. He longed to be able to sit down in the evening and discuss school and the world and his job with us. He was certain it would not be too much longer before he got to see his family. He could not stand to think about a longer separation. It was now getting close to eighteen months since he had left us behind.

In September 1945, Nick was promoted from director of field operations of the UNRRA Yugoslav Mission to director of field operations and distribution. The chief of the Yugoslav Mission, Mikhail Sergeichic, depended on him for his good judgment, his excellent interpersonal skills, and his ability to get things done. Trust and respect grew strong between the two men.

The new job doubled Nick's responsibilities and gave him little down time. This was fine with him because he missed his family terribly when he had time on his hands.

In a letter dated October 6, 1945, Nick related a fantastic story about a bridge in Yugoslavia. The war had started in Yugoslavia in late 1941. By early 1942, the Yugoslav partisans had fled to the mountains to wage a guerilla war against the invading Nazis. Some of these partisans had hidden in the village of Mostar above the Neretva River valley. They had hardly any food, their clothing was inadequate, and they had no war materiel with which to fight.

One day one of the partisan scouts raced back to Mostar to report that a huge German convoy of trucks was winding its way slowly through the mountain roads toward the village. The convoy would have to cross the Mostar Bridge over the Neretva River in order to proceed to supply the Nazi army in Sarajevo. It looked to the scout as if the convoy had about one hundred trucks, which contained food, weapons, ammunition, and other supplies, as well as about five hundred Nazi troops.

The leader of the partisans made a careful plan. He sent a few men to plant explosives (which they *did* possess) under the bridge, which spanned a deep gorge above the river. He instructed his men that they must wait until the last minute to blow the bridge so as not to warn the enemy too soon.

Then the partisan leader detailed a few more men to a spot where the road wound through a narrow pass with sheer walls rising high above the road a few miles away from the bridge. The German convoy would have to traverse this pass as it approached Mostar. The men in this detail had no weapons. Their job was to allow the convoy to travel through the pass and continue for a time until out of ear shot and then to roll boulders down the steep mountain sides to block the road and prevent a Nazi retreat.

Another group of men armed with hunting rifles, the only weapons they had, were assigned to the mountain ridges above the road between the narrow pass and the bridge. Their responsibility was to shoot the Germans caught in the ambush.

After the convoy traveled through the narrow pass, the partisans sent boulders cascading down the steep slopes, blocking the road and cutting off retreat. When the convoy was a few hundred yards from the bridge, it blew up right in front of them. Then the panicking Nazis were trapped in a withering barrage of hunting rifle fire. Every one of them was killed. Not a single partisan soldier was wounded.

In addition, the partisans were rewarded for their efforts with the German trucks, hundreds of gallons of fuel, rifles, ammunition, machine guns, food supplies, and clothing. It was a truly impressive haul, and the partisans were exceedingly proud of it. They delighted in relating the details to the newly arrived mission personnel.

At the other end of the spectrum, Nick had been told stories of battles between the Yugoslav partisans and the Germans where only 10 percent of the partisan fighters survived. Sometimes for weeks the partisans had little to eat except grass. And in spite of capturing convoys like this one, they were woefully equipped to fight the mechanized, well-supplied Nazi war machine.

The bridge that the partisans had blown up was so critical to the Nazi supply lines that the Germans rebuilt it. Thereafter they guarded it and its approaches to prevent a recurrence of the partisan attack. When the war was ending and the Germans were retreating north, they themselves blew it up again so they could not be pursued. One of Nick's jobs was to procure a Bailey bridge for the site.

The Bailey bridge allowed for the passage of thousands of tons of food to the people of Sarajevo and the villages and towns between Mostar and there. One such village had changed hands between the partisans and the

Germans fifty-two times during the course of the four years of war. Only four houses out of about five hundred were left standing in this town at the end of the war.

The partisans forced the Germans to expend considerable resources in Yugoslavia that they did not have to allocate to surrendered countries such as France, Belgium, the Netherlands, Poland, Austria, and Hungary. Nick became more and more impressed with what the partisans had accomplished. As already noted, he greatly admired the Yugoslav people.

By this point, October 1945, with several months in Italy and Yugoslavia, Nick was fluent in Italian and Serbo-Croat in addition to English and Arabic. He found the Serbo-Croat language much more challenging than the others. Before his assignment was completed in 1947, he had interacted with enough French and Russian colleagues to be able to function in their languages as well. He had become a citizen of the world while doing this meaningful work.

On October 8, Nick wrote a letter that he had been anticipating for months. Correspondence was slow and agonizing, but permission had finally been granted for the UNRRA personnel to bring their families over to Yugoslavia! Nick was thrilled and wanted us with him as soon as possible. He wrote to tell us two things.

The first was that he would be coming home for the first time in eighteen months for a period of about three weeks, during which he would need to spend a few days in Washington. The rest of the time he was certain we would enjoy together at home in Rome, New York. He expected to be home during the year-end holiday season and to return to Yugoslavia in January 1946.

Then came the *big* news: around the first of March, in order to allow spring to approach, Nick wanted us to join him in Yugoslavia! He expected that by midsummer his job would be wrapped up, and then we all could return to the States.

Nick further explained in the letter how all this had come about. He had gone to see the chief of mission on the morning of October 8 to tell him that he hadn't been home in almost eighteen months and that he was resigning in order to return to his family. Sergeichic had refused to accept his resignation, telling him that he could go home for a time instead and then bring his family over.

Nick was concerned that he had made a major decision for his family without consulting his partner. He had agreed to remain under those conditions without discussion with Polly. He only hoped that she would want to experience the Balkans with him prior to his returning home. The next portion of Nick's letter is quite insightful regarding their relationship.

> I know that you will probably object to my making this plan altogether without consulting with you, but by the time I wrote and received an answer more than a month would have elapsed and I didn't feel that I could delay Chief for such a long time particularly as the holiday season is only seven weeks away. Please be excited about this and not angry. I know that it means a frightful amount of work for you but hire all the help you need for the packing away of the furniture and bring all your clothes and buy a lot of new things so you can wow the local citizenry.
>
> Quick, have a drink—who would have thought two or three years ago that we would be discussing so casually moving ourselves half way around the world. But it would be good for you to be able to say in the future when I say when I was in ———, "Oh, yes and do you remember . . . ?"

As I was growing up in Syracuse after the war, my observation was that Nick ruled at home. The cautious persuasiveness of Nick's pleading letter was a pleasant surprise to me when I reread the letter many years later.

Nick was scheduled to travel to Washington, DC, to the UNRRA headquarters with Chief Sergeichic of the Yugoslav Mission. The upside of this experience was that he would be able to spend a few days with us in Rome, New York. The assignment in Washington was to negotiate for more trains, trucks, and manufacturing machinery for Yugoslavia.

His travel authorization home did not come through channels until December 17. Nick was to take a plane from London, stop for refueling in the Azores and again in Goose Bay, Canada, and ultimately arrive in Rome (Griffiss Air Force Base) on Christmas Eve. War priorities took precedence again, however, and the entire planeload of passengers (all trying to make it home for Christmas) was bumped in the Azores. The group eventually spent Christmas Eve in Goose Bay. Nick managed to arrive in Rome on Christmas Day and was able to spend a few happy days with us.

I was five years old and had not seen my father for eighteen months. I was apparently quite uncertain regarding who this Daddy person was. At the end of the visit, Nick was just *beginning* to reinsert himself into my life—not an unusual experience for American fathers and their children during the war.

After a few days in Washington, Sergeichic, who had never been to America before, decided that because he had a knowledgeable guide, he would like to spend a couple of days in New York City before returning to Europe. It was an eye-opening experience for Nick to see someone from a nonconsumer country go "buying berserk" in New York. In addition to awe at the availability of every product under the sun, the Russian was filled with wonder at the harbor's capacity, Manhattan's skyscrapers, and all the hustle and bustle that made up the city.

They sailed from New York to Southampton, England, on HMS *Queen Elizabeth* at the end of the year. Nick had been able to spend his tenth wedding anniversary with Polly, but it was not enough for either of them.

19

The Yugoslav Rezaks

NICK AND HIS UNRRA COLLEAGUES continued their efforts to rebuild the war-torn societies of Europe. This task became much easier after the war was over. By early 1946, plans had been laid and work was in progress toward returning the ravaged nations to prosperity.

On April 15, 1946, Nick made a shortwave radio broadcast to report on UNRRA progress since its entry into Yugoslavia approximately eighteen months earlier. He pointed out that when he and his colleagues had landed in Split, the Nazis still occupied most of the country. By the time the war ended in May 1945, the extent of the devastation was obvious.

Hundreds of villages and towns were destroyed. Farms were demolished, livestock killed or driven off. Railroads were disrupted or bombed; roads and bridges were blown up; and telephone and telegraph communication was a thing of the past. A large portion of the population was starving and desperately short of clothing. Industry and manufacturing capability had been decimated. The government was struggling because most records and systems had been destroyed.

Against this backdrop, Nick outlined in his broadcast the story of the village of Nevesinje, Herzegovina.

> It is a half-destroyed village on the western side of a wide bowl of rich ploughland in the very heart of the barren rocky mountains of Hercegovina [sic]. When I first saw the village last March there was deep snow on either side of the road that had been cleared to supply the [Allied] army moving forward in their advance on Sarajevo, which was still in German hands. The road was littered with German equipment and trucks. Down in the wide valley beneath the circle of white peaks, the snow had melted and the river was full—a lovely river that leaps down

through narrow gorges to spread out in the valley and then disappear suddenly underground like so many rivers here in this curious Karst country.

I was told that in summer the river is usually dry so that there was no water to turn the wheels of the water mills set along its banks. Then the people had to walk 40 kilometers over the mountain passes to mill their grain which they carried on the backs of horses and mules. In the meantime, they were living on UNRRA imported flour and grain—very little, five or six pounds per person per month, but enough to keep them alive until harvest.

In June, July and August came the drought, the worst in 90 years. The entire crop was ruined. Since the river was dry, the UNRRA grain had to be milled in Mostar before it came over the mountains in trucks to the village. The whole length and breadth of Hercegovina was dried up. Yet the people were still anxious about their mill so that next year would see them self-sufficient with their own grain and their own mill. They wanted seed immediately for the autumn sowing.

Just a few weeks ago, the villagers of Nevesinje had their fields plowed by oxen for spring planting. A new mill arrived from UNRRA so they would no longer need to transport their grain to Mostar for milling. We are confident that UNRRA supplies are being distributed equitably. I want to say to the people of America and the contributing UNRRA nations that your supplies have been put to excellent use. They have saved millions of people from cold and starvation. They have given new hope and new life to the war-weary but energetic people of Yugoslavia.

Polly and I left Rome, New York, on May 9, 1946, and traveled by rail to New York City. We spent two days touring New York and then embarked from Jersey City, New Jersey, on May 11 on the Italian ocean liner *Vulcania*. The ship had been built by Cantiere Navale Triestino in Montfalcone, Italy, and set sail in 1928. It weighed almost twenty-four thousand tons. The *Vulcania* sailed successfully until the 1960s, when it caught fire and burned in Hong Kong Harbor. During the war years, the *Vulcania* had been converted to troop-style accommodations.

The passage for the two of us cost $345. We sailed with two other UNRRA wives and their children—three mothers and four children. All seven of us were assigned to a small fifteen-by-fifteen-foot stateroom with four bunk beds and no room for any other furniture—no chairs or tables, etc. The stateroom did have a private bath and a narrow veranda, also with no chairs. We ate twenty-five to thirty people at a table in the main dining salon.

The four of us children had great fun together racing around the ship playing tag, hide-and-seek, and other games in this new setting. The other children were Peter and Eric Gangloff and Cathy Ross. Seven days into the voyage I began to feel ill.

"Mommy, I don't feel good," I complained.

"Maybe you're seasick, honey. Tell me what's wrong, can you?" Polly was concerned.

"I feel tired, and my tummy hurts. I itch in lots of different places," I responded.

"Let me look at you a minute." Polly lifted my shirt and observed that I had a rash on my torso, both front and back.

"Oh boy, I hope it's not measles!" she exclaimed.

Polly told the other mothers, Edith Gangloff and Melanie Ross, that she was concerned that I might have a highly contagious case of measles.

"You'd better notify the captain," suggested Edith.

"I know, and I'm dreading it! He may quarantine us," worried Polly.

Sure enough, with no doctor aboard to confirm her diagnosis, the captain was taking no chances. He insisted that not only Polly and I be quarantined, but also the other children and their mothers. All seven of us were confined to our cabin for the three days remaining in the trip. No one else succumbed, and I began to feel better and was fine by the time we reached Naples. I was, however, not the favorite of the others in the group, who could not leave our quarters for several days.

In the meantime, Nick and his colleagues, Perry Gangloff and Irv Ross, drove from Belgrade to Naples (about one thousand miles) in a three vehicle caravan. Nick drove a jeep (always his preferred mode of travel in Yugoslavia) pulling a trailer, and the other two drove sedans. They met the ship in Naples on May 21 and learned of the quarantine.

Polly and I were taken directly by US Army ambulance to an army hospital located atop a hill high above the city with a fabulous view of

Naples Harbor and Mount Vesuvius. Almost six at the time, I thought the ambulance ride ranked right up there with the most fun things I had ever experienced. I asked the driver if he could turn on the siren. The driver was more than willing to accommodate, so we roared through Naples to the hospital with the siren announcing our arrival.

Polly and I remained in the hospital for four days until the Italian doctors were satisfied that I was fully recovered. Nick stayed in a local hotel and did some work on the side. He and Polly were so excited to be together again that he spent most of the time with us in the hospital—not the romantic reunion they might have planned for their first few days together after so long a separation.

During their stay, Nick began to introduce card games to the son he had seen so rarely for the past two years. I learned how to play the card game war and the board game *Battleship,* and Polly and Nick played gin rummy for hours on end.

On May 25, I was released from the hospital, and we Rezaks, together again at last, started our long motor trip back to Yugoslavia. We drove north through the Italian countryside to Rome, Milan, Pisa, Venice, and Trieste.

In Rome, we went to the ancient Coliseum, which the Emperor Vespasiano had built in 72 CE. It was a circus 160 feet high seating 50,000. Nick remarked that it was larger the 35,000-seat Archibald Stadium at Syracuse University and a good bit older!

I was fascinated by the slopping floor in the Leaning Tower of Pisa. This gorgeous example of Romanesque architecture was a free-standing bell tower for the adjacent Cathedral of Pisa. It stood 180 feet tall and was 52 feet in diameter. There was a 294-step spiral staircase to the bell chamber, but by 1946 the public was no longer allowed to climb up. I was disappointed.

Paddling through the Venice canals was exciting as well. The mind of a young child attaches to some of the less beautiful sights, however. I was disturbed by the many dead rats, floating swollen, belly up, and by the Bridge of Sighs at one end of St. Marks Square which, Nick explained, was aptly named as the connecting way between the Venetian jail and its execution chamber.

I loved feeding the hundreds of pigeons in the square. We stayed in the Danieli while in Venice, one of the truly grand hotels of the world.

Then it was back to the drive to Yugoslavia, this time riding in the Jeep with the top down and the windshield folded forward to enjoy the warm springtime mountain air. Nick drove with no shirt, welcoming the sunshine—that is, until he drove into an unhappy wasp, which nailed him square in the midsection.

The roads were earthen and wound up the steep mountains with no guard rails. There was little vegetation, and one could look over the edge of the roadway, straight down for hundreds of feet. This sight also made a lasting impression on me.

We arrived in Belgrade on June 2. Belgrade means "White City," so called owing to the predominance of white stucco buildings. It had about 250,000 residents at the time. We moved into the Nedic family villa in the Dedjinje section of town, where Nick had been residing.

The Yugoslav king's palace was located on a large city block across from the Nedic house. It had extensive gardens and lawns around it. On each corner was a concrete pill box occupied by armed guards and bristling with guns. One day when I was out playing with my next door neighbor and good friend, eight-year-old Draggon, we crossed over to the palace lawn. "Nieht, nieht!" screamed the excited guards, and off we ran, frightened half out of our wits. We did not make that mistake again!

We lived on the second floor of the beautiful villa. We enjoyed a dining room, a living room, a large terrace, and two large bedrooms, the master with a balcony. Dave Leff moved upstairs to the third floor, which had another terrace with a shower.

Mr. and Mrs. Nedic were older than Polly and Nick and had three daughters ranging from their late teens to early twenties. The three young women gave the Rezaks built-in baby-sitters. Mrs. Nedic cooked and delivered all the food. The only kitchen was downstairs. The Nedics also provided a maid for housework and laundry chores.

Nick was assigned a Jeep of his own. Polly had only to call the motor pool for a Jeep and a driver to take her shopping or to the hair dresser—life was good! She and Nick enjoyed swimming in the Sava River and going to the horse races and Kola dances.

We ate most of our meals on the veranda in good weather. The climate in Yugoslavia is much like that in the northeastern United States. Behind the house was a large yard or garden or pasture that contained a good-size vegetable garden, goats, pigs, and chickens.

Draggon spoke no English, and I spoke only a bit of Serbo-Croat, but we got along just fine. Draggon's house was not as grand as the Nedics', and it had a huge ten-foot-wide bomb hole in the side at ground level. Draggon's family was no stranger to the ravages of war.

The winters in Belgrade were quite fierce. Draggon and I were able to sled and ski right down the street in front of the houses. Polly home-schooled me for the year we were there.

Nick agreed to remain in Yugoslavia until mid-1947 to help dismantle the mission, for which he received a nice bonus.

Life was returning to normal. In the Yugoslav business day, offices opened from 7:00 AM to 1:00 PM in the summer and from 8:00 AM to 2:00 PM in winter. In the summer, everyone had lunch at 2:00 PM, then took a nap. Everyone went for a stroll between 7:00 and 8:00 in the evening. Dinner was served from 8:00 to 9:00 PM. Stores were open for shopping between 8:00 AM and 12:00 and again from 4:00 to 7:00 PM. UNRRA worked from 9:00 to 5:00 in winter and from 8:00 to 3:00 in the summer.

Polly had a hard time getting dinner served as early as 6:30 PM until she mentioned to Mrs. Nedic that I was too tired to eat well at 8:00 PM. Then there was no problem, for all the Nedics *loved* me!

We took a vacation starting at 5:00 AM on August 17, 1946. We made the ten-hour drive to Sarajevo, where Nick spent three days working at Yugoslav Mission headquarters. Sarajevo was a Muslim town located in a deep valley between steep mountain slopes. I remember marveling at the women wearing burkas.

From Sarajevo, we made the day's drive to Split on the Adriatic Coast. The drive followed a road along the Neretva River in an eight-hundred-foot-deep gorge. We traveled over mountain roads with no pavement and no guard rails at speeds of twenty miles per hour tops. Polly wrote to friends that "everyone should follow the Neretva all the way to the Adriatic (Dalmation) Coast." She explained that most of the stone cutters who helped build the Empire State Building were Dalmations—they had learned their skill by carving rocks out of the mountains along the Adriatic coast and were quite used to working at great heights.

We spent five days in Split, a lovely small port with a Diocleasian Palace dating from the fourth century CE. The streets were six to eight feet wide, and the architecture had an Italian continental influence.

The sculptor Ivan Mestrovic's home in Split was situated on a beautiful spot overlooking the Adriatic Sea. It was constructed of white Dalmation stone and featured a *cozy* 150-foot-long dining room. Mestrovic was an illiterate Dalmation stone cutter who lived from 1883 to 1962. He was discovered at the age of sixteen by a mentoring stone cutter, who arranged for him to go to Germany to be educated and learn sculpture. He was the first *living* person to have a one-man show at the Metropolitan Museum of Art in New York City. He moved to the United States in 1946 as a professor at Syracuse University. It was said that he could carve anything in stone or wood.

From Split, it was a six-hour drive along a scenic mountain road two to three thousand feet above the Adriatic Sea, with no trees all the way to Dubrovnik. The Venetians had cut all the trees to build ships, and the soil then washed away to expose rocks upon which nothing could grow.

We remained in Dubrovnik, in Nick's opinion the world's most beautiful city, for three weeks and celebrated my sixth birthday along the way. According to Polly, after we checked into the Argentina Hotel and were scanning the Adriatic Sea from the window of our suite, I exclaimed, "Let's stay here for 155 days!" It *must* have been gorgeous to so focus a six-year-old's attention! The Dubrovnik walled city, also known as Ragusa, was built in about 1400 CE.

Nick began to teach me how to swim in the Adriatic. We fished in water so clear that we could see the fish at a depth of seventy feet!

We returned to Belgrade (a two-day drive from Dubrovnik to Sarajevo to home) in mid-September. On November 9, 1946, we celebrated the third anniversary of the creation of UNRRA.

Polly and Nick ever after believed that their experience in Europe was the highlight of their lives in terms of making a meaningful contribution to society, promoting cross-cultural understanding, and gaining an appreciation for another nation and its people. There was great camaraderie among the Yugoslavs and the UNRRA mission personnel from all over the world. It changed the lives of everyone involved in a fine and positive way. The way this war-shattered country began to recover and the way its tough, caring people rebuilt their lives and homes were amazing displays of strength.

Bill Curnick died suddenly in his sleep of a massive heart attack in January 1947 at age seventy-one. He had come to Canada at the age of ten all alone and had built a successful life. He and Florence had been able to retire in 1942 and live on their Social Security checks.

Bill's proudest accomplishments were his daughter, a solid professional woman and a terrific parent, and his grandson. His marriage had not been the Aunty and Uncle Serviss ideal that he had hoped for, but he knew that few were. His last years were spent in contentment. He is interred in Section S-2 of Rome Cemetery.

Polly, age thirty-six, was devastated. She received a telegram at the Nedics' home in Belgrade from a neighbor of her parents informing her of Bill's passing. She cried so much that it badly frightened me.

"Mommy, Mommy, what's the matter?" I cried.

Polly could not respond.

"Your gramp died, Billy." Nick was holding Polly. There was no place for me to be comforted. I clung to my mother's skirt until she regained her composure enough to explain what that meant.

"I feel so badly that I have missed the funeral and can't provide any support for Mother!" Polly lamented. "She's all alone dealing with this."

20

Home to Syracuse

BY THE EARLY 1940S, it had been more than thirty years since Habeeb, Radia, Daoud (Dave), and N'cola (Nick) had left the old country. Still, those left behind were not forgotten. Letters were regularly exchanged and eagerly awaited. They were sealed with a drop of wax, and personalized seals were pressed into the wax to identify the sender. Dave's son Louis Rezak keeps Habeeb's seal in his treasure box to this day.

Dave remembered firsthand what was and wasn't available in Nazareth. He would periodically pack a large carton with canned foods, soaps, toiletries, and so on and ship it to family there. The Nazarenes, naively believing America was truly the land of milk and honey, requested instead a new car. Not a Cadillac, of course, a Chevrolet would be fine. Dave, annoyed at this request, stopped sending the boxes, and the letters diminished.

The late 1940s were a special time for Dave's family. The war ended, and the store prospered. Mary's and his life revolved around their children, the store, the church, and the extended family of siblings, aunts, uncles, and cousins.

Habeeb, as mentioned previously, was one of the founders of St. Elias Church, and Dave was also active on the parish council for years, serving as president (1940, 1958, and 1959) and treasurer and chairing the annual Mahrajan festival many times.

The Mahrajan from the 1930s through the 1960s was a closed, private church family event. It is now a fund-raising celebration of Arabic culture that is open to the public. Radia and Mary prepared food for days in advance—rolled grape leaves, kibbe, rolled cabbage leaves, tabbouleh, pocket bread, platters of cut vegetables, and bowls of *laban* (homemade yogurt)and hummus.

Families arrived early to get the best tables under the big open-sided tent near the stage and entertainment. They came with all they needed to spend the day—coolers full of beer and soda, picnic baskets of dishes, silverware, tablecloths and napkins, and kettles of steaming food.

Of course, the ever-present *argeeli* (water pipe) was included to smoke the perfumed Turkish leaf tobacco that burned in the top over charcoal. Also present were bottles (or jugs) of arak, which many members of the Arab American community distilled at home.

The Mahrajan was the original Rezak family reunion, an annual event to this day. Aunts, uncles, and cousins arrived from near and far and spent the day visiting and enjoying the entertainment. Arabic entertainers were booked from New York City or Boston or Detroit—areas with large Arab American populations. Along with male and female vocalists were instrumentalists: violin, oud (lute), *kanun* (autoharp), *derbucki* (hand drums), and the shrill, double-barreled oriental flute.

Radia and Mary were founding members of the Ladies Auxiliary at St. Elias Church. The women met once a month, and it was an upscale social event. Members took turns hosting the meeting in their homes, and preparation took days. Everything had to be perfect: the house spotless, sweets baked flawlessly, Turkish coffee brewed and served perfectly, and, of course, several *argeeli* spaced around the parlor to accommodate the twenty or thirty women who would attend and smoke.

The Ladies Auxiliary was more than just a social group. Their hard work cooking and baking helped support the church. During the war years, they made socks to send to the armed forces. They also knitted mittens to be sent to orphanages in the old country.

Radia was of course expert at needlepoint. In the fall, she made comforters for her grandchildren's beds to keep them warm in the long, cold Syracuse winters. She also created a cloth covering for the altar at St. Elias Church. It had a cross in the front, with an angel kneeling and praying on each side.

The St. Elias Ladies Auxiliary formed a Red Cross Auxiliary in the church during the war. The women met weekly to generate funds in support of the war effort and the families of young male parishioners who were fighting for their country.

Thanksgiving and Christmas holidays were major family events for Mary and Dave. Everyone would gather at their home. Dave cut the turkey and passed out gifts, with the entire family present. He was never happier than in his role as host, father, brother, and patriarch.

The year 1950 was a prolific one for the extended Rezak family. Mary, her second-oldest daughter, Helen, and Dick's wife, Hifa, were pregnant and due to deliver at about the same time. Dave and Mary's youngest child, Barbara Joy Rezak, was born on August 16, 1950, two days after Helen's oldest (Rick Abdo) and about a month before Dick and Hi's first and only (Chris). There were new babies everywhere you turned, and Taita Radia was in her glory once again. She had two new grandchildren and her first great-grandchild.

In the summer of 1945, Charlie Ryan found a large house for Dave and Mary to purchase at 328 West Kennedy Street, across and down a bit from his own house and half a block east of the store. That stretch of West Kennedy Street was still paved with cobblestones and remained so until the early 1950s.

Dave's family moved into their new home after Bill Robitoe finished painting and wallpapering. It was a beautiful old house with high ceilings and lots of woodwork, wainscoting, and dish rails. The stairway off to the left of the large entry hall went to a landing that had a window seat in front of three stained-glass windows built out bow style. The landing also had a small door on the right that led to another set of stairs going down to the kitchen in the back of the house. It was a great place for us kids to hide!

The house had a large living room on the right and spacious parlor on the left in front of the stairs as you entered. There was an enormous porch across the front.

The kitchen was the large eat-in variety with a butler's pantry between it and a large dining room. On the second floor were four large bedrooms and a bath, all around a spacious center hall. The house also had a large attic with two finished bedrooms and a full basement that Dave finished into a bar and game room. Dave and Mary occupied the second-floor master bedroom. On this same floor, Radia had her own bedroom, Laurice and Helen shared one, and Louis had one of his own. Bob and Jack lived in the bedrooms in the attic.

There was an enclosed porch across the back of the house looking out onto an expansive backyard that featured a grape arbor. It was a terrific house, suitable for the throngs of family and friends who always gathered there.

Holidays, especially religious ones, saw the extended Rezak family come together at Dave and Mary's because the largest portion of the family already lived there, because the house was so large, and because it was so obvious that they loved any such gathering at their home. Radia and Mary would prepare exotic Arabic meals and desserts for days in advance.

Then the crowd would descend upon them. Huge meals were the order of the day, followed by various games. The meals consisted of an assortment of Arabic delights—large steaming platters of kibbe, *koosa*, grape leaves stuffed with rice, plenty of *laban,* flat bread with homemade hummus, tabbouleh, and then the wondrous Middle Eastern deserts, such as baklava and *khak.*

The dining room could accommodate about twenty around the huge table. If more needed to be served, card tables were set up in the parlor and living room for the overflow. The rooms were filled with chatter and laughter—it was a marvelous celebration on each occasion.

After the meal, the men frequently adjourned to the basement to play poker, pitch, or some such. The women sat in the living room, smoked the *argeeli* and visited.

Mary loved life on Kennedy Street. You could tell that as she washed dishes and worked in her kitchen singing "God Bless America" along with Kate Smith on the radio, one of them terribly off-key!

While Dick was awaiting assignment in Syracuse in early 1942, a friend of the Rezaks, George Khoury (no relation), who owned a liquor store in town, introduced Dick to a friend of his daughter's, Hifa Hider. Hifa ("Hi" to family and friends) lived in Binghamton. She was Lebanese, bright and beautiful, with a warm sense of humor.

Dick fell hard for Hifa. They corresponded as he rotated from training site to training site. She came to visit him on occasion, and he spent his leaves in Binghamton more than in Syracuse. They were married in July

1944, and Hi joined him at his various duty stations during the rest of his wartime assignments in the navy.

Hifa's family wanted her wedding to be held in an Episcopal church in Binghamton, which caused some stress in the Eastern Orthodox Rezak family, who wanted the wedding at St. Elias in Syracuse. It was finally agreed that the ceremony would be performed in the Episcopal church in Binghamton, with both the Episcopal priest and Father Karim from St. Elias presiding.

After the war, Hi and Dick returned to Syracuse so Dick could finish college. They lived in married student housing in Quonset huts off Skyline Drive just to the south of Colvin Street, between Comstock Avenue and Nottingham Road. Dick graduated from Syracuse University with a bachelor's of science degree in geology in 1947.

He wanted to undertake graduate studies and was referred by his adviser to a well-reputed geology program at Washington University in St. Louis, Missouri. He and Hi headed west for this undertaking. Dick's intention was to pursue a doctorate at Washington; however, after arriving there, he discovered that the Geology Department was not what he expected, but he earned his master's degree in geology there in 1949.

Toward the end of his second year at Washington, Dick telephoned his geology mentor at Syracuse University. "This department is in chaos," Dick lamented. "I don't think that I can remain here for the PhD program."

"Well, why don't you contact my colleague at St. Lawrence University in Canton, New York? They have a teaching position open. Maybe you can hang out there while you figure out your next move. I'll call him and put in a good word for you," encouraged Dick's mentor.

So Dick and Hi returned east, and he taught for a year at St. Lawrence while he applied for admission to Syracuse University's doctoral program in geology. Dick entered the program in 1950, living again in married student housing on Skyline Drive.

Hi became pregnant during the year in Canton (there's not much to do up there in the winter!) and gave birth to a beautiful daughter on September 21, 1950. They named her Christine Sara Rezak.

Dick graduated from Syracuse University with his PhD in geology in 1957. His dissertation in the field of micropaleontology required that he do research in Glacier National Park in Montana. He and his family spent two wonderful summers there as he collected data and samples. During that experience, he became close to the park ranger with whom he worked.

By the time Dick completed his PhD coursework, his ranger friend had moved to the US Geological Survey in Denver, Colorado. He offered Dick a job, and so off Dick, Hi, and Chris went to Denver in 1954. Dick finished his dissertation while working in Denver.

Dick began flying again in earnest with the US Naval Reserve. At first, he flew the Grumman F8F Bearcat, which was a propeller-driven transonic aircraft. The Bearcat had the same 2,000-HP Pratt & Whitney engine as the Hellcat and was lighter than the earlier Hellcat and Tigercat. Dick loved these powerful little fighters and their incredible speed and maneuverability.

He subsequently moved on to jet-powered aircraft, flying the Grumman F9F Cougar, which featured a swept wing design. He also flew the twin-engine McDonnell F2H Banshee, which utilized two jet engines, each with 3,250 feet-pounds of thrust. The Banshee had a maximum speed of 525 miles per hour and could cruise all day at 460 miles per hour.

Dick flew the Banshee into Syracuse's Hancock Field in 1955. He took me, fifteen at the time, out to see the plane. I sat in the incredibly complex-looking cockpit as Dick explained everything. The main thing I remember was the red ejection lever beside the seat. When he flew back to Denver, Dick arrived before he left Syracuse, what with the time change.

While with US Geological Survey, Dick published several geological papers. They were well received by the oil industry, and in 1958 he was offered a position with Shell Oil Company in Houston.

The family moved to Houston, and Dick remained with Shell for nine years. In 1967, he left Shell to become professor and head of the Oceanography Department at Texas A&M University in Bryan, a position he retired from in 1991.

Dick and Hifa's marriage had soured in Houston, though, and they split in 1965. Shortly thereafter, Dick married Anna Lucille (Jerry) Nesselrode, who was several years his senior.

The breakup was stressful for young Chris, who was fifteen at the time. She remained with her mother but stayed close to her father even though she saw him only a couple of times a year until Hifa died in 1997. Jerry passed away in 1995.

Dick lived with daughter, Chris, and her family in Houston at the end of his life. He died in November 2006 at the age of eighty-six.

The loss of Bill Curnick focused Polly and Nick regarding their plans for the future. Nick, with his six languages and familiarity with American, European, and Middle Eastern cultures, was in demand. He had several job offers to remain in Europe—one from an American movie distributor that wanted him to promote motion pictures in the region.

The two finally decided that with two widowed mothers and Nick's large family in Syracuse, they would be happiest there. Both were fed up with the itinerant life they had led up to this point in their twelve years of marriage. They wanted stability and another child.

Polly and I immediately made plans to return to Rome to be with Florence, who, although she had seemed content having her husband spend his evenings at the Masonic Temple for years, was now distraught without him.

Our UNRRA travel authorization papers were issued on February 24, 1947. Nick followed in the summer of 1947 after wrapping up things in Yugoslavia. There was, however, a dilemma—the only jobs that seemed available in social services were in New York City or Europe and involved extensive travel.

Dave Rezak came to the rescue. He had long wanted Nick to join him in the store. With Habeeb gone and Radia now sixty-seven, the full responsibility for operating the increasingly successful business rested with Dave, now forty-four. His children were beginning to take on some of the load, but Dave had bigger plans in mind. He believed that he could double the size of the business. He asked Nick to buy in and become a partner with him. This option seemed to be the route to the stability and "rootedness" that Polly and Nick sought. So back to Syracuse we came, and Nick began to run the meat market portion of the store.

With so many war veterans returning home, though, there was no housing to be had. Dave came to the rescue again. He owned several apartment buildings on the south side of town. One such was on the northwest corner of South Avenue and Crescent Street at 919 South Avenue. Izzi's Drug Store was on the first floor, and there was a large three-bedroom apartment on the second. There were tenants there, but Dave somehow figured out how to get them to move, so Nick, Polly, and I could take over.

Nick started networking with people in town who he knew were in the social services field. In the fall of 1948, he accepted a half-time position as budget director of the Syracuse Community Chest. He continued to work at the store several days per week, including Saturdays.

In the late fall of 1947, Nick bought a used (1935–40) Lionel electric train set. It was a terrific setup, with four trains, which Nick doled out one Christmas or birthday at a time for a couple of years. We crafted mountains and streams and other landscaping for the layout. A highlight of the postwar years for me was to go up in the attic over our apartment and operate the magnificent train set that covered every square inch of floor space. Nick and I had laid out what seemed like miles of track, multiple switches, and separate sets of track on two levels, complete with tunnels, bridges, railyards, and the four separately operated trains. That train set today occupies the loft in my barn.

Polly became pregnant in early 1948, and another son, David (after Nick's brother) Mark Rezak, was born on November 10. David was the image of Nick, so now each parent had a look-alike child.

This Dave Rezak is currently a faculty member and director of the Bandier Music Business Program at Syracuse University. He also took after his namesake and became a successful real estate investor in the Syracuse University section of the east side of town.

After two years in Dave's apartment, Polly and Nick purchased their first and only home at 102 Euclid Terrace in 1949. The Terrace, as the street was known to its inhabitants, was a large cul-de-sac fringed by fourteen lovely homes built in the 1920s. We neighborhood children played in the small, parklike grassy space in the middle of the cul-de-sac.

Our place had a small, narrow lot with a detached garage in back. It had a full unfinished basement. The main floor consisted of a large living room with a small sun room toward the street. Through a wide archway to the rear was a good-size dining room. Florence and Bill's sideboard nicely covered the twelve-foot rear wall. The room included Polly and Nick's cherry dining set (which I enjoy in my home) and Polly's spinet piano, which she never played, but with which she could not part. Behind the living room and next to the dining room was a large eat-in kitchen with a half bath. In the extreme rear was an enclosed television "Florida room."

Upstairs were three good-size bedrooms, a full bath, and an unheated but enclosed sleeping porch across the rear. The full attic with pull-down ladder-stairs in the second floor hall housed the relocated train layout, which Nick and I had painstakingly moved and reassembled.

Epilogue

IN 1951, Radia, age seventy-one, was diagnosed with liver cancer. Cancer has raised its ugly head frequently in the Rezak family. Radia's last weeks were not pretty. She was in a great deal of pain, but, consistent with her character, she never complained. She died in Crouse-Irving Hospital with her family around her and was buried next to Habeeb in Morningside Cemetery in Syracuse.

Radia went with the knowledge that she had provided her family with a fresh start and that they were becoming eminently successful. She never returned to Nazareth and never saw her parents or family there again. She was a woman of great substance and courage. It was the end of an era for the Rezak family.

Radia's determination, dedication to bettering her family, adventuresome spirit, and tenacity have always been a marvel to her descendants. How could people who did not even speak the language of their adopted land leave everything and everyone they knew and loved to relocate halfway around the world? Things must have been *bad* in Palestine! It is sad that they still are, albeit for different reasons.

In 1994, the extended Rezak family established the Radia Khouri Rezak Family Scholarship at Alfred State College in Alfred, New York. It has assisted worthy students with financial need ever since.

Radia's three sons were highly successful. Dave was an enterprising businessman and real estate investor. In the early 1960s, he purchased several building lots in Onondaga Hill, outside Syracuse. He and Mary built a modern and spacious home on one of them. Dave retired from the store, turning it over to sons Bob, Jack, and Louis. Louis bought out his brothers and ran the entire operation himself until selling it in 1988. Dave passed on (more cancer) in 1980 at age seventy-seven, and Mary in 1991.

In 1952, Nick decided that he wanted to purchase a cabin cruiser to keep on Lake Ontario. At the same time, probably in response to Nick's interest in a large boat, Polly expressed an interest in acquiring a vacation cottage. After a couple of years renting cottages on Tuscarora Lake, they purchased a vacation place there, about twenty-five miles southeast of Syracuse. My brother, Dave, and his family still enjoy this lovely spot.

Nick's job at the Community Chest evolved into a full-time commitment, and he eventually sold his interest in Rezak's Silver Star Supermarket back to Dave. The Community Chest became the United Way of Syracuse and Onondaga County, and Nick became its associate executive director and then executive director. He was with the Chest/United Way for twenty-six years.

Polly went back to work in 1958 for various social service agencies. She was almost as well known as Nick in the social service professions around Syracuse. In 1977, the Syracuse Federation of Women's Clubs selected her as a "Woman of Achievement" for her volunteer leadership in 1976. She was ever so proud of this well-deserved recognition.

Nick retired as executive director of the Syracuse and Onondaga County United Way in 1974, but both he and Polly served as volunteers on several social service agency boards of directors for many years of their retirement. Nick passed away in 1996, Polly in 1998, both at age eighty-seven.

Dick retired as a well-known oil industry researcher, professor, and author, to say nothing of his accomplishments as a navy pilot. He passed away in 2006 at age eighty-six.

Florence Elsie Belcher Curnick lived longer than all the others in her generation who had immigrated to the United States. She died of "old age" in 1966 at age seventy-eight. She is buried next to Bill Curnick in Rome Cemetery.

Hers was a troubled, bitter life. Nevertheless, she helped to raise successfully a competent, loving daughter who was unmarred by her mother's unhappiness. Florence loved her grandchildren dearly, although she always favored me over David because I look like my mother, whereas David is the spitting image of Nick. Some hurts run deep.

Afterword

BETWEEN ABOUT 1890 AND 1924, more than 20 million immigrants entered the United States via Ellis Island in New York City Harbor. Almost half of the people living in America today (about 150 million of us) trace their heritage through this portal. That's more than 1,600 immigrants processed every day for thirty-four years! And this task was accomplished manually, with no sophisticated computing equipment to support record keeping.

The United States has long known how to process immigrants, how to integrate them into society, and how to benefit from their contributions. Many of our historical enterprises have been built on the backs of immigrants—manufacturing, construction, agriculture, food processing, and shipping, to name a few.

Indeed, this is still the case. Food would literally not reach our tables were it not for immigrant labor. Why then is the United States having such a problem dealing with immigration?

We seem to have forgotten our history. No other nation has the benefit of the cultural diversity that exists in America. This diversity allows us to function effectively almost any place on the planet. Opening our borders to immigrants who seek work and who are willing to undertake jobs and wages that most Americans won't accept is smart business. If there are no such jobs, immigrants will no longer wish to come. Protecting the borders requires the kind of immigration policy and processing at which we were so successful for decades.

The immigration debate in the United States today is baffling to those of us whose families arrived in this great country so recently. The two immigrant families in this story and their descendants have made significant contributions to the societies into which they integrated. People with the fortitude to immigrate have the courage and tenacity to succeed in creating wealth and contributing to society. Immigration isn't easy—it's incredibly challenging, even when one comes *legally*. Think how desperate those people must be who come *illegally* just to try to get a foothold to a better life!

My guess is that merely opening our borders would eliminate the immigration controversy. Immigrants would come only if jobs are available. The recession of 2008–2009 has proven that. Those who do come will make meaningful contributions, and America will continue to prosper.

America would be wise to expend the resources we invest in keeping people *out* on processing them for legal entry. This processing provides the opportunity to identify criminals, people with contagious diseases, and individuals on terrorist watch lists prior to allowing entrance into the country.

Immigrants want to come to America to find opportunity for their families to live a better life. Our nation has been built on this concept. If we turn our backs on this proven economic engine, we risk a decline in our worldwide competitiveness at a time when China, India, Brazil, and Turkey, to name only a few countries, are literally beginning to eat our lunch.

We know how to do immigration! We have just forgotten.

And what of Palestine today? The Israelis have allowed the Palestinian organization Hamas to control the Gaza Strip. They and the United States, however, consider Hamas a terrorist organization.

It is true that Hamas has perpetrated violence in Israel. The reason that the Palestinian people still favor an organization that practices terrorism is that their government is relatively ineffective. The central state government does not have total control. Hamas provides the average Palestinian with security, health care, educational services, and the like.

A more peaceful political arm, Fatah, provides Palestinian leadership in the West Bank region. Fatah is equally ineffective, though. The Palestinian people are caught between ineffectual government and Israeli oppression.

The Israelis justify oppression by pointing out some Palestinians' terrorist activities. And so the vicious cycle continues. If the Arabs were able to master the strategy of nonviolent resistance, they would soon have world opinion on their side. Alas, that doesn't seem to be in the cards.

For its part, Israel utilizes largely ineffectual Palestinian rocket attacks to justify its apartheid approach to oppressing the Arabs. The Israeli lobby is so strong in the United States that the American government usually turns a blind eye to Israeli oppression.

In the meantime, the United States added to the instability of the region by invading Iraq, which was the single deterrent to Iran in that part of the world. With a weak Iraq, Iran is now flexing its muscles and has become an international pariah, thanks primarily to US policies in the region.

I used to discuss these issues at length with Nick. His ultimate resolution of the Palestinian situation regarding Israel was that "sooner or later 350 million Arabs will overcome 6 million Israelis." This is a fatalistic outcome, and one I don't condone; however, it will be more and more difficult for Israel to continue to call itself a democracy when a minority of Jewish citizens rule a majority of disenfranchised Palestinians.

Appendix

Bibliography

Appendix

The Middle East

Much of early human history transpired in the arc of territory at the eastern end of the Mediterranean Sea. This stretch of land running about five hundred miles from north to south and seventy-five miles east to west was known to Westerners as "the Levant." At various times, the great powers of the ancient world fought over and occupied this region—now Israel/Palestine, Lebanon, and western portions of Jordan and Syria. The Levant contains some of the oldest continuously inhabited cities on earth and, of course, many historically significant religious sites of Judaism, Christianity, and Islam.[1]

From the dawn of recorded history, three thousand years before Christ and until about 1500 CE, the Levant was the center of the world. As the capital of the Arab Empire and the origin of three great religions, the region was the perpetual victim of foreign invasion. This constant subjugation to foreign rule assumed a pattern, endlessly repeated for more than five millennia. This pattern is still in evidence today.

The Levant, under Ottoman Turk control from Constantinople beginning in the early sixteenth century, was locally governed by independent *bedou* tribal leadership. The Turks collected taxes from this local leadership and its citizens in order to support their occupation and to send treasure home to Constantinople. The lack of a unified system of government failed to provide the public security required to create a strong society, respected leadership, or any sense of nationalism.

It is the lack of nationalism that confuses Western nations today. Arab loyalty is to family, tribe, clan, and religion—not to nation. Aside from this fact, the current-day Arab nations and their borders were created by Western colonial powers, not by Arabs.

1. See Peter Mansfield, *A History of the Middle East* (New York: Penguin Books, 1992), 2.

Over the centuries in the Middle East, Jews, Christians, and Muslims lived together peacefully. They seemed to accept Moses, Jesus, and Mohammed as religious prophets, respecting one another's right to worship as they pleased.

Tensions began to arise thanks to meddling by the Allies after World War I as they defined arbitrary countries according to their own interests, which were centered mainly on assuring access to oil and the Suez Canal. These tensions were escalated dramatically by the atrocities that the Nazis perpetrated on the Jews before and during World War II. The Allies, trying to appease the horrors experienced by Jews at the Nazis' hands, brought chaos to the region by unilaterally creating a Jewish state that to this day most Arabs still have not accepted.

After escaping Egypt around 1300 BCE, the Hebrews invaded Canaan (now northern Israel). About the same time, the Philistines also invaded the region. The name "Palestine" ("Falastin" in Arabic) derives from the Philistines.[2] These people came by sea from Crete or Cyprus.

By 600 CE, the civilized world (omitting India and China) was divided between the Roman Empire on the west and the Persian Empire on the east. The Arabian Peninsula lay south of the boundary between the two and was in contact with both. Most of this peninsula consisted of barren desert inhabited by nomadic *bedou* tribes—wandering breeders of camels, sheep, and goats. The camel provided the only means of transport in the desert. Travel on horseback or on foot was not viable in this inhospitable environment.

The official religion of the Roman and Byzantine empires, which included the Levant, in 600 CE was Christianity.

Palestinians have historically been lumped with those people now known as "Syrians" (the northern Arabs), in contrast to the people of Saudi Arabia. For most of five thousand years of intermingling and assimilation of outside cultures in what are now Iraq, Israel/Palestine, Jordan, Lebanon, and Syria, the Arabian Peninsula to the south (now Saudi Arabia and its several tiny neighbors) remained relatively unmixed.[3] Foreign invaders were not attracted to the peninsula's inhospitable central deserts.

The Arabian Peninsula is more than twelve hundred miles wide at the southern end, where Yemen and Oman today border the Indian Ocean, and about fifteen hundred miles from the southern reaches to the Mediterranean Sea in the north.

2. Ibid., 4.

3. Ibid., 6.

Three thousand years ago caravans of camels and Bedouins transported frankincense, myrrh, gold, pearls, ivory, cinnamon, silk, tortoise shell, and lapis lazuli from Asia across the desert wastes from south to north. Ships sailed to the southern coast of the peninsula from India and China bearing these commodities, which were then carried north by caravan for sale in the Levant, Persia, and Europe.

These goods were less vital than the amenities provided to caravan travelers by the tax-levying Arab camps and villages along the route north. The Arabs made handsome trades—water, food, and safe passage in exchange for a portion of the shipment. This pirating was the livelihood of many Arabs residing along the caravan routes.

By the eighth century CE, the Arab Empire had achieved glory and wealth comparable to western Europe. Baghdad, the capital, was the richest city in the world. Constantinople was the only other city in the same class for luxury and refinement. Arab merchants did business in China, Indonesia, India, and East Africa. Their ships were the largest and best in the world. Because of the highly developed banking system, an Arab businessman could cash a check in Canton, China, on his bank in Baghdad.

In Baghdad, there was an abundance of gold. Ornate structures were plastered with it. In Europe, Charlemagne, emperor of the Holy Roman Empire and a contemporary of the Arab leader Haroon, was unable to mint gold currency because the precious metal was unobtainable.

Medical schools were prevalent in Baghdad. Doctors, chemists (pharmacists), barbers, and orthopedists were subject to government certification and regulation.

Arab sailors ruled the Mediterranean Sea. They invaded and conquered all of North Africa, much of Spain and France, the Balkan countries, and some of Russia and Persia.

If the Arabs' splendid qualities were widely diffused by their exploits, their faults also penetrated the many cultures they encountered. Their mutual jealousies, their pursuit of private honor, and their love of personal freedom resulted in endless internal feuds and rivalries.

From the time of Mohammad (d. 632 CE), Arabs had enjoyed centuries of splendor and power. Arab armies conquered the vast region from the western Mediterranean to India and China as well as Spain and southern France. Not only was their empire the most extensive up until that time, but Arabs enjoyed world leadership in military power, wealth, culture, science, and literature.

The economic results of the Arab conquests were as striking as the religious and cultural. Under the Romans, the Mediterranean Sea had been a Roman lake.

For seven hundred years, it never saw a naval battle and played the peaceful role of highway for commerce. Thus, Asian trade reached Europe unhindered. The extension of the Arab Empire from the Atlantic to China cut off western Europe from world trade.[4]

In Roman times, Italy, France, Spain, and Britain had been a region of wealthy commercial entrepreneurs. Arab naval command of the Mediterranean succeeding the Romans, however, destroyed overseas trade for Europe. European cities fell into decay, and the West became an agricultural region, with land replacing cash as the standard of wealth. These years are sometimes called the "Dark Ages," but the darkness was only in Europe. For Arab lands, the period was one of wealth, progress, and enlightenment.[5]

With the collapse of the Arab Empire, starting in the twelfth century CE, the West's trade slowly recovered, but the belief that landowners were a social class superior to traders has continued down to our own times. Thus, the social development of Europe for more than one thousand years was affected by the four centuries of Arab power. If we assume that the British Empire lasted from about 1700 to 1940, we see that Arab predominance was no flash in the pan.

The Arabs were so prosperous that they adopted a shortened work week. With the remains of the accumulated wealth of centuries, they introduced the welfare system with which we are familiar. Universities and colleges were built in every city; instruction was free, and students received a government grant to cover their living expenses. In the larger towns, free hospitals treated patients at government expense, and medical students received a four-year course of training free of charge.

In 1498, Vasco da Gama discovered the Cape of Good Hope, and the expanding fleets and commerce of Europe began to bypass the Middle East to reach India and China by sailing around Africa. After that, the Middle East began to decline in terms of its influence on the world stage.[6]

Fear of Arabs was strong, which seems to have resulted in historians' minimization of Western society's indebtedness to Arab civilization. Credit was given to the Greeks and Romans for knowledge and art that in truth either derived from the Arabs or was improved by the Arabs.

4. Ibid., 9.

5. Sir John B. Glubb, *A Short History of the Arab Peoples* (New York: Stein and Day, 1969), 136.

6. Mansfield, *A History of the Middle East*, 33.

The most outstanding contributions by Arabs were probably in the field of mathematics. Arabs introduced our present system of writing units—tens, hundreds, thousands, and so on—and the concept of zero. Having introduced those numerals, which we still call "Arabic numerals," the Arabs went on to invent logarithms, algebra (the word *algebra* itself is an Arabic word), plane and solid geometry, and trigonometry.[7]

In the same manner, they studied and improved on the Greeks' medical work. Arab medical treatises remained standard textbooks for students in Europe for centuries. In botany, geography, natural history, and zoology, they were centuries ahead of Europe. Astronomy was advanced to the point that *The Compendium of Astronomy*, an Arabic work published around 1000 CE, was in use as a textbook in Europe until the sixteenth century.

Their textiles, silk, embroideries, glassware, weapons, and metalwork were superior to anything that Europe could produce. They introduced, to the West, the use and manufacture of paper (which they had learned from the Chinese). Arabs were also innovators in the field of poetry and romance literature. They brought rhyming verse, unknown to the Greeks and Latins, to Europe.

Today, even with current uprisings by Arabs in Tunisia, Egypt, Yemen, Libya, and Syria, most Arab governments are not democracies. Rather, they operate as dynastic kingdoms, with leadership passing from father to son. For the most part, they are corrupt and ineffectual. The provision of basic social services such as security, health care, and education to the populace falls to shadow governments such as Hamas and Hezbollah—which is why the Arab populations support these groups.

Current conditions in the Middle East are the result of Western powers' interventions in the region. This meddling by westerners stems from the need for a reliable source of oil and the security of Israel. It will continue until oil is no longer such a valuable resource and until the Israelis address their undemocratic approach to governing Palestinians.

Yugoslavia

In the sixteenth century, the Ottoman Turks invaded and conquered the region that in 1945 was Yugoslavia. They ruled it for three hundred years, much as they had in Palestine, by collecting taxes from the people and generally oppressing them.

---

7. Glubb, *A Short History of the Arab Peoples*, 109.

Although the Turks conquered the country, they were not able to conquer the people. Many natives fled to the mountains, where they could live, worship, and raise their families as they pleased. This difficult life in the rugged mountains bred a tough-minded people over three centuries. They were a resilient, adventurous lot who were willing to struggle to survive in the wilderness rather than succumb to the invaders.

In the late nineteenth century, with the help of the Austrians and Hungarians, the Serbs regained control of the country and established a monarchy that lasted through World War I. After that war, the Allies helped set up the country of Yugoslavia in hopes of developing a democracy in the Balkan region. A dictatorship developed instead (much like Iraq under Saddam Hussein) to hold together disparate ethnic and religious groups, and at the start of World War II the government aligned itself with the Axis powers.

The *citizens* of Yugoslavia, however, did not accept this alignment, and they rebelled. The Nazis, therefore, invaded the country, and the partisans again fled to the mountains, where they fought the Germans fiercely for four years.

After World War II, Josep Broz Tito became the leader of Yugoslavia. He was challenged with organizing the diverse population of Serbs and Croats of various religious persuasions.

Great Britain

London in the second half of the nineteenth century was struggling to cope with the effects of the Industrial Revolution. The population had expanded dramatically, and much of the increase was concentrated in the east end of town, where the factories were located. Overcrowding, poor housing, unemployment, poverty, and disease were pervasive.

An extensive railroad system provided a solid foundation for the increase in manufacturing and distribution and made travel easier for those who could afford it. Despite the affluence attained by the land owners and captains of industry and commerce, education was still not available to the masses. Those with money sent their children to private schools; those without did what they could at home to educate their offspring. Illiteracy was the norm.

In addition to the expansive rail system, Great Britain built other infrastructure to support commerce and make its cities inviting. Sewers, potable water, and an underground rail system enhanced the attractiveness of city dwelling.

Democracy, feminism, unionization of workers, socialism, Marxism, Darwinism, and the thinking of Sigmund Freud shaped the fast-evolving social environment. Those with the means to help others began to accept their social responsibilities for the first time. There were also significant advances in medicine, science, and technology.

In the last quarter of the nineteenth century, Great Britain enjoyed the largest world empire ever amassed, consisting of more than 25 percent of the world's population and geographic area. The British Empire included India, Australia, Canada, New Zealand, South Africa, Rhodesia, Hong Kong, Gibraltar, several islands in the West Indies, and various colonies on the African coast. At the end of her more than sixty-year reign, Queen Victoria ruled more than four hundred million people.

Family Tree

I. Radia Khouri, born 1880, married Habeeb Rezak, born 1866, in 1901.
Children of Radia and Habeeb:
A. David Habeeb Rezak, born January 1, 1903, married Mary L. Habeeb, born February 2, 1907, on May 26, 1929.
Children of David and Mary:
  1. Laurice Rezak, born November 30, 1930, married Harry Karim on February 17, 1952.
  Children of Laurice and Harry:
  (a) Michael Karim, born June 30, 1953, married Adrienne Cardellini on October 31, 1981, divorced; married Linda Hadeed on February 7, 2004.
  (b) Rhonda Karim, born July 31, 1958, married William Cook on December 31, 1988, divorced; married Peter Fox on March 27, 2010.
  Children of Rhonda and William:
     (i) Sam Cook, born July 26, 1994.
  2. Helen Rezak, born April 24, 1932, married Fred Abdo on September 11, 1949, divorced.
  Children of Helen and Fred:
  (a) Richard Shelby Abdo, born August 14, 1950, married Donna Allen on February 8, 1981, divorced; married Theresa Olson on November 10, 2001.

Children of Rick and Donna:

(i) Sean Curtis Abdo, born January 25, 1970.

(ii) Shane Curtis Abdo, born December 3, 1971.

(iii) Eric Wadu Abdo, born May 30, 1982.

(iv) Tashina Jane Abdo, born October 31, 1983.

(b) Nadine Ruth Abdo, born June 19, 1955, married to James Canby Kerr on May 19, 1985.

Children of Nadine and James:

(i) Madison Canby Kerr, born December 14, 1988.

(ii) Sawyer Canby Kerr, born May 28, 1990.

(c) Janice Abdo, born January 20, 1958, married John Joseph Rott on February 19, 1994.

Children of Janice and John:

(i) Trevor David Rott, born October 15, 1994.

(ii) Natalie Marie Rott, born April 20, 1997.

3. Robert Rezak, born March 2, 1934, married Lucille Karim in 1956, divorced.

Children of Robert and Lucille:

(a) Dawn Rezak, born June 21, 1959.

(b) Laurie Rezak, born December 7, 1961, married Gino Baldino on November 14, 1987.

Children of Laurie and Gino:

(i) Michael J. Baldino, born May 25, 1990.

(ii) Kristen L. Baldino, born February 20, 1992.

(c) David George Rezak, born June 8, 1967.

4. John (Jack) Rezak, born June 12, 1935, married Deanna Young on July 17, 1960.

Children of Jack and Deanna:

(a) Kathy Rezak, born September 5, 1963, married Robert Fedrizzi on May 15, 1992.

Children of Kathy and Robert:

(i) Kyle Fedrizzi, born November 7, 1993.

(b) Debra Rezak, born October 28, 1965, married Gary (Chip) George on May 27, 1994.

Children of Debra and Chip:

(i) Zakary George, born September 23, 1995.

(ii) Elizabeth George, born January 11, 1999.

(iii) Grace George, born April 20, 2002.

5. Louis Rezak, born October 22, 1940, married Antonette Mathar, December 16, 1963.

Children of Louis and Antonette:

(a) John Christopher Rezak, born March 24, 1967, married Deborah Ann Blair on December 31, 1994.

Children of John and Deborah Ann:

(i) Crystal Starr Rezak, born March 30, 1990.

(ii) Sierrah Allesse Rezak, born January 9, 1997.

(iii) Taylor Blair Rezak, born December 6, 1999.

(b) Renee Michelle Rezak, born April 9, 1970, married Mark Baker on August 15, 1997.

Children of Renee and Mark:

(i) Jason Tabor Baker, born June 13, 1999.

(ii) Steven Louis Baker, born August 20, 2001.

(iii) Michael Patrick Baker, born November 21, 2003.

(c) Amy Lynn Rezak, born June 22, 1974, married Kevin E. Alger on September 28, 2012.

(d) Kristen Marie Rezak, born June 22, 1974.

6. Barbara Joy Rezak, born August 16, 1950, married Arthur Charles Just on June 1, 1969, divorced; married Paul Laurence Windhausen on August 1, 1990.

Children of Barbara and Arthur:

(a) Julie Marie Just, born April 7, 1973, married Lawrence Metcalf on August 14, 1993.

Children of Julie and Lawrence:

(i) Victoria Marie Metcalf, born March 20, 1994.

(ii) Kristina Leigh Metcalf, born July 31, 1995.

(iii) Lawrence Edward Metcalf, born February 6, 1998.

(b) Kelly Michelle Just, born October 13, 1975, married Charles Bruce Balcom on October 15, 2005.

Children of Kelly and Charles:

(i) Andrew Charles Balcom, born April 3, 1988.

(ii) Carson James Balcom, born November 5, 1992.

(iii) Cameron Charles Paul Balcom, born February 12, 2002.

B. Nicholas Habeeb Rezak, born February 22, 1909, married Frances Pauline (Polly) Curnick on December 28, 1935.

Children of Nick and Polly:

1. William David Rezak, born August 30, 1940, married Eleanor Pauline (Paula) Burroughs on September 28, 1968.

    Children of Bill and Paula:

    (a) David Todd Rezak, born April 10, 1969, married Achirya Tanya Stone on July 20, 2002.

        Children of David and Achirya:

        (i) Alba Sophia Rezak, born February 10, 2005.

    (b) Sarah Beth Rezak, born September 1, 1971, married Christopher Glasgow on May 3, 2008.

2. David Mark Rezak, born November 10, 1948, married Linda Marchione McCauley on April 16, 1978.

    Children of David and Linda:

    (a) Jennifer McCauley, born March 3, 1973.

    (b) Nikki Michelle Rezak, born December 20, 1979, married Jeffery Petties on June 22, 2011.

        Children of Nikki and Jeffery:

        (i) Jaylen Edwards, born November 27, 2003.

        (ii) Jeffery Petties, born July 2, 2008.

C. Richard Habeeb Rezak, born April 26, 1920, married Hifa Hider on July 21, 1944, divorced; married Anna Lucille (Jerry) Nesselrode in March 1965.

Children of Dick and Hifa:

1. Christine Sara Rezak, born September 21, 1950, married James Barker on October 24, 1990.

    Children of Christine and James:

    (a) Christy Barker, born August 8, 1989.

II. John Robert Milton Curnick, born 1854, married Sarah Patience Cooke, born December 30, 1854, on July 24, 1875.

Children of John and Sarah:

A. William John Thomas Curnick, born May 26, 1876, married Florence Elsie Belcher on June 25, 1907.

    Children of Bill and Florence:

1. Frances Pauline (Polly) Curnick, born November 25, 1910. Married Nicholas H. Rezak on December 28, 1935. See her offspring under Rezak Family.

B. Ellen Mary (Nell) Curnick, born January 3, 1878, married Arthur Glassford.

Children of Nell and Arthur:

1. Cecil Glassford, born 1903, married Irene Cobb in 1926. Had two daughters.

2. Violet Glassford, born 1907, married Roy Harrigan in 1930.

Children of Violet and Roy:

(a) Jack Harrigan, married a woman named Judy from Rochester, had four daughters.

C. Harry Cecil Curnick, born August 11, 1879, married a woman named Jen from Watertown, New York.

Children of Harry and Jen:

1. Cecil Curnick, born 1906, married, with one son.

2. Catherine Curnick, date of birth unknown.

3. Mary Curnick, date of birth unknown, married a man named Bauerschmidt in Rochester and had four or five children.

4. Paul Curnick, date of birth unknown.

D. Ada Louise (Lou) Curnick, born August 18, 1883, married Frederick Spraggins in Cardinal, Ontario, settled in Rome, New York.

Children of Lou and Fred:

1. Emma Louise Spraggins, date of birth unknown, married Clifford Cobb.

Children of Emma and Clifford:

(a) William Cobb, born 1941.

(b) Cynthia Cobb, date of birth unknown, married Roy Snyder, one son.

(c) Robert Cobb, date of birth unknown.

2. Irene Spraggins, date of birth unknown, married a man named McArdle in Syracuse, New York.

3. Victor Spraggins, date of birth unknown, married, with one son in Albany area.

4. Harry Spraggins, date of birth unknown.

III. Hannah (Annie) Belcher, born November 18, 1866, married Eli Stimpson in 1890.

Children of Annie:

A. Florence Elsie Belcher, born June 24, 1888, married William John Thomas Curnick on June 25, 1907. See Curnick Family for listing of their offspring.

B. Ellen Stimpson, born in 1891, remained in Great Britain.

C. Alice May Stimpson, born in 1892, died in 1900 in Great Britain.

D. Charles Eli Stimpson, born in 1894, remained in Great Britain.

E. Elsie Stimpson, born in 1896; remained in Great Britain.

F. Daisy Stimpson, born in 1897, married Timothy Staple of Lee Center, New York.

Children of Daisy and Timothy:

1. Ronald Staple, date of birth unknown.

2. Betty Staple, date of birth unknown, married Oliver Frost of Onieda, New York.

Children of Betty and Oliver:

(a) Linda Frost, date of birth unknown.

(b) Laurie Frost, date of birth unknown.

(c) Four other children, names unknown.

3. Jack Staple, date of birth unknown, married a woman named Joan in Rome, New York.

Children of Jack and Joan:

(a) Sheila Staple, date of birth unknown.

(b) Tina Staple, date of birth unknown.

(c) Jay Staple, date of birth unknown.

Bibliography

Barnardo's, Jim Jarvis, and the Biggest Family in the World. Hertford, UK: Barnardo's School of Printing, n.d.

Emmett, Chad F. *Beyond the Basilica*. Chicago: University of Chicago Press, 1995.

Glubb, Sir John B. *A Short History of the Arab Peoples*. New York: Stein and Day, 1969.

Lowe, Nicholas. *The Barnardo Story*. Barkingside, UK: Barnardo's, n.d.

Mansfield, Peter. *A History of the Middle East*. New York: Penguin Books, 1992.

Mansour, Rev. Asa'ad. *The History of Nazareth*. Cairo: Al Hilal Press, 1924.

Rezak, Nicholas, Richard Rezak, William Rezak, and David M. Rezak. *The Rezaks of Syracuse*. Syracuse, NY: self-published, 1983.